Urban Housing
and
Neighborhood Revitalization

URBAN HOUSING

AND

NEIGHBORHOOD REVITALIZATION

Turning a Federal Program into Local Projects

DONALD B. ROSENTHAL

Contributions in Political Science, Number 208

GREENWOOD PRESS

New York • Westport, Connecticut • London

Library of Congress Cataloging-in-Publication Data

Rosenthal, Donald B., 1937–
  Urban housing and neighborhood revitalization : turning a federal
program into local projects / Donald B. Rosenthal.
    p. cm. — (Contributions in political science, ISSN 0147–1066
; no. 208)
  Bibliography: p.
  Includes index.
  ISBN 0–313–26148–2 (lib. bdg. : alk. paper)
  1. Community development, Urban—United States—Citizen
participation. 2. Urban policy—United States. 3. Federal aid to
community development—United States. 4. Housing policy—United
States. I. Title. II. Series.
HN90.C6R67 1988
307.1′4′0973—dc19   87–32259

British Library Cataloguing in Publication Data is available.

Library of Congress Catalog Card Number: 87–32259
ISBN: 0–313–26148–2
ISSN: 0147–1066

First published in 1988

Greenwood Press, Inc.
88 Post Road West, Westport, Connecticut 06881

Printed in the United States of America

Copyright Acknowledgments

The author and publisher gratefully acknowledge the following for granting permission
to reprint the author's previously published materials, revised for the present volume:

"The Politics of Decentralization: Creating a Local Government Role in Federal
Housing Programs," *The Urban Interest* 4 (Fall 1982): 90–104, is used with
permission from the *The Urban Interest*.

"Joining Housing Rehabilitation to Neighborhood Revitalization: The Neighborhood
Strategy Area Program," in Robert Eyestone, (ed.), *Public Policy Formation*, pp.325–
357, is used with permission from JAI Press, copyright © 1984.

"Forms of Local Participation in a Neighborhood-Based Federal Program," *Policy
Studies Review* 3 (February 1984): 279–295, is used with permission from the Policy
Studies Organization.

CONTENTS

PREFACE

This study grew out of an opportunity provided to me by the National Association of Schools of Public Affairs and Administration to serve as a faculty fellow at the Department of Housing and Urban Development (HUD) in 1977–1978. I spent the greater part of that time as a member of the staff engaged in developing a program design for what came to be known as the Section 8 Neighborhood Strategy Area (NSA) Program.

I wish to thank the extraordinarily dedicated members of that HUD group, including Amy Jones, James Flemming, Cheryl Patton, John Bohm, and, most of all, John (Jack) Kerry, whose enormous dedication to the development and implementation of the NSA program belied conventional images of government lethargy or timidity.

In the course of my experience at HUD, I became aware that involvement in the NSA program would provide me with an unusual opportunity to do research in several areas of academic interest: intergovernmental relations; policy analysis; and housing and community development policies including those directed at revitalizing urban areas. My stay in Washington familiarized me particularly with the process by which the NSA program was formulated and the initial steps taken to implement it.

Upon my return to teaching in the fall of 1978, I continued to maintain occasional contact with persons responsible for the program in Washington. As time permitted, I did research at the NSA office in Washington. However, my principal research efforts shifted to examining the behavior of HUD field offices and local governments engaged in implementing the program. Even during the period while I was in Washington, I began to interview a number of local officials involved in the process of applying for program participation and some individuals in HUD field offices responsible for program administration. That part of my research effort became more extensive, however, during a year's sabbatical from the State University of New York at Buffalo in 1980–1981. At that time, I visited program sites throughout the nation. It is from this period that much of the data that deal with the early stages of program implementation come.

The NSA program was designed to be a five-year program (to end in September 1983) but it took longer to be implemented than its supporters had hoped it would. This occurred for a number of reasons, the main one being problems in the general economy that made it difficult to finance the housing rehabilitation projects at the core of the program's design. By 1981, the Reagan administration was also trying to bring the rather expensive program to a swift conclusion.

The story might well have ended there except that in the spring of 1983, I spent some time in Albany, New York, as a senior fellow at the Nelson A. Rockefeller Institute of Government. This provided me with incentive to do additional field work on local implementation experiences, particularly in upstate New York and Massachusetts. Since localities in those two states had been the most active participants in the program, that research was intended merely to update information on certain local efforts. Somewhat to my surprise, I found that in a number of places where implementation efforts had appeared to be dying in 1981, a considerable number of projects had returned to life. Even where implementation of core aspects of the program had not been successful in producing federally financed housing projects, other "good things" were taking place in the targeted neighborhoods that were worth noting.

These discoveries led me to spend that summer visiting additional sites, particularly in New England. Early in 1984, visits were also paid to New York City, and Washington, D.C. Finally, a trip to the West Coast in January 1985 permitted me to update materials collected earlier on neighborhoods in Los Angeles and San Francisco.

These visits revealed that activities were still being initiated in some neighborhoods, occasionally as a direct consequence of program participation. Indeed, it can be argued that an adequate evaluation of the program will be impossible for some years to come or at least until the full impact can be felt from the investments made.

Because the complexity of program histories varied enormously, it was possible to understand something about some local program performances on the basis of a single visit. In other instances, three or four visits did not provide adequate coverage of all the issues involved. Nevertheless, the findings reported in this volume are based on data collected over a six-year period from approximately 87 local jurisdictions out of the 118 that participated in the program. Both for these localities as well as those not visited, written materials were collected (such as program reports, intergovernmental communications, and local press coverage of events bearing on NSA program activities). These are drawn on in the following study along with interview materials.

Simply counting the number of program sites visited is not entirely revealing since some of the most telling interviews about a local program might not be gathered in the locality itself. Interviews were held, for example, with HUD field office personnel and professional developers located hundreds of miles from the site of a project. Thus, important insights about a program in Savannah, Georgia, might be gathered from a developer's staff member in Columbus, Ohio, or a HUD official in Atlanta.

Given the considerable variation in the quality and quantity of information available for each locality—and sometimes for different neighborhoods within the same jurisdiction—I have not attempted to present this analysis in quantitative terms. No standardized questionnaire was employed. Rather my questions were shaped to the particular circumstances of each local government and target neighborhood.

In the course of interviewing in the field, some HUD offices were highly cooperative in making materials available to me while others were less so. As a result of such difficulties, much of the information gathered from the seventeen field offices visited (with some notable exceptions) was in the form of interviews rather than written documentation. In terms of interpersonal contacts, I found the overwhelming majority of HUD personnel both cooperative and more forthright on sometimes controversial matters than I had anticipated from their reluctance to make written materials available.

Yet, if HUD personnel were friendly, interviews with them tended to last no more than an hour and to be rather general in character. In comparison, many of the over 250 other interviews conducted with local government officials, representatives of neighborhood organizations, developers, and others knowledgeable about aspects of the NSA program were long and detailed. Furthermore, in forty-six instances the same persons were interviewed more than once—in eleven cases as many as three or four times—over the course of the program's history. Obviously, it would be difficult to thank each one of these persons individually—and in some cases I am not sure that they would want to be mentioned by name. In the course of the following research report, however, I have occasionally cited sources where I felt remarks would not betray any confidence.

Three points need to be made in this connection. First, while some informants requested and were assured of personal anonymity, few made that a condition of their interviews. In a few instances, informants did ask that specific pieces of information not be attributed directly to them. I have honored those requests. In contrast, where written communications were drawn upon, I have cited the correspondents without necessarily identifying the person who provided the document.

Second, nearly all interviews were taped and later transcribed, so that remarks quoted are practically verbatim. On occasion, I have edited comments (either in the process of transcription or in the final text) so they read more smoothly in print. I have also inserted information in brackets where such interpolations may help clarify references made by the speaker.

Finally, as an aid to the reader, I have provided a summary list in Appendix A of the number and kinds of interviews conducted, and in Appendix B of designated NSA localities and neighborhoods, the dates of my visits (if any), and some additional program information.

Along the way, I have received assistance from a number of students who have worked on some of the data. In particular, I wish to thank Peter Baxter, Roy Fitzgerald, David Goldfischer, Sa-Myung Park, and Blake Strack. I also want to thank Arthur Johnson, William Mishler, and Dennis Woods for commenting on earlier drafts, and David Scott for helping to put the index together.

ABBREVIATIONS

APO	Advocacy Planning Organization
BHDC	Berkshire Housing Development Corporation
CAP	Community Action Program
CBD	Central Business District
CD NSA	Community Development Neighborhood Strategy Area (Program)
CDBG	Community Development Block Grant
CDC	Community Development Corporation
CETA	Comprehensive Employment and Training Act
CPD	(HUD) Office of Community Planning and Development
Demo Rehab	Demonstration Rehabilitation (Program)
EPA	Environmental Protection Agency
FAF	Financial Adjustment Factor.
FHA	Federal Housing Administration
FMR	Fair Market Rent
FY	Fiscal Year
GNMA	Governmental National Mortgage Association
GRS	General Revenue Sharing
HFDA	(State) Housing Finance and Development Agencies
HUD	Department of Housing and Urban Development
IGR	Intergovernmental Relations
LMI	Low- and Moderate-Income
LSC	Legal Services Corporation
MHFA	Massachusetts Housing Finance Agency

Mod Rehab	(Section 8) Moderate Rehabilitation (Program)
NBO	Neighborhood-Based Organization
NHP	National (Corporation for) Housing Partnerships
NHRA	National Housing Rehabilitation Association
NHS	Neighborhood Housing Services
NPO	Neighborhood Preservation Office
NSA	(Section 8) Neighborhood Strategy Area (Program)
OEO	Office of Economic Opportunity
RAP	Rehabilitation Assistance Program
SHPO	State Historic Preservation Office
SRO	Single-Room Occupancy
Sub Rehab	(Section 8) Substantial Rehabilitation (Program)
TRIP	Troy Rehabilitation and Improvement Program
UDAG	Urban Development Action Grant (Program)
USCM	U.S. Conference of Mayors

1

STUDYING THE INTERGOVERNMENTAL POLICY PROCESS

This volume is designed to contribute to an understanding of three aspects of political and policy behaviors during the Carter and Reagan administrations: (1) the character of political relations among national and local government participants in the American federal system; (2) the way such relations were expressed through the policy process; and (3) the operation of intergovernmental programs aimed at promoting neighborhood revitalization and housing rehabilitation for low-income people.

These three themes are treated by focusing on the Section 8 Neighborhood Strategy Area (NSA) Program initiated by the Department of Housing and Urban Development (HUD) in 1978. The NSA program ultimately involved 118 local governments in projects in 155 neighborhoods before its termination in 1983. These case materials provide an excellent source for studying intergovernmental relations during the Carter era; they also permit us to compare local performances by drawing on data from a variety of circumstances and from different stages of the policy process.

Before focusing in chapter 2 on factors that led to the creation of the NSA program, the principal dimensions of this study will be introduced. First, five analytical models from the literature of intergovernmental relations (IGR) will be described, against which the actions of governmental participants in the NSA program will be assessed. Second, the approach to the policy process employed is detailed. Third, recent themes in urban policy—particularly those concerned with housing and community development programs—are drawn upon to identify the ideological and political constraints within which programs like NSA have operated. Finally, the scope of the study is delineated by identifying the stages of NSA policy development.

A TYPOLOGY OF INTERGOVERNMENTAL RELATIONS

Two major traditions exist in the study of American federalism and intergovernmental relations (IGR): (1) a normative tradition that proceeds from a reading of constitutional design and associated "intent" to the identification of deviations from constitutional design; and (2) a behavioral tradition that describes the actions of governmental officeholders (as well as nongovernmental participants) in those political and policy processes associated with the interactions between two or more governments.

The first tradition is incorporated particularly in notions of dual federalism. This model posits the existence of distinct spheres of national and state activity based on strict interpretations of the words and putative "intentions" of the framers of the Constitution.[1] Not only has such an approach served as a normative benchmark for judging the performance of IGR, but it has also been used to describe and understand relations among governments—particularly prior to the New Deal. The image of separateness fundamental to dual federalism finds its expression most recently in the writings of theorists supportive of the attitudes of the Reagan administration.[2]

Despite this emphasis on distinct constitutional spheres of activity, some students of federal history began to argue in the 1950s that from the founding of the Republic there was a significant measure of cooperation in practical matters among governments. According to one such interpretation, cooperation resulted from the initiatives of state and local governments seeking to exploit resources (including technical skills) in the possession of the national government as much as from the ambitions of national actors attempting to expand their influence.[3] This is not the place to review the debate about how significant such acts of cooperation were before the twentieth century (given the limited nature of governmental activity); nor do we need to examine the massive growth in both formal and informal cooperation since the New Deal, including the role that local governments came increasingly to play in the intergovernmental "partnership" from the 1930s onwards.[4]

Whatever its descriptive value, the cooperative model opposed the dual federalism tradition by treating the existing pattern of IGR in the 1950s as a legitimate expression of political values—whatever their deviation from supposed constitutional intentions. In a sense, what began as a behavioral descriptive model assumed the role of a normative standard in its own right. The cooperative model still assumed the existence of constitutional and political norms that protected the autonomy of state and local governments from the incursions of national power.

By the late 1960s, however, questions about boundaries came to concern students of IGR from both the dual and cooperative federalism schools. The central question was whether the system had moved too sharply away from a cooperative approach to one that fostered centralized power during the Johnson administration.[5] Even persons otherwise sympathetic to the substantive program goals of the period recognized the potentially centralizing effects of providing resources and federally mandated opportunities for minorities and the poor to participate in subnational political arenas.[6] At that point both the normative (dual federalism) and cooperative approaches had to contend with the direction the system appeared to be taking.

One issue for behavioral theorists was whether what was happening represented a significant shift away from what Daniel J. Elazar has called "non-centralization"—a situation in which state and local governments maintained significant areas of political and functional autonomy from federal control—to a system that might be better understood as a nationally dominated form of decentralization, in which local governments functioned essentially as administrative units of an increasingly centralized intergovernmental system.[7] According to this perspective, the situation did not change significantly as a result of the replacement of the Johnson administration by both Nixon's and Ford's. For while those administrations professed a concern with autonomy for state and local governments, the policy actions taken during those years—as much due to congressional initiatives as to presidential leadership—did not substantially move the national role in IGR in a less interventionist direction.

Indeed, it has been argued that programs like General Revenue Sharing (GRS) in 1972 and block grants—particularly, the Community Development Block Grant of 1974—made national resources available to deal with a variety of local needs in a fashion that drew additional governmental units into the web of IGR. In other words, localities which had been nonparticipants or only minor participants in the highly fragmented intergovernmental processes of the past came increasingly in the 1970s to play a part in a more "organized" intergovernmental system.[8] Furthermore, Democratic Congresses added a variety of regulatory "strings" to these and other resource-rich programs, thus reinforcing centralizing effects.

Having described the nature of the historical debate up to the Carter administration, it is useful to sort out these and other analytical possibilities by positing five behavioral models of intergovernmental relations; in subsequent chapters, we shall attempt to match these models against behaviors observed during the various stages of the Section 8 Neighborhood Strategy Area (NSA) Program. The five models are as follows:

1. a conflict model reflective of the dual federalism tradition which presupposes the existence of distinct governmental centers operating autonomously in large spheres of action but occasionally coming into conflict when matters of independent concern occur;

2. a pork barrel model which perceives the federal government essentially as the possessor of valuable resources that may be exploited by local and state (as well as nongovernmental) interests without substantial costs in power to the recipient;

3. a bargaining model which assumes the continuing vitality of noncentralizing forces in American political life and emphasizes the way both broad programmatic principles

and administrative particulars are continuously refined through the interactions of persons from a variety of governmental and nongovernmental arenas;

4. a sharing model which emphasizes the notion that there is an intermingling of policy goals and program activities among governments; and

5. a view of IGR which draws on images of hierarchy to emphasize a notion of control or centralization in which components of the national government direct the behaviors of others in the policy process.

While the dual federalism approach emphasized the constitutional boundaries between national and state governments, it largely ignored the role of local governments save as creatures of their respective state governments. In contrast, all five of these behavioral models allow for involvement in intergovernmental relations of local political and governmental actors, though in regard to the control model, one might argue that neither the states nor local governments are of much independent significance; at best they may function as administrative units (along with quasi-governmental creatures of the federal government) in carrying out federal programs.

Reflections of each of the five models may be found in recent intergovernmental experiences. Thus, the conflict model is present in the guardedness of state and local governments in protecting what they perceive to be their legal and political integrity against the incursions of national power. Resort to the courts, in particular, points to the failure of other means to resolve political and administrative differences.[9]

Given the large number of contemporary intergovernmental transactions, however, those which are in serious conflict at any one time are relatively few. That may be as much a function of unwillingness among institutional actors to expend the necessary resources to press fundamental issues, however, as it is a reflection of an essential harmony in the system. Nor is it easy to deny that among transactions that do not result in judicial actions there are many that are steeped in controversy.

In contrast, the significance of the pork barrel in generating and sustaining intergovernmental relations may have been undervalued. Present in notions of "distributive" decision making, state and local participants in IGR historically have sought to obtain a share in the resources vested in the domain of the national government.[10] Thus Beer, writing of the importance of the pork barrel in understanding nineteenth-century politics and its continuing presence as a factor in policy making, paraphrases an argument made by Philip Monypenny in 1960. Beer suggests that some of the claims made for federal programs as centralizing instrumentalities are misplaced, for

each program is the product of a specific coalition consisting of members with very different objects, who therefore could not agree on an all-federal program and so concerted their pressure to get money from the federal government with such vague requirements that each member of the coalition could use it pretty much as he liked within his own jurisdiction.[11]

In sum, as much as conflict informs some aspects of intergovernmental experiences, so does pork barrel politics. Whether one speaks of programs of the 1950s like urban renewal or highway construction, or programs of the 1970s like GRS or block grants, federal resources have been made available to subnational governments to carry out program activities that largely conformed to state or local definitions of need.

In contrast, the bargaining model proceeds from the assumption that actors in IGR are moved by a complex mixture of motives. On the one hand, there may be willingness to cooperate in the pursuit of common goals but conflict may arise over the means by which those goals are pursued. On the other hand, while goals may be markedly different in particular situations, participants may seek the advantages gained by participating in intergovernmental programs in order to achieve their distinct ends—much as in the pork barrel model. In contrast to the control model, which tends to see nationalizing tendencies everywhere, bargains over "details" of program administration may be as important to maintaining effective state and local autonomy as bargains struck over broad principles. Indeed, within this framework, and consistent with the Monypenny argument, nationalizing rhetoric may merely be a "cover" for allowing state and local governments to run federal programs in quite localized fashion. Furthermore, there need be no expectation that political power and policy outcomes will necessarily be linked to the primacy of national agencies over state and local governments.

While the bargaining model is appealing to many political scientists, it is too easy to overlook some of its deficiencies.[12] The vision of two or more sets of governmental actors explicitly negotiating differences over program issues squares less with reality than one might expect.[13] Indeed, in some instances, the parties to intergovernmental transactions may value ambiguity. If the conflicting goals and diverse value premises held by relevant actors were actually spelled out through bargaining, in fact, many of the agreements reached as a result of participants talking past each other would collapse. This is not to argue against the theoretical utility of something like a bargaining model in describing many intergovernmental transactions. Rather, it is to recognize that much bargaining is implicit and is shaped by forces that undermine clarification of ends and means through the bargaining process itself.

In contrast, the sharing model, originally explicated by Grodzins and elaborated by Elazar as part of their effort to develop a "cooperative" alternative to dual federalism, stresses a harmony of goals among participants.[14] In its original version, at least, it appeared to perceive the existence of a frictionless world, if only for the purpose of contrasting that world with the one present in conflict theory. The reality of political life, of course, is that even in the most harmonious of centralized organizations there are likely to be interpersonal and intra-organizational differences over goals and the means for reaching those goals.

How much more likely, then, that distinct governments made up of individuals owing only tenuous political loyalty to each other would experience disagreements about goals and means. Even where some values are shared among program professionals based in different government arenas, as in the case of the "picket fences" about which Deil Wright has written, it may be necessary to strike bargains on other matters.[15] Nonetheless, what is useful about the model is its assertion that responsible governmental actors can interact in good faith in the pursuit of shared goals.

Finally, the control model assumes a nationalized system in which identifiable national actors have developed programs that create clear-cut power dependencies by other governments. Some shadings of this model recognize that considerable fragmentation exists at the national level, thus diffusing the impact of nationalizing tendencies. Writers who draw on the control model argue that federal grants and the regulatory "strings" attached to them have had extensive nationalizing effects on state and local governments—even where the programs in question are nominally directed to serving decentralizing or noncentralizing purposes.[16]

These models provide a framework within which the federal and local experiences associated with the evolution of the NSA program will be subsequently reviewed. Before doing so, we shall introduce the terminological approach to the policy process that will be used in the present study.

DIMENSIONS OF THE POLICY PROCESS

It is useful to begin with a relatively simple distinction among the terms *policy*, *program*, and *project* that will be employed in tracing the life history of the Section 8 NSA program. The term *policy* is sometimes used in an inclusive way as it is in much public policy literature to designate the various elements of inquiry involved in the study of governmental activity. It is also used more narrowly here to mean the specification of values and goals with respect to a particular segment of societal concern. Such a statement may be either explicit, that is, incorporated in a public pronouncement (such as legislation) or implicit, that is, derived from observation of the behaviors of actors engaged in "policy-related" activities. However determined, one is then able to speak of the existence of an "education policy" or a "health policy."

In theory, *programs* are premised on policies. They identify the means by which a portion or the totality of a policy is expected to be converted into action. In practice, the relationship between the two is not clear-cut, for most programs emerge out of political processes in which the connections between the actions authorized and the policy goals being pursued may be only tenuous at best. In some circumstances, a program will reflect one aspect of a policy while ignoring or contradicting other elements of that policy. The situation is further complicated when programs attempt to incorporate multiple goals. Thus, the Community Development Block Grant (CDBG) proclaims as its principal goals "benefit[ing] low- and moderate-income families" and "aid[ing] in the prevention or elimination of slums or blight. . . . ''[17] In practice, these are two distinct program goals that lead to distinct sets of activities sometimes pursued in contradiction to one another.

While programs identify the actions that their designers wish to promote, many programs are administered through intergovernmental or nongovernmental means. Therefore, program designs must be adjusted to local circumstances in order to achieve their stipulated purposes. The result is that programs, which may be viewed as consisting of general statements of actions to be taken, must be converted into *projects*: specific actions taken either in pursuit of the goals represented in a particular program or under the guise of pursuing those goals. Ideally, projects should be carried out in such a way as to translate program goals directly into activities, but one of the major findings of the implementation literature is that there is considerable slippage between program design and project implementation.

One of the complications involved in analyzing the connection between policy and program activity is that programs are likely to require the construction of political coalitions whose participants seek project benefits—pork barrel—but do not necessarily agree about policy goals. While ambiguity of policy goals may provide an incentive to program participation precisely because participants are free to develop projects with only minimal accountability to other actors, difficulties arise for the policy analyst in drawing the connections between program, policy, and project when not one but several sets of purposes are served by a particular program.

These definitional distinctions obviously have implications for the lessons one draws from studying governmental behaviors. A case in point is the endless controversy over the much studied war on poverty. Part of the problem with analyses of that program—or, more specifically, that *set* of programs and projects—has been the lack of consensus about what the policy or policies were that were supposed to be translated into programs within the framework of the Economic Opportunity Act of 1964. Without any agreement about the goals such programs were intended to serve, it was difficult later to generate agreement about the standards against which the programs and projects carried out under them could be evaluated. That has not prevented many critics from labeling the overall effort a ''failure,'' though even among them there is considerable disagreement about the proper understanding of the nature of that failure.

Thus, ''failure'' has been variously ascribed to: (1) disagreements among policy makers about the character of poverty in American society and how to alter it; (2) fundamental differences about the purposes programmatic efforts were intended to serve; (3) inadequacies in the particular program designs intended to respond to the defects perceived in previous approaches; (4) deficiencies in the organizational mechanisms through which project designers attempted to implement programs; (5) insufficient resources available to support the projects designed and administered by locally based agencies; (6) the opposition of local political actors to challenges to their authority by newly mobilized interests; and, ultimately, (7) deterioration in the foreign and domestic political environment of the 1960s that limited the effects of projects.[18]

THE URBAN POLICY ENVIRONMENT

In understanding the background to the Section 8 NSA program, it is necessary to review three sets of problems related to the analysis of policy making for urban areas in the United States: (1) the distinction between ideology and interest; (2) the relationship between forms of power in society and the products of the urban policy process; and (3) the linkage between forms of urban power and patterns of intergovernmental relations.

Ideology and Interest

It is not necessary to explore the difficult question of the priority between ideology and interest in the evolution of public policy. Nonetheless, recent examinations of the subject have demonstrated how closely intertwined these dimensions of analysis are. The recent work of R. Allen Hays, for example, treats the evolution of urban housing and community development programs over the past fifty years by contrasting what he characterizes as "liberal" and "conservative" ideologies operating in those policy arenas.[19] For the purposes of that analysis, Hays defines ideology as "a widely shared set of interrelated assertions about the world which guides the behavior of individuals and groups."[20] In contrast, "interest" is "1) an [sic] need experienced by an individual or group; and 2) an external object or state of affairs which is seen by the individual or group as fulfilling their need."[21]

Recognizing the insufficiency of these distinctions, Hays introduces the notion of an "operational ideology," which he characterizes as a set of ideas that has a "direct influence on political behavior."[22] In the course of specifying the characteristics of the American operational ideology, however, he concedes that both "liberal" and "conservative" value systems are subsumed under an overarching market ideology that leaves out of the policy debate a range of options for government action.

What results is a fairly narrow set of distinctions between conservatives and liberals in which the former are seen as accepting certain government interventions as a way of encouraging "productive activity by those economic actors who are already winners in the private market struggle. . . . "[23] Liberals have supported the private market, Hays suggests, but have deviated in certain respects from the market ideology by tending "to view a government which more actively plans and orders social relationships as essential . . . " to preserving that market.[24]

Although Hays employs these ideological distinctions in his program survey, he recognizes the extent to which ideological tendencies have been modified by interest. Thus, supporters of the conservative ideology might have been expected to oppose government interventions in housing policy; in fact, they have often supported interventions that benefited the construction and finance industries.

To go beyond Hays, a result of this interest-based policy process has been to create a coalition that cut across liberal and conservative ideological lines. That coalition dominated housing and community development program making from the late 1930s through the 1970s. While the makeup of the coalition and its concerns changed over time, those changes occurred slowly and then only in response to alterations in the balance of socioeconomic forces in the larger society.

Forms of Power and the Urban Policy Process

For present purposes, we may distinguish two interest-based interpretations of the urban policy process in the United States: one that emphasizes determinist explanations of policy behaviors; the other that reflects political indeterminacy. Included among the first kind are those approaches based on Marxist analyses of the disposition of economic forces in society. Whether framed in Marxist or in neo-Marxist terms—the latter recognizing a degree of autonomy for institutions of the state—the thrust of such approaches is that public policies and the specific programs derived from them substantially reflect the character of class relations in society.[25] For some neo-Marxist writers, however, considerable room remains for translating general economic forces into governmental actions. Just how much room is problematic. Indeed, of late, some neo-Marxists have begun to describe a kind of political indeterminancy that might warrant characterizing them as neopluralists.

In contrast to the pluralists who held that policies, programs, and specific projects emerged from interactions among elites and interested publics, the neo-pluralists proceed on the assumption that policy making is substantially shaped by political elites.[26] These elites have some discretion in responding to the demands of other elites, but are likely to accord only limited attention to the desires of the public.[27] While political elites reflect the class currents dominant in their society, they also have independent interests that they serve through the political process.

Two types of neopluralist models may be identified in recent urban policy analyses: the policy subgovernment and the political entrepreneurial approaches. The first focuses on the existence of a coalition of interest groups that take part in program development and implementation.[28] In housing and community development, such coalitions include the construction and lending industries, politicians who have chosen to take an interest in this policy sector including members of relevant committees in Congress, and bureaucratic specialists, notably decision makers in HUD and related state and local government agencies.

These interests would be expected to participate in the formulation of new programs or in the alteration of existing ones. They would also have a voice in the translation of legislative designs into administrative procedures. While the subgovernment incorporates economic interests, its importance also lies in its influence over organizational and political resources.

A related but more specifically politician-centered approach is represented by the political entrepreneurial model. The concept of politician-centered policy making is not, of course, new. Indeed, the model developed twenty-five years ago by Robert Dahl in his theory of pluralism focused on an "executive-centered coalition" led by the mayor of New Haven, Richard C. Lee. Similarly, Edward C. Banfield's description of Chicago politics in the same era centered on the critical role played by Mayor Richard C. Daley, though given the Daley style, the mayor's contribution to the local policy process was perhaps less entrepreneurial than seigneurial.[29] Nonetheless, in the 1960s, students of federal programs and urban politics identified the emergence of what later came to be called "growth machines" or local "progrowth coalitions" in which political leadership played a critical independent role.[30]

While it is possible to treat local decision making as primarily a product of local forces, the growth of intergovernmental program relations since the 1960s and the involvement of private market forces tied only tentatively to territory suggests the importance of viewing urban programs from a national and intergovernmental perspective.

Intergovernmental Urban Policy Coalitions

Extending neopluralist arguments to the national level, John H. Mollenkopf has described the New Deal coalition put together by Franklin D. Roosevelt largely in terms of political entrepreneurship.[31] Mollenkopf's argument is that the intergovernmental coalition assembled by Roosevelt was held together by a combination of pork barrel and electoral incentives that served the political interests of coalition partners for the next forty years.[32]

Mollenkopf argues that this political arrangement worked well during the Depression, when forces resistant to government intervention were weak. With the return of economic prosperity following World War II, the dominant electoral coalition was beset increasingly by internal contradictions that led eventually to the defection of white working-class and lower-middle-class segments of the population. Efforts to renew the Democratic electoral coalition during the Kennedy–Johnson years by extending participatory opportunities to previously non-mobilized minorities were only temporarily successful, for they exacerbated local and intergovernmental conflicts.[33]

This is not the place to trace the decline of the New Deal coalition, particularly since Mollenkopf undertakes that task in some detail. What he essentially argues is that a new progrowth intergovernmental coalition especially well-represented in the more conservative sections of the nation—suburbia and the Sunbelt—and drawing support from the more conservative elements of the Republican party, emerged during the 1960s to counter the political and material interests of the dominant Democratic coalition, though the full impact of these forces was felt only with the election of Ronald Reagan.

Mollenkopf associates the behavior of national and local political entrepreneurs with intergovernmentally linked program coalitions that brought together ideologically diverse interests in pursuit of political and economic benefits. He illustrates the argument with cases drawn from the Boston and San Francisco urban renewal experiences. Thus, while the urban renewal program was created during the presidency of Harry S. Truman as a product of compromises among liberal and conservative interests, it was not fully implemented until modifications were introduced in 1954 that shifted the program away from "a nationally directed program focusing on housing to a locally-directed program which allowed downtown businesses, developers, and their political allies, who had little interest in housing, to use federal power to advance their own ends."[34]

The urban renewal program was then seized upon in the late 1950s by local progrowth coalitions—some of which were dominated as in Boston and San Francisco by political entrepreneurs including bureaucratic politicians like Edward J. Logue and M. Justin Herman.[35] As urban renewal projects proceeded, however, they created strains within the Democratic electoral base; minorities and neighborhood interests, in particular, reacted strongly to policies of wholesale clearance and consequent displacement, thereby contributing to the turbulent urban politics of the 1960s.

The Johnson administration, Mollenkopf argues, attempted to expand its coalitional base both by extending opportunities for program participation to some of those aggrieved with local progrowth coalitions and by attempting to buy the support of construction and other business interests through various subsidy programs. Such efforts did not effectively restore the support of those interests to a New Deal-style coalition. Instead, political and economic power continued to move to the suburbs and to the Sunbelt which were little concerned with integrating the interests of minorities and urban neighborhoods into their growth coalitions.

The Carter administration failed to reverse this process. Summarizing those failures, Mollenkopf writes:

At heart, the traditional liberal approach rests on subsidies to the agency administrators, local elected officials, developers and their allies who benefit directly from the development process. It thus tends to ignore the accountability of these development interests to the neighborhoods, underemployed minority groups, or the public interest as a whole, who are supposed to benefit from the growth. . . .

The Carter administration's version of tradition liberalism . . . failed because it lacked a political strategy. The Carter programs offered nothing designed to mobilize such rising metropolitan electoral constituencies as central-city young professionals or the suburban, unionized labor force. Nor did Carter attempt to appeal to the minority groups living in newer cities like those in the Southwest who have not yet been mobilized as a force in urban politics. . . . [36]

In sum, Mollenkopf suggests that "rather than modernizing the local political coalitions on which national Democratic majorities must rest, the 'new partnership' [espoused by the Carter administration] played to the same old crowd."[37]

These judgments seem harsh, though Mollenkopf's estimation of the result may be correct. Mollenkopf ignores the struggles that went on in the Carter administration to reach those constituencies he identifies. As he indicates, the baggage from past program coalitions proved to be a major encumbrance that Carter administration policy makers were unable to overcome. It is in this light that the problems experienced by the NSA program may prove to be particularly illuminating.

PHASES IN THE NSA POLICY PROCESS

One way many studies of the policy process have proceeded is through the specification of the "passages" from policy to program to project. I have followed that procedure in presenting the materials from the research reported here. Thus, in chapter 2, we will introduce the agenda setting process that led to the creation of the NSA program.[38] We review the programmatic history and political environment that shaped the NSA program design. In regard to the former, we identify earlier assisted housing, housing rehabilitation, community development, and neighborhood revitalization programs that contributed to the formulation of the Section 8 NSA program. That examination is followed by an exploration of more proximate political factors that shaped the program.

While certain programmatic and political goals accounted for the creation of the NSA program, they did not prescribe the form that the program took. Details of program design are discussed in chapter 3. For reasons indicated there, that phase of program development was peculiarly insulated from intergovernmental participation. The result was a design that was unusually clear in its specification of preferred projects but weak in its political base.

Once the program design was developed within HUD, it became necessary to convert that design into an implementable program. The attendant conversion process—the translation of general program definitions into specific projects— is part of what Paul Berman has called the "macro-implementation" process.[39] Chapters 4 and 5 deal with different aspects of that process. The former examines a federal dimension by outlining the efforts made by HUD to promote local participation in the NSA program and to develop procedures for dealing with plans for participation submitted by localities. Chapter 5 treats the macro-implementation problem from the local viewpoint as local governments or their agents sought to implement the program in ways that would meet their particular needs.

Berman also writes of "micro-implementation" which involves a second conversion process. In that case what is at issue is the conversion of a local plan of action into "do-able" projects that can be carried out under the auspices of designated local agencies. As Berman argues:

Implementing national policy . . . consists of not one but two classes of problems. The federal government must execute its policy so as to influence local delivery organizations to behave in desired ways; we call this the *macro-implementation* problem. In response to federal actions, the local organizations have to devise and carry out their own internal policies; we call this the *micro-implementation* problem.[40]

It is not clear whether Berman is assuming too much about the degree to which national programs should be understood in federally controlled terms rather than in terms of intergovernmental bargaining or independent local decision-making processes. Yet such matters are at the heart of chapters 6–8, which illustrate some of the problems local actors experienced in the course of micro-implementation. Chapter 6 highlights the diverse ways political and administrative arrangements were worked out within local jurisdictions in order to enhance the prospect for implementation.

In contrast, chapter 7 emphasizes certain difficulties that actors from outside the local government (including HUD officials) set in the way of project implementation. As part of that chapter, we describe efforts localities made to overcome those obstacles. Chapter 8 then identifies strategies that went into realizing projects that overcame barriers to micro-implementation.

Although the NSA program was an early target of the Reagan administration's cutback policies, project monitoring and program evaluation activities continued until the formal conclusion of the program in 1983. Consistent with an effort to understand the achievements and weaknesses of the NSA approach, in chapter 9 we undertake what might be termed a macro-evaluation of the NSA program, drawing on materials from a formal evaluation of the program initiated by HUD during the Carter years as well as on materials collected for the present study. In chapter 10, we take a more disaggregated view of NSA experiences—what might be characterized as micro-evaluations of particular local programs.

Finally, in chapter 11 we conclude with a reconsideration of the NSA program in informing our understanding of the urban policy process and the condition of intergovernmental relations during the period of this study. We also touch briefly on several subsidiary themes related to issues of housing and community development policy.

NOTES

1. On the original understandings associated with American federalism, see Rozann Rothman, "The Ambiguity of American Federal Theory," *Publius* 8 (Summer 1978), 103–22; and Herbert F. Storing, *What the Anti-Federalists Were For* (Chicago: University of Chicago Press, 1981). For a historical overview of the experience with "dual federalism," see David B. Walker, *Toward a Functioning Federalism* (Cambridge, Mass.: Winthrop, 1981), esp. 46–65.

2. See, for example, the contributions to Robert B. Hawkins, ed., *American Federalism* (San Francisco: Institute for Contemporary Studies, 1982).

3. Daniel J. Elazar, *The American Partnership* (Chicago: University of Chicago Press, 1962).

4. Morton Grodzins, *The American System* (Chicago: Rand-McNally, 1966). See also Walker, *Toward a Functioning Federalism*, 65–95.

5. See the fears expressed, for example, by Daniel J. Elazar in the various editions of his *American Federalism: A View from the States*, including the 3d ed. (New York: Harper and Row, 1984).

6. See Samuel H. Beer, "The Modernization of American Federalism," *Publius* 3 (Fall 1973), 49–95; and Michael D. Reagan and John G. Sanzone, *The New Federalism*, 2d ed. (New York: Oxford University Press, 1981).

7. See Daniel J. Elazar, "Federalism vs. Decentralization," *Publius* 6 (Fall 1976), 9–19; and his *American Federalism*.

8. In addition to Elazar, see William Hudson, "The Federal Aid Crutch," *The Urban Interest* 2 (Spring 1980), 34–44.

9. For reviews of judicial interventions in areas of intergovernmental conflict, see A. E. Dick Howard, "Judicial Federalism: The States and the Supreme Court," in Hawkins, *American Federalism*, 215–37; and Walker, *Toward a Functioning Federalism*, 135–57. Most recently, see the controversy surrounding *Garcia v. San Antonio Metropolitan Transit Authority* (1985). This Supreme Court decision removed certain constitutional protections for state and local autonomy and left to the political process responsibility for maintaining subnational autonomy. See Paul J. Hartman and Thomas R. McCoy, "Garcia: The Latest Retreat on the States' Rights' Front," and A. E. Dick Howard, "Garcia: Federalism's Principles Forgotten," *Intergovernmental Perspective* 11 (Spring–Summer 1985), 8–14.

10. For the original formulation of the typology from which the notion of "distributive" policy was derived, see Theodore J. Lowi, "American Business, Public Policy, Case Studies and Political Theory," *World Politics* 16 (July 1964), 677–715. For a recent reformulation of the concept, see Paul E. Peterson, Barry G. Rabe, and Kenneth K. Wong, *When Federalism Works* (Washington, D.C.: Brookings Institution, 1986).

11. Beer, "Modernization of American Federalism", 59. Also see David Stockman, "The Social Pork Barrel," *The Public Interest* 39 (Spring 1975), 3–30.

12. See Eugene Bardach, *The Implementation Game* (Cambridge, Mass.: MIT Press, 1977); Helen Ingram, "Policy Implementation Through Bargaining," *Public Policy* 25 (Fall 1973), 499–526; and, Jeffrey L. Pressman, *Federal Programs and City Politics* (Berkeley, Calif.: University of California Press, 1975).

13. Donald B. Rosenthal, "Bargaining Analysis in Intergovernmental Relations," *Publius* 10 (Summer 1980), 5–44.

14. Elazar has hesitated since the 1960s to treat "sharing" as a core descriptive model for IGR, though it still occasionally appears in his writing. In the most recent edition of *American Federalism*, for example, he strikes an uneasy balance between the sharing and bargaining models in describing the present situation while expressing fears about continuing tendencies toward federal control.

15. Deil S. Wright, *Understanding Intergovernmental Relations*, 2d ed. (Monterey, Calif.: Brooks-Cole, 1982), esp. 63–65.

16. At the same time, they may disagree about the degree to which the tendency has manifested itself and whether it is reversible. For the most extreme perspective on this, see the comments of W. S. Moore, "A Pessimistic Note," in Hawkins, *American Federalism*, 239–43. For a different approach that supports notions of increasing control

of state and local behaviors by the federal government, see Catherine Lovell and Charles Tobin, "The Mandate Issue," *Public Administration Review* 41 (May–June 1981), 318–31.

17. Raymond Rosenfeld, "Who Benefits and Who Decides? The Uses of Community Development Block Grants," in *Urban Revitalization*, edited by Donald B. Rosenthal (Beverly Hills, Calif.: Sage, 1980), 214.

18. Representative of the different understandings of what the poverty program was intended to do and what it actually achieved are the following: J. David Greenstone and Paul Peterson, *Race and Authority in Urban Politics* (New York: Russell Sage, 1973); Ira Katznelson, *City Trenches* (Chicago: University of Chicago Press, 1981); Peter Marris and Martin Rein, *Dilemmas of Social Reform* (New York: Atherton, 1969); Daniel P. Moynihan, *Maximum Feasible Misunderstanding* (New York: Free Press, 1969); Francis Fox Piven and Richard Cloward, *Regulating the Poor* (New York: Vintage, 1971); John Strange, "Community Action in North Carolina: Maximum Feasible Misunderstanding? Mistake? or Magic Formula?" *Publius* 2 (Fall 1972), 51–73; and James L. Sundquist, *Making Federalism Work* (Washington, D. C.: Brookings Institution, 1969).

19. R. Allen Hays, *The Federal Government and Urban Housing* (Albany: State University of New York Press, 1985).

20. Ibid., 3.

21. Ibid., 5.

22. Ibid., 4.

23. Ibid., 21.

24. Ibid., 22.

25. See for example, Katznelson, *City Trenches*; Michael P. Smith (ed.), *Cities in Transformation* (Beverly Hills, Calif.: Sage, 1984); and, William K. Tabb and Larry Sawers (eds.) *Marxism and the Metropolis* (New York: Oxford University Press, 1978).

26. For example, see Robert A. Dahl, *Who Governs?* (New Haven, Conn.: Yale University Press, 1961); and Raymond Wolfinger, *The Politics of Progress* (Englewood Cliffs, N.J.: Prentice-Hall, 1974).

27. It is difficult to draw a line between those I have characterized as neo-Marxists and neopluralists, particularly since the same writers on different occasions appear to emphasize one or the other perspective. Nonetheless, in the latter category, I would place the works of Susan S. Fainstein, Norman I. Fainstein, and contributors to their recent *Restructuring the City* (New York: Longman, 1983). See also Clarence N. Stone, "Systemic Power in Community Decision Making," *American Political Science Review* 74 (December 1980), 978–90.

28. On the theory and practice of policy subgovernments, see Donald C. Baumer and Carol E. Van Horn, *The Politics of Unemployment* (Washington, D.C.: Congressional Quarterly Press, 1985); on the related concepts of "iron triangles" see Harold Seidman, *Politics, Position and Power*, 3d ed. (New York: Oxford University Press, 1980).

29. Edward C. Banfield, *Political Influence* (New York: Free Press, 1961).

30. See, in particular, Robert Salisbury, "Urban Politics: The New Convergence of Power," *Journal of Politics* 26 (November 1964), 775–97. On "growth machines," see Harvey Molotch, "The City as a Growth Machine," *American Journal of Sociology* 74 (September 1976), 309–32; for local progrowth coalitions, see John H. Mollenkopf, *The Contested City* (Princeton, N.J.: Princeton University Press, 1983).

31. For a recent neo-Marxist critique of the Mollenkopf approach, see Joe R. Feagin,

"The Corporate Center Strategy," *Urban Affairs Quarterly* 21 (June 1986), esp. 619–21.

32. To the extent that he highlights issues related to the urban base of the national coalition created by the New Deal, Mollenkopf understates the role that rural interests played in generating a series of programs to serve the needs of the South and Southwest. While the latter programs strengthened the national Democratic coalition at the time, Mollenkopf argues that they ultimately contributed to the decline of the coalition after the 1950s.

33. See Piven and Cloward, *Regulating the Poor*.

34. Mollenkopf, *Contested City*, 117.

35. An even stronger example of this genus was Robert Moses. See Robert A. Caro, *The Power Broker* (New York: Alfred A. Knopf, 1974).

36. Mollenkopf, *Contested City*, 280.

37. Ibid., 281.

38. On agenda setting, see, Roger W. Cobb and Charles D. Elder, *Participation in American Politics: The Dynamics of Agenda Building*, 2d ed. (Baltimore: Johns Hopkins University Press, 1983).

39. Paul Berman, "The Study of Macro- and Micro-Implementation," *Public Policy* 26 (Spring 1978), 157–84.

40. Ibid., 164. Characteristically, Berman's treatment of the policy process blurs distinctions among "policies," "programs," and "projects" of the kind we highlight in this study.

2

CREATING THE CONDITIONS FOR PROGRAM MAKING

For almost fifty years, the national government has made resources available to localities in support of two major policy goals: (1) the improvement of housing opportunities for a limited number of low- and moderate-income households; and (2) the redevelopment of urban areas. The first goal was pursued initially through the construction of public housing and, later, through rental and home ownership subsidy programs. The second goal was one of the original goals of the urban renewal program and, more recently, of programs to revitalize neighborhoods. Rather than harnessing these two policy goals to the same program instrument, however, the Department of Housing and Urban Development (HUD) and the various administrative entities that preceded its creation in 1965, pursued the two goals in relative isolation.

The creation of the Section 8 Neighborhood Strategy Area (NSA) Program in 1978 reflected dissatisfaction with this separation. Equally important, it was designed both as an intellectually coherent response to certain deficiencies in prior assisted housing and community development programs and as an opportunity to improve the residential environments of low- and moderate-income households.

This chapter identifies factors that shaped the creation of the NSA program. Those factors included experiences with existing housing and community development programs as well as more immediate socioeconomic and political considerations.

THE PROGRAM ENVIRONMENT

The Evolution of Assisted Housing Programs

The public housing program resulting from the landmark National Housing Act of 1937 provided housing opportunities to low-income households in units that met prevailing construction standards. Rather than linking those efforts to improvements in existing neighborhoods, many structures were built as free-standing entities. Many of the social problems found in the slums they were intended to replace carried over to such housing "projects." A few projects became neighborhoods in their own right—particularly those that involved low-rise construction—but in others, issues such as personal safety and privacy gave that form of housing a poor reputation.[1]

In reaction to what were judged to be the mistakes of public housing, the federal government devised a series of programs beginning in the early 1960s intended either to subsidize low-income tenants directly through rents, or, more commonly, indirectly through the provision of financial assistance to private developers or nonprofit organizations willing to undertake construction or re-habilitation of units for eligible low- and moderate-income households.

Thus, the Kennedy administration initiated the 221 (d)(3) program which encouraged the construction of rental housing by providing below-market–interest rate subsidies to nonprofit development organizations. However, as one writer remarked:

Nonprofit groups—churches, fraternal societies, and ad hoc civic committees—had the strength of charitable motivation. But they were amateurs. They knew little about home building, mortgage finance, FHA [Federal Housing Administration] procedures, and economic realities; they knew little about how to manage a rental housing project. On the other hand, the professional home builder knew the complexities of building and financing, but his experience and his commercial motivations were not always compatible with the social purposes of the program. He knew little about managing housing for this type of tenant.[2]

In 1968, the Johnson administration introduced two programs: the Section 235 program, designed to assist low- and moderate-income (LMI) families in purchasing new or existing houses; and the 236 program, an effort to create rental units by providing subsidies to developers to support mortgage loans. Regarding the former program, Roger Starr notes:

Builders who would buy up older buildings and remodel them in a very sketchy way could make the plea to the local FHA office that the government was saving the cost of subsidization by approving mortgage insurance on the properties. Because the federal government in 1970 and 1971 was placing great emphasis on the brute number of housing starts, some FHA employees were able to convince themselves that in bending property standards . . . they were actually helping to support the national economy and the administration's housing goals. In Detroit and in Nassau County, New York, major scandals broke out in the wake of this pressure. . . . Buildings started to deteriorate rapidly, thanks to inadequate reconditioning. Investigation revealed that the buildings had been greatly overappraised by officials who had been paid to make mistakes.[3]

The scandals were associated principally with the mishandling of mortgage insurance by HUD personnel rather than with the inherent logic of the program.

The record under the Section 236 program was not nearly so bad. Nevertheless, these experiences made the FHA extremely wary of program approaches that involved providing mortgage insurance for structures proposed for rehabilitation.

Innovations introduced by the Johnson administration subsidized rents in privately owned units of LMI tenants. Beginning in 1965, the Section 23 program placed eligible tenants in older residential structures as well as in newer buildings. The program was gradually expanded to include newly constructed housing. Section 23 established a model for making rental housing available to LMI households by using the private construction and rental market. While this may have contributed to enhancing support within the private rental market for the program, it weakened the capacity of public sector agencies like public housing authorities to act as major vehicles for the delivery of assisted housing services.

The Section 23 approach was later expanded through the Section 8 program which became a central feature of the Housing and Community Development Act of 1974. Section 8 subsidies were designed to generate property owner interest in providing rental opportunities to LMI households by guaranteeing owners payments at levels consistent with the cost of standard rental units in the vicinity—"fair market rents" (FMRs). At the same time, eligible households were assured that they would be required to pay no more than 25 percent of their income toward rent. HUD would make up any difference between that figure and the FMR.[4] Not only would such an approach leave much of the operational responsibility for the construction and management of housing units in private hands—consistent with the private-market orientation of the Nixon–Ford administration—but it was also expected to promote the "deconcentration" of LMI households, thus contributing to the breakup of low-income and minority "ghettoes."

At the outset of the Section 8 program, there were three components: (1) direct subsidization of the rents of LMI households in standard dwelling units in buildings where the household already resided or to which it moved (the Existing Housing Program); (2) assurances of rental subsidies to developers who undertook the construction of new residential structures in which some or all of the units were made available to LMI households (the New Construction Program); and (3) the Substantial Rehabilitation Program, which would provide rental assistance to tenants in deteriorated structures whose owners brought those structures up to HUD-approved standards.[5]

In the last two programs, not only did HUD provide guaranteed rents at levels that some critics regarded as excessively favorable to private interests, but in some cases it also made mortgage insurance available to support private loans when lenders might otherwise have been reluctant to invest in the construction or rehabilitation of properties in central cities. Financing for these projects might also come from private lenders without federal insurance (though this was rare) or through public organizations including state housing finance and development agencies which were becoming increasingly active in the housing field in the 1970s.[6]

While the Existing Housing Program was well received because it was easily adaptable to a variety of local situations, and the New Construction Program provided a popular vehicle for spurring construction (especially for the elderly and handicapped), activity under the Substantial Rehabilitation (Sub Rehab) Program through 1976 was limited. The reasons for this are in dispute. Some observers suggest that the rental subsidy was not sufficiently attractive, despite its apparent generosity, because of delays and complexities associated with HUD procedures for processing applications for subsidies and mortgage insurance; others stressed the problems inherent in doing rehabilitation in central cities.

In regard to the last point, the tasks associated with rehabilitation are complex and the probability of success considerably lower than would be the case for new construction undertaken in an undeveloped suburban area or on a vacant central city site. An account of one early program effort HUD made to encourage rehabilitation highlights such problems:

Many more parties are involved in rehabilitation than in new construction of a similar scale. . . . Community complaints and problems of relocation can cause disastrous delays to a project. . . . Rehabilitation takes place usually in an inner-city neighborhood. Not only are there risks of vandalism, but also movement of materials is more difficult, storage of materials becomes a problem, and generally the cramped conditions preclude the efficiency of an open and new construction site. Because of the nature of the process, work tasks are more vague and scheduling less clearcut in rehabilitation. The repetition of tasks and the ability to schedule work activities accurately is less complex with residential new construction. . . . Constant on-site supervision and direction is required. . . . Materials of differing conditions and qualities must be handled. Building elements have to be fitted together and the movement of manpower and materials is involved and time consuming.[7]

Thus, by 15 July 1977, when planning for the NSA program got underway, only 8,272 units of Section 8 Sub Rehab housing were in the process of rehabilitation or were already completed.[8] One HUD official described the level of activity up to August 1977 in the following terms:

26 cities have accounted for 73 percent of all insured rehabilitation loans. The implications for all aspects of the Section 8 Substantial Rehabilitation Program, including . . . [the Neighborhood Strategy Area Program] are serious. Unless interest in rehabilitation becomes more widespread, it appears that it will be impossible to meet the FY [Fiscal Year] 1978 goal of 21,000 Section 8 Substantial Rehab units.[9]

These comments are especially interesting for two reasons. First, despite the poor performance record of Sub Rehab, a target figure of twenty one thousand units had been set by the Carter administration; this reflected a desire to move forward vigorously. Second, that desire stimulated the search for an approach that would increase the use of those resources.

The Evolution of Community Development Programs

While the realm of housing programs is relatively distinct, the scope of community development is considerably less clear-cut. Perhaps the most common thread is that such programs have sought to assist in the revitalization of urban areas and to improve the quality of life for persons living in them. At the same time, housing and construction-oriented community development programs have included among their less explicit goals: (1) the use of construction as a countercyclical instrument for spurring the national economy; (2) meeting the needs of the construction industry (both private developers and construction unions) by allowing them to play a significant role in setting many of the standards that have contributed to the high costs of publicly assisted construction; and (3) providing a major voice to lending institutions and other financial interests in defining how financial benefits should flow to public investment programs.[10]

The urban renewal program typifies a program with mixed policy motives. Emerging in 1949 as a compromise between liberal and conservative interests, it was seen by liberal supporters as a method for fighting slums and blight through acquisition, clearance, and the construction of new residential structures.[11] Housing opportunities would be provided to households displaced by such activities. That goal gave way after 1954, however, to an emphasis on profit making through nonresidential redevelopment; residential development became more concerned with creating market-rate residential opportunities for middle-income households than supplying housing to LMI populations.

There were numerous attacks on the program before its demise in 1974, particularly because of its displacement effects on poor people and racial minorities.[12,13] There is some evidence that the program began in the mid-1960s to put more of an emphasis on providing housing to LMI persons. Greater attention was also given to the rehabilitation of existing structures rather than clearance for new construction.[14] But it was too late.

One reaction to the "bricks-and-mortar" emphasis of urban renewal was the Model Cities Program designed in 1966 to target federal resources to selected neighborhoods in which LMI populations were predominant. As Frieden and Kaplan observe:

Two distinct points of view about the defects in federal urban policies shaped the initial conception of the Model Cities Program. The first stressed the growing difficulty of coordinating and managing the rapidly growing number of federal aid programs for the cities; the second focused on the neglect of social concerns in urban renewal and its failure to improve living conditions for the poor and for minority groups. Different people advanced these two viewpoints, basing them on different sets of values and concerns and on different political priorities.[15]

The implementation achieved during the program's troubled history, however, was limited more to the expansion of social services than to improving the physical environment or the residential units of persons living in targeted neighborhoods.[16]

As Frieden and Kaplan indicate, if some of those who designed the Model Cities Program were concerned about meeting the needs of minorities and LMI households, others were more interested in dealing with a set of managerial concerns about the most effective instrumentalities for delivering urban programs. The support of progrowth coalitions (including local government agencies that designed and implemented project plans) was limited. At the same time, greater support among them for urban renewal was unsuccessful in preserving that program in the face of the Nixon administration's effort to consolidate community development grants. The result was the melding in 1974 of seven community development programs (including urban renewal and Model Cities) into the Community Development Block Grant (CDBG).

Part of the motivation behind this effort was to decentralize decision-making responsibilities to general purpose local governments from the national government rather than siphoning funds to special interest local bureaucracies like urban renewal agencies. Furthermore, larger jurisdictions would receive their grants on an "entitlement" basis and would then apply them to locally preferred purposes rather than operating according to the stricter guidelines that characterized previous federal grants.[17] To a significant degree, CDBG was intended to strengthen general purpose local governments both at the expense of the federal bureaucracy and in relation to other actors in local progrowth coalitions. How successfully it achieved the latter purpose is problematic, since localities varied in the extent to which the exercise of greater discretion by mayors and councils shifted the actual balance of influence over public investment decisions away from private interests.[18]

Many local governments responded to the opportunities provided by CDBG by putting their funds into such projects as resurfacing streets, upgrading parks and play areas, and renovating sewers. As early as 1976, housing rehabilitation emerged as one of the leading uses of CDBG but mainly in the form of grants or subsidized loans to home owners. That use continued to increase over the following years.[19] Little use was made of CDBG as a vehicle for promoting the rehabilitation of rental units.

There was concern from the outset of planning for CDBG among liberal interest groups that program resources would not be targeted sufficiently to benefiting LMI populations as opposed to assisting in the eradication of slums and blight even though Congress identified these as the two principal goals of the program. Indeed, the relative weights to be assigned to the two goals remained a matter of dispute in later years.[20]

Efforts by the Ford administration to leave to local governments major decisions about the allocation of resources within their jurisdictions were modified by the Carter administration. The latter feared that local governments might overrespond to those interests that had the most political "clout"—downtown in relation to neighborhoods; better organized (i.e., middle-income) neighborhoods rather than lower-income ones.[21] As a result, an early action of the Carter administration required local recipients of CDBG funds to concentrate a substantial portion of their grants in LMI areas designated as Community Development Neighborhood Strategy Areas.[22]

While the 1974 act sought to make local governments more responsible for setting agendas for community development activities, and also provided a mechanism for subsidizing LMI tenants through Section 8, efforts to integrate the two sets of activities were more a matter of form than substance. The principal formal means provided in the act was the Housing Assistance Plan mandated for entitlement communities. In these plans, localities were expected to identify the needs of their populations for assisted housing and how those needs were to be met through the use of Section 8 and related housing program resources.[23] Aside from serving as a basis for determining aggregate demand for assisted housing among entitlement communities, only a limited linkage was ever established between aggregation of these "wish lists" and the decisions made within HUD about allocating housing resources to particular neighborhoods.

Instead, HUD adopted an approach to the allocation of New Construction and Sub Rehab resources under Section 8 that ran counter to the decentralization principle. Under that approach, HUD allocated resources to HUD field offices on what was termed a "fair share" basis for distribution within designated "allocation areas"—areas of upwards of 150,000 population. Developers were then required to take the initiative in submitting plans for specific projects to HUD field offices in response to notices of fund availability.[24]

This approach largely bypassed the interests local governments or target neighborhoods might have had in participating in project designs. Critics argued that it largely reaffirmed a "project mentality" at HUD and among developers. The latter might be attracted to program participation because of the profit-making incentives provided by the federal government, but this system would allow them to ignore the impacts of their projects on affected neighborhoods.[25]

Nonetheless, this approach was actually regarded as an improvement over previous practices in which construction programs had been driven even more by the preferences of developers. One HUD informant argued that the shift to a "fair share" approach represented a "dramatic change" from earlier programs "in which many communities did not get any or many units because developers didn't want to go there." At least, after 1974, "projects were funded on an 'over-the-counter' or 'first-come, first-served' basis" within allocation areas. While this assured more dispersion of housing resources and also provided opportunities for central city neighborhoods to benefit from federal construction and rehabilitation funds, it still placed the initiative for projects in the hands of private developers.[26]

Putting an Emphasis on Rehabilitation

By the time of the Carter administration, housing and community development activities had become concerned increasingly with the conservation of existing structures relative to clearance. Even under urban renewal, there had been the glimmerings of such an emphasis under the Johnson administration's Neighborhood Development Program.[27]

The involvement of the federal government in promoting residential rehabilitation was not a novel concept. As early as Title I of the 1934 Housing Act, the federal government had encouraged maintenance of the existing housing stock by providing low-interest loans to owners of single-family homes. That program continued to be available in the 1970s, although it was supplanted largely by private consumer credit.[28]

In addition to Title I, assistance to owner-occupants had been a major component of government housing policy since the 1930s, mainly in the form of mortgage interest deductions on income taxes and insurance programs administered by the FHA since 1934 and the Veterans Administration since World War II.[29] For the most part, these agencies' activities stimulated the construction of single-family homes in suburban areas or in newly developed sections of central cities rather than rehabilitation.

Rehabilitation financing was particularly hard to get for multifamily structures since such structures were likely to be located in neighborhoods that were regarded by lending institutions as poor risks. HUD and its bureaucratic forebears occasionally attempted to intervene by providing insurance (as in the Section 235 program) or construction subsidies but with limited impact. Thus, one estimate of total units insured by HUD up to 1977 reported that only 5.8 percent involved rehabilitation.[30] While such figures reflected, in part, the biases of the federal government against subsidizing the redevelopment of rental housing, they also indicated the difficulties involved in attracting builders and investors to central city rehabilitation.

Despite these drawbacks, HUD occasionally attempted to encourage rehabilitation in multifamily structures. In the 1960s, several demonstration programs were undertaken. One in New York City involved a highly publicized effort at "Instant Rehab" that experimented with lowering unitized bathrooms and kitchens through holes in the roofs of high-rise buildings. That experiment proved to be extremely costly and was not pursued.[31]

HUD later provided a special allocation of below-market interest rate subsidies to Pittsburgh's ACTION Housing, Inc., which coordinated the various activities necessary to make rehabilitation in multifamily structures work: selection of neighborhoods; acquisition of property; developing and funding of nonprofit sponsors; obtaining finance; dealing with the community; supervising construction; and administering relocation. Production under that program was limited.[32]

HUD also financed a demonstration program in Boston in 1967 to promote rapid rehabilitation of 2,000 housing units in 101 buildings in the Roxbury–Dorchester area. Originally seen as a way to encourage the development of a rehabilitation industry by maximizing contractor involvement, only 5 developers participated in the program and one of these assumed responsibility for approximately 55 percent of the total units. An evaluation of that effort showed that the program was unusually successful in meeting production goals: 1,400 units were rehabilitated in less than 10 months. Nevertheless, that study emphasized some of the problems associated with the program:

Critics have judged that the social cost and neighborhood resentment was too high a price to pay for more standard housing—there was lack of community involvement, displacement, and lack of participation in the construction by the black community. The quality of workmanship was also highly criticized.[33]

Despite the limited achievements of these ventures, Nixon's first HUD Secretary, George Romney, was convinced that techniques for mass production could be applied to housing rehabilitation. As a result, in 1969, HUD initiated Project Rehab which sought to encourage large-scale rehabilitation in fourteen cities; that number later was increased to twenty-six. The department was expected to work with large firms that would undertake the rehabilitation of inner-city multifamily structures. The agency anticipated that thirty seven thousand units would be rehabilitated in the first two years of the program. According to a subsequent program evaluation, the most that may be credited to Project Rehab by the time of its termination (around 1971–1972) was ten–fifteen thousand units.[34]

Under the program, HUD's central office was expected to provide technical assistance both to its own field staff and to developers, or to local governments or nonprofit organizations where the latter were involved. The formal program evaluation done by Arthur D. Little in 1971 identified reasons why only eight cities had any rehabilitation underway twenty months after the program's start. Many failures were attributed to confusions, slippages, and inadequacies in the organization of both HUD's central office and its field staff. Others had to do with problems that developed in trying to elicit and then coordinate commitments from builders, contractors, local governments, citizen groups, and nonprofit organizations. By the time the evaluation was received and fully digested at HUD in mid–1971, the program was being phased out.

Another ill-fated venture was the Demonstration Rehabilitation (Demo Rehab) Program initiated by the Ford administration in mid–1976 under which the National Housing Rehabilitation Association—the elite association of rehabilitation developers—reached an agreement with seven major construction unions to develop special wage rates and conditions for a set of rehabilitation projects. Cities were then invited to submit project proposals that would include a labor agreement and a strategy for rehabilitation of an area within the city. The agreement reached among national organizations broke down, however, during conversion into local project designs. A variety of issues were involved, including the discovery by union locals that there were no guarantees under the national agreement that union workers would be employed on projects whatever the wage rates agreed upon.

As a result of conflicts over the program, the first Carter-appointed HUD

Secretary, Patricia R. Harris, announced on 20 July 1977, that Demo Rehab would be phased out in those sixteen cities where agreements had already been signed and would not be pursued elsewhere. In her announcement, she indicated that the program would be replaced by another—what was to become the Section 8 NSA program. Consequently, in some places where contracts had been signed (Hoboken, New Jersey; Washington Heights in New York City; Lowell and Lynn, Massachusetts), the Demo Rehab Program was still in the process of being implemented even as plans for Section 8 NSAs in the same neighborhoods were being developed and carried out.

In addition to these direct programmatic stimuli, rehabilitation was promoted increasingly during the 1970s through provisions of the tax code. In particular, the Tax Reform Act of 1969 introduced Section 167(k) which provided incentives to investors to finance rehabilitation in targeted redevelopment areas. The scope of tax benefits was enhanced when structures also qualified for designation as historic places.[35]

A New Concern with Neighborhoods

Despite bureaucratic separation among programs, HUD critics were well aware of the connection between housing and neighborhood redevelopment. As Alvin Schorr noted:

The fate of a building depends upon the fate of a neighborhood—whether it has police and sanitation services, is relatively free of crime and other adverse conditions, and has jobs or convenient transportation. Any number of demonstration buildings in which heavy investment was made have gone down because neighborhood circumstances overwhelmed them.[36]

Despite the reasonableness of such comments, federally funded programs such as urban renewal and highways initially paid little attention to the neighborhood impacts of their projects. Nor did the federal government do much to reverse the course of disinvestment eating away at the foundations of many neighborhoods. Neighborhood-based efforts to fight federally sponsored redevelopment projects were accorded procedural recognition in the 1960s in the form of enhanced participatory rights for residents of affected neighborhoods, but such federal requirements were often treated grudgingly by local agencies.

Probably more important in gaining attention for neighborhoods was the emergence of organizations representing neighborhood interests—some based in particular neighborhoods, others serving broader constituencies. Some groups adopted the militant posture of Saul Alinsky;[37] others were organized along less confrontational lines with the intent of delivering a variety of services. Whatever the origin of such groups, they became increasingly important in the 1960s as resources were made available to them by the Johnson administration.

The Model Cities Program represented the height of such attention during this period. Yet, an analysis of program procedures indicates that neighborhoods were actually treated as peripheral participants in the program development process. The program basically reflected the administration's desire to target resources to meet the service needs of minorities and poor people in urban areas; working with the social and organizational fabric of target neighborhoods was marginal to the program's concerns. Indeed, an important aspect of the program's design involved an effort to avoid the kind of participatory mobilization associated with the War on Poverty.

One can see this remoteness from neighborhood organizations and residents in the recommendations put forward by the task force that devised Model Cities.[38] Much emphasis was placed on "coordination," which meant focusing national program resources more effectively in dealing with urban problems. The local role in coordination was to involve centering responsibility in "a new city demonstration agency which would serve as the coordinator for all federal funds of flowing into the selected neighborhood."[39]

Similarly, while program planners spoke of mobilizing local leadership, what they apparently had in mind involved charging local governments with greater responsibility for program design and implementation. As Haar writes, "There was an implicit assumption that the participation of local residents would be cooperative rather than competitive with, or threatening to, existing agencies. . . . " In line with that assumption, Haar explained, citizen participation would be "contained without necessarily being controlled." This approach was intended to counter a "specter" of "OEO-CAP antagonism and chaos."[40] In spite of this effort to "contain" conflict, some localities' Model Cities planning processes were occasions for major battles between neighborhood-based organizations and city governments.[41]

This brief review of some of the characteristics of the Model Cities Program is intended to serve two purposes. First, it points to the limited acceptance of neighborhood residents and organizations as participants in the urban policy process prior to the Carter administration. Second, it foreshadowed aspects of the design and some of the problems of the NSA program.

With the demise of Model Cities, a concern with neighborhoods seemed fated to fade away. At the time the CDBG program was created, some critics feared that even the limited role that neighborhood groups had staked out in local program designs would be severely compromised. Such fears were reinforced by the inclusion of only a weak requirement for public hearings in the program, consistent with the posture of the Nixon and Ford administrations which wished to withdraw from serving as a referee among actors in local politics.

Yet, contrary to the misgivings of the critics of CDBG, studies over the first four years of the program showed that an increasing share of funds were being put into neighborhood projects and that neighborhood residents were exercising considerable influence in such expenditures. By the fourth year, one study noted that the jurisdictions sampled were spending, on the average, 52 percent of their allocations on a combination of housing and conservation activities directed to neighborhoods.[42] At a minimum, such expenditures reflected the interest and political effectiveness of home owners in using CDBG to promote their particular brand of neighborhood revitalization. As a result, by the time of the Carter administration, neighborhoods around the country were beginning to show positive results.

At about the same time, neighborhood residents were becoming more influential in the development of intergovernmental urban programs. Notably, in reaction to experiences with the disinvestment or "redlining" process, National Peoples Action was formed in March 1972. It pressured Congress for legislation to alter lending institutions' antipathy to providing mortgage money to urban neighborhoods. The legislative results were the Federal Home Mortgage Disclosure Act of 1975 and the Community Reinvestment Act of 1977.[43]

Neighborhood reinvestment was also promoted by the creation of Neighborhood Housing Service (NHS) units in many cities after 1974.[44] Each NHS consisted of a nonprofit corporation designed to work with local home owners to upgrade their properties either through arrangements with local lending institutions or by drawing on revolving loan funds made available by the NHS itself. NHS boards were made up of representatives from the targeted neighborhood, from local lending institutions, and from the local government; neighborhood representatives constituted a majority of the board's membership.

As a result of these and related activities, a new assertiveness on the part of neighborhoods and some responsiveness by national policy leadership were apparent at the time that Carter ran for president.[45]

IMMEDIATE INFLUENCES IN THE DESIGN OF NSA

Among the considerations that contributed directly to the creation of the Section 8 NSA program were the following: (1) a change in the national mood toward prospects for neighborhood revitalization; (2) the political environment of the Carter administration; and (3) the appointment of personnel to positions in the administration who were sympathetic to initiatives in housing and community development.

Changing Attitudes Toward Central City Neighborhoods

Lyndon Johnson served as president during a time when older cities were viewed as centers of societal "crisis." Richard Nixon heralded the end of that crisis, perhaps prematurely. Nonetheless, by 1976 the notion that some neighborhoods were beginning to experience a "renaissance" was no longer so farfetched as it might have seemed a few years earlier. Not only was CDBG assisting in revitalizing neighborhoods, but private investment was becoming more common.

The causes of this turnabout are in dispute. Whether attributable to the effectiveness of neighborhoods in promoting themselves through such vehicles as the anti-redlining campaign, or to socioeconomic factors such as rapid increases in the costs of new construction or the coming of age of the "baby boom" generation, some urban neighborhoods were beginning to experience improvements.[46] Whatever the causes, evidence began to emerge of what came to be called "incumbent upgrading," in some instances, and "gentrification" in others.[47]

Prospects for many urban neighborhoods may have been some distance from the mythology of "gentrification" and "upgrading," but no longer was the future of older cities and their neighborhoods seen simply in terms of decay and decline. As a result of this attitudinal shift, new attention was being focused on housing rehabilitation. Some of this attention came from the housing industry itself. Reviewing the situation in the summer of 1977, an internal HUD memorandum reported:

Within the last two months, the Mortgage Bankers Association formed a committee made up of members who are experienced in working in inner cities. Their mission is to exchange ideas . . . and tell other members of the Association how to get involved in what the Association perceives to be a growing and potentially major new market area. Committees with similar missions have recently been formed in the Home Builders Association and the National Board of Realtors, and other industry associations. The Home Loan Bank Board (whose constituent S[savings] and L[oan] associations have assets of over 400 billion dollars) has started the Neighborhood Housing Services programs in 40 neighborhoods and they expect that number to grow to over 100 by the end of next year. These groups recognize that there is a growing market which they must come to understand better before they can serve it.[48]

Major downtown redevelopment projects like Boston's Quincy Market and Baltimore's Harborplace, which owed their origins to the urban renewal program, were also beginning to serve as models of successful projects that were beginning to attract middle-class attention to downtown and to feed back into neighborhood reinvestment, especially when neighborhoods contained attractive features in their own right such as access to desirable central city locations or structures of historic interest.

The Changing Political Climate

In attempting to build a political coalition sufficient to win the 1976 presidential election, Carter made a major effort to appeal to urban residents in the Frost Belt by arguing in favor of a "coordinated urban policy from a federal government committed to develop[ing] a creative partnership with our cities."[49] Part of that urban policy would reflect a greater concern with neighborhoods, whether they were predominantly minority in composition or of a more "ethnic" character. Nevertheless, Carter stressed that his approach would involve working with and through local governments in the development and implementation of programs.

The new administration kept some of the president's campaign promises by taking a series of early, largely symbolic initiatives. One such action was the creation of an interdepartmental task force in March 1977, headed by HUD Secretary Patricia R. Harris, charged with developing a national urban policy; another was the formation of a National Commission on Neighborhoods in December 1977, which was assigned the task of "investigating the causes of neighborhood decline and recommending policies which would support revitalization."[50]

While these efforts were getting underway, HUD established an Office of Neighborhoods, Voluntary Associations, and Consumer Protection. A leading figure in community organization, Monsignor Geno Baroni, became its first assistant secretary.[51] Baroni later described the mission of that office as serving "as an advocate for community organizations and other self-help associations within the federal government and . . . encourag[ing] agencies to revise, coordinate, and expand their programs to assist them."[52]

Criticisms of project-oriented approaches to rental rehabilitation had already received preliminary attention in the Ford administration, when discussions were conducted within HUD about developing a program that would decentralize responsibility to local governments for administering assisted housing programs in a fashion analogous to CDBG. Public attention was first drawn to this effort in a brief preamble to regulations published in the *Federal Register* on 26 April 1976, which dealt with administration of the Section 8 Sub Rehab program.

That statement merely indicated that HUD was interested in developing special procedures to assist local governments already receiving funds under CDBG to use Section 8 in implementing local rehabilitation programs "that are integral parts of neighborhood renewal strategies."[53] Not only would those neighborhoods receive an allocation of Sub Rehab units, but the local government would be expected to make sure that owner-occupied units were maintained and that neighborhood social and physical services were in good condition. HUD would approve neighborhood renewal strategies as part of its annual review of CDBG applications and encourage governments receiving block grants to work with owners of neighborhood properties to submit applications for Section 8 subsidies.

It was not until 31 January 1977, however, during the presidential transition, that the outgoing administration published "for comment" procedures for implementing "neighborhood renewal strategy areas."[54] While important changes in design would occur from this time to the point exactly one year later when Section 8 NSA regulations were published "for effect," the pivotal design element in both documents was the promise to extend to local governments a much greater voice in the use of federal resources.

HUD's New Program Personnel

On the whole, the Carter administration accepted the same bureaucratic split personality in administrative organization that had marked earlier HUD regimes.

Thus, community development activities, particularly CDBG, were located under
the Office of Community Planning and Development (CPD). At the same time,
the needs of the financial markets and construction industry continued to be well
served within the FHA, while separate units administered the construction and
management of public housing and other assisted housing programs. All of these
housing-related responsibilities were formally placed under the Office of Housing.

CPD encouraged neighborhood revitalization both by supporting physical improvements for community facilities and low-interest loan or grant programs to
promote the rehabilitation of single-family housing. In addition to CDBG, it
promoted rehabilitation efforts through the 312 program which provided loans,
principally for single-family homes, at 3 percent interest over a twenty-year
period.[55]

Robert C. Embry, Jr., the new Assistant Secretary for CPD in the Carter
administration, had previously been responsible for promoting both downtown
and waterfront renewal projects and significant neighborhood revitalization efforts in Baltimore.[56] Nonetheless, his earliest concerns at HUD included assuring
that the needs of LMI persons were being met by exercising closer oversight of
that aspect of CDBG implementation. At the same time, CPD expressed its
continuing concern with business district revitalization by promoting creation of
the Urban Development Action Grant Program (UDAG).

Lawrence B. Simons, the Assistant Secretary for Housing, brought to his
position experience as a major private developer in New York City, involvement
in a variety of builders' associations in that city, and service as a director of
public authorities in New York State and New York City. Despite the traditional
problems of the Office of Housing in balancing the organizational claims of
those interested in assuring the reliability of mortgage insurance programs against
those concerned with providing more assisted housing, Simons later described
his efforts during this period as intended to create a better linkage between
housing programs and local governments:

When we assumed office in 1977 and looked at housing and housing programs, there
was obviously a missing link: the support of local government. . . . It became quite obvious
that one of the most important constituencies for housing did not understand and was not
interested in government housing programs. They viewed federal housing programs as
purely federal programs in which they had no part. The only programs they were really
interested in were those programs that gave them block grant funds.[57]

While arguing that it was desirable to move in the direction of a housing block
grant analogous to CDBG, Simons contended that local governments needed
first to generate an administrative capacity in housing development that they had
never had before—skills in such areas as developer and site selection. In his
view, therefore, it was necessary to weave a careful line between local responsibility and federal oversight.

[I]t was my theory that as long as HUD kept a programmatic design that was basically uniform throughout the country, we could give to local governments the responsibility for how they allocated their funding within those areas and the areas they wanted to work in and even how they selected developers.

To achieve that, it was important to maximize the commitment of local officials to the neighborhood selected.

The judgment of what neighborhood will go and what will not is a very difficult judgment to make, but we could enhance that expectation by looking at what commitments the cities were prepared to make to those neighborhoods. If a city was really willing to say that it was going to use enough resources to make a neighborhood fly and I am willing to commit other resources to it, the housing will be successful. Housing per se is not sufficient. It is the environment that you create that is important. . . . At the same time, cities have political problems in trying to allocate their resources to neighborhoods, because they have been spreading their housing and CDBG and 312. . . . I wanted to give them an excuse so they could target resources.

The assignment for developing a neighborhood-oriented housing rehabilitation program might well have gone to CPD. Through its oversight of CDBG, it was already involved in such programs, although not in rental rehabilitation. Nonetheless, Secretary Harris accepted the argument put forward by Simons that primary program design responsibility ought to go to the Office of Housing in order to sensitize personnel (particularly those in the FHA) to the needs of local governments and neighborhoods. Furthermore, the availability of untapped resources from the Sub Rehab program and the experience of the Office of Housing in operating the Section 8 program strengthened Simons's argument.

Once design responsibility was given to Simons, he assigned to his Deputy Assistant Secretary for Assisted Housing, Nancy Chisholm, a career civil servant, a leading role in developing what was to become the Section 8 NSA program.

It was not until the late spring of 1978, however, that focused attention was given to turning the design suggested in the proposed regulations issued by the Ford administration into a full-fledged program. That responsibility was given primarily to John (Jack) Kerry, a specialist in neighborhood programs. Prior to his service at HUD, Kerry had been involved in a number of private and public planning and development organizations, serving most recently as head of a neighborhood revitalization program in Louisville, Kentucky. An unusually dynamic person, Kerry played a pivotal role in the development of the NSA program and in selling it to local governments. How he pursued those tasks is the subject of the next chapter.

CONCLUSIONS

The Section 8 Neighborhood Strategy Area Program emerged out of an ideological consensus among liberal Democrats and moderate Republicans that the federal government had an obligation to provide some assisted housing units to low and moderate-income households. That consensus was reflected in the creation of the Section 8 program which made rental subsidies available to eligible households by building political support among participants in the private housing market—owners of existing dwelling units in the case of the Existing Housing Program; property owners, developers, construction unions, and financial institutions in the cases of the New Construction and Substantial Rehabilitation Programs. The Carter administration accepted the policy and program consensus built on behalf of Section 8 and simply sought to commit greater resources to that effort.

At the same time, the new administration reached beyond the constituent elements of the existing housing subgovernment to include more participants in local program coalitions. This emerged as a focus of special attention in the NSA program where an otherwise developer-oriented assistant secretary was eager to generate support for housing programs by enlisting local government officials as major participants.

The model for such an effort already existed in community development where earlier federal attempts to actively guide local planning and implementation efforts had been judged failures. The Nixon administration led the way toward disengagement from extensive program intervention in areas such as urban renewal and Model Cities. The result was CDBG which left to local government decision makers primary responsibility for resource allocations.

While minority and neighborhood interest groups initially viewed the coming of CDBG with concern, the 1960s left behind an important stratum of local organizations and participatory expectations that made it possible for such groups to take part in allocational decisions in a meaningful way in many cities, particularly where officeholding cadres had undergone significant alterations in response to the inclusionary politics of the 1960s. At the same time, the designation of general purpose local governments as the recipients of CDBG strengthened elected officials both in relation to existing quasi-independent agencies like urban renewal agencies and with respect to other participants in local politics. The result was to build enormous political support for CDBG among municipal and county officials, especially after the claims of business interests were met separately through the creation of Urban Development Action Grants.

The Carter administration espoused a willingness to exercise greater influence than the Ford administration in assuring that program benefits from CDBG reached lower-income segments of the population. It also claimed a commitment to cooperation with neighborhood interests that opened the policy process not only to local progrowth coalitions (including local government officials) but to neighborhood-related interests and organizations claiming to represent the interests of minorities and the poor. Attempts to generate a national urban policy and a distinct neighborhood policy foundered, however, on the inability or unwillingness of the administration to go beyond the rhetoric of "cooperation" and "partnership" to deal with the hard choices of resource allocations and procedural constraints.

In that respect, one might agree with Mollenkopf that Carter attempted in large part to re-create and expand the existing Democratic coalition to assure the continued support of minorities as well as of ethnic residents of urban neighborhoods and a variety of neighborhood interests ranging from the liberal to the conservative ends of the ideological spectrum. Characteristically, then, in the NSA program, the administration sought to maximize support from a variety of constituencies including local governments and representatives of neighborhood groups along with members of local progrowth coalitions. Targeting local governments for leadership in project development was a new step in housing but one already pioneered in CDBG. Much less certain was the role that neighborhoods would play. That remained to be determined during the process of elaborating a program design and in implementation efforts.

NOTES

1. For overviews of assisted housing programs, see R. Allen Hays, *The Federal Government and Urban Housing* (Albany: State University of New York Press, 1985); and Eugene J. Meehan, "The Rise and Fall of Public Housing: Condemnation Without Trial," in *A Decent Home and Environment*, edited by Donald Phares (Cambridge, Mass.: Ballinger, 1977), 3–42.

2. M. Carter McFarland, *Federal Government and Urban Problems* (Boulder, Colo.: Westview Press, 1978), 136.

3. Roger Starr, *Housing and the Money Market* (New York: Basic Books, 1975), 176–77. Also see McFarland, *Federal Government*, 138–45.

4. On the theory and practice of Section 8, see Hays, *Federal Government and Urban Housing*, 145–63.

5. In 1978, a fourth element was added—the Moderate Rehabilitation Program—which attempted to reach those rental units that required some upgrading but did not demand replacement of major structural systems or other work associated with the Substantial Rehabilitation Program.

6. See Nathan S. Betnun, *Housing Finance Agencies: A Comparison Between the States and HUD* (New York: Praeger, 1976); and Starr, *Housing and the Money Market*, 149–64.

7. Arthur D. Little, Inc., *Project Rehab Monitoring Report: Overview* (Washington, D.C.: U.S. Department of Housing and Urban Development, 1971), 66.

8. At about the same date, construction starts under New Construction were about 10 times that number; over 240,000 units of Existing Housing were under lease by 31 January 1978.

9. Memorandum from Jack Kerry, Special Assistant, to Nancy S. Chisholm, Deputy Assistant Secretary for Assisted Housing, 3 August 1977.

10. See Michael E. Stone, "Housing, Mortgage Lending, and the Contradictions of Capitalism," *Marxism and the Metropolis*, edited by William K. Tabb and Larry Sawers (New York: Oxford University Press, 1978), 179–207.

11. See, Hays, *Federal Government and Urban Housing*, 174–91; and John H. Mol-

lenkopf, *The Contested City* (Princeton, N.J.: Princeton University Press, 1983), esp. 115–19.

12. For early critiques of the program, see Martin Anderson, *The Federal Bulldozer* (Cambridge, Mass.: MIT Press, 1964); and contributions to James Q. Wilson (ed.), *Urban Renewal: The Record and the Controversy* (Cambridge, Mass.: MIT Press, 1966).

13. For early displacement experiences, see Robert A. Caro, *The Power Broker* (New York: Alfred A. Knopf, 1974), esp. 961–83; and Herbert Gans, *The Urban Villagers* (New York: Free Press, 1961).

14. Heywood T. Sanders, "Urban Renewal and the Revitalized City: A Reconsideration of Recent History," in *Urban Revitalization* edited by Donald B. Rosenthal (Beverly Hills, Calif.: Sage, 1980), 103–26. Despite the evidence presented by Sanders, experiences late in the history of the program continued to display behaviors by local renewal agencies of the kind criticized earlier. See, in particular, Chester Hartman, *The Transformation of San Francisco* (Totowa, N.J.: Rowman and Allenheld, 1984).

15. Bernard J. Frieden and Marshall Kaplan, *The Politics of Neglect* (Cambridge, Mass.: MIT Press, 1975), 15. Also see Charles M. Haar, *Between the Idea and the Reality* (Boston: Little, Brown and Co., 1975).

16. Problems in Model Cities planning and program implementation are dealt with in a variety of works including Dennis R. Judd and Robert E. Mendelson, *The Politics of Urban Planning* (Urbana, Ill.: University of Illinois Press, 1973), esp. chap. 4; "Citizen Action in Model Cities and the CAP Programs," *Public Administration Review*, Special Issue, 32 (September 1972), 377–408; and James L. Sundquist, *Making Federalism Work* (Washington, D.C.: Brookings Institution, 1969), 79–129.

17. Municipal governments of more than fifty thousand population or "urban counties" of two hundred thousand or more people qualified as entitlement communities. HUD continued to operate a more centralized grant program for smaller communities until 1982 when administration of that program was turned over to the states.

18. For examples of the range of forces that influenced particular localities' CDBG decisions, see Paul R. Dommel et al., *Decentralizing Urban Policy* (Washington, D.C.: Brookings Institution, 1982); Susan S. Fainstein et al., *Restructuring the City* (New York: Longman, 1983); and Donald F. Kettl, *Managing Community Development in the New Federalism* (New York: Praeger, 1980).

19. According to Dommel, housing activities were the single leading planned expenditure category during the first four years of the program. These figures increased from 23 to 28 percent of planned expenditures with over 70 percent of the funds being targeted for rehabilitation (Paul R. Dommel et al., *Targeting Community Development* [Washington, D.C.: U.S. Department of Housing and Urban Development, January 1980, 121–22). Housing rehabilitation programs were slow to get underway, however, so that actual expenditures were less successful in meeting spending targets than other types of programs.

20. Raymond Rosenfeld, "Who Benefits and Who Decides?," in Rosenthal, *Urban Revitalization*, 211–35; and the various volumes produced by Dommel et al. including *Deregulating Community Development* (Washington, D.C.: U.S. Department of Housing and Urban Development, October 1983.

21. On the issue of targeting CDBG, see, Rosenfeld, "Who Benefits and Who Decides?" and, Dommel et al, *Targeting Community Development*.

22. To avoid confusion, in a few places where references may be unclear, I have distinguished between the two types of NSAs. For the most part, references in this study

are to the Section 8 NSA program. No one interviewed at HUD ever satisfactorily explained why steps were never taken to change the name of one of the two programs to avoid confusion.

23. Many suburban entitlement communities sought to meet their obligations under the plans by providing housing to senior citizens and the handicapped and then, only reluctantly, to families. See Karen S. Christensen and Michael B. Teitz, "The Housing Assistance Plan: Promise and Reality," in *Housing Policy for the 1980s*, edited by Roger Montgomery and Dale Rogers Marshall (Lexington, Mass.: Lexington Books, 1980), 185–202.

24. Responsibility for local administration of the Existing Housing Program and later for the Moderate Rehabilitation element of Section 8 were given to local housing agencies.

25. In principle, HUD field offices were supposed to take into account HUD's socially and environmentally sensitive "site and neighborhood standards" in reviewing projects for mortgage insurance or awards of Section 8 subsidies. Too often, critics charged, they failed to make careful analyses of the circumstances of a project—the social and economic conditions of an area as well as any prospectively negative project impacts.

26. While local governments had the formal right to review project plans before they were approved by HUD in respect to compliance with local building codes or eligibility for local tax exemptions, they were often brought into the process quite late, so that their options were constrained: either go along with a project proposed by a developer or lose the private investment and the federal subsidies.

27. Haar, *Between the Idea and the Reality*, 19–20; Sanders, "Urban Renewal."

28. According to Arthur D. Little, Inc., *Title I Property Improvement Program* (Washington, D.C.: U.S. Department of Housing and Urban Development, June 1977) 4, thirty million loans totalling over $25 billion had been made up to that time. By 1976, however, less than 3 percent of total home improvement expenditures (representing 16 percent of all home improvement loans) were being made under Title I.

29. McFarland, *Federal Government*, esp. chap. 7; and Starr, *Housing and the Money Market*, esp. chap. 12.

30. These data come from the files of the Office of Assisted Housing Development at HUD in 1978.

31. U.S. Department of Housing and Urban Development, Office of Loan Origination, *HUD/FHA Rehabilitation Programs: Multifamily*, 1 May 1977, 1–2. All seven projects carried out under the program (involving a total of 882 units) had either been foreclosed by HUD or were in default by 1977.

32. Ibid., 2; and Arthur D. Little, Inc., *Project Rehab*, 74.

33. *HUD/FHA Rehabilitation Programs*, 2. Also see Langley C. Keyes, *The Boston Rehabilitation Program* (Cambridge, Mass.: Joint Center for Urban Studies of Harvard-MIT, 1970).

34. *HUD/FHA Rehabilitation Programs*, 3–4.

35. On the use of tax shelters to encourage investment in rehabilitated structures, see Joseph Miller Blew and Howard H. Stevenson, "How to Understand a Subsidized-Housing Syndication," *Housing Urban America*, 2d ed., edited by John Pynoos et al. (New York: Aldine, 1980), 574–84; and Sally G. Oldham and H. Ward Jandl, "Preservation Tax Incentives: New Investment Opportunities Under the Economic Recovery Tax Act," in *Housing Rehabilitation*, edited by David Listokin (New Brunswick, N.J.: Center for Urban Policy Research, Rutgers University, 1983), 136–45.

36. "Trapping Welfare Tenants," *New York Times*, 7 January 1979.

37. For examples of organizations that followed the Alinsky approach, see Robert Bailey, *Radicals in Urban Politics* (Chicago: University of Chicago Press, 1974); and John Hall Fish, *Black Power/White Control* (Princeton, N.J.: Princeton University Press, 1973). Also see Robert Fisher, *Let the People Decide* (Boston: G.K. Hall, 1984), esp. 46–59.

38. Haar, *Between the Idea and the Reality*, 44.

39. Ibid., 47.

40. Ibid., 48. The latter reference is to strained relations between the Office of Economic Opportunity, the federal agency responsible for overseeing poverty programs, and local Community Action Programs responsible for designing and implementing those programs.

41. On participatory conflicts in Model Cities, see the items in n. 19; and, Fish, *Black Power/White Control*, esp. 235–83.

42. Dommel et al., *Targeting Community Development*, 118. This contrasted with 39 percent of planned expenditures in the first year of the program.

43. On redlining and the reaction to it, see Richard Hula, "Lending Institutions and Public Policy," in Rosenthal, *Urban Revitalization*, 77–99; Peter Marcuse, "The Deceptive Consensus on Redlining," *Journal of the American Planning Association*, 45 (October 1979), 549–56; and Lynne Beyer Sagalyn, "Mortgage Lending in Older Urban Neighborhoods," *Annals of the American Academy* 465 (January 1983), 98–108.

44. In that year, a cooperative agreement between HUD and the Federal Home Loan Bank Board created the Urban Reinvestment Task Force. The task force was converted in 1978 into a public corporation—the Neighborhood Reinvestment Corporation. By 1980, it was working through eighty-three neighborhood-based units to promote neighborhood revitalization in areas composed predominantly of home owners. For some of the background to NHS, see Roger S. Ahlbrandt, Jr., and Paul C. Brophy, *Neighborhood Revitalization* (Lexington, Mass.: Lexington Books, 1975), esp. 127–50.

45. For one perspective from that period, see Janice Perlman, "Grassrooting the System," *Social Policy* 7 (September–October 1976), 4–20.

46. On these debates, see the contributions to Phillip L. Clay and Robert M. Hollister (eds.), *Neighborhood Policy and Planning* (Lexington, Mass.: Lexington Books, 1983).

47. The former term was popularized by Phillip L. Clay in *Neighborhood Renewal* (Lexington, Mass.: Lexington Books, 1979). On gentrification, see the contributions to Rosenthal, *Urban Revitalization*; Michael H. Schill and Richard P. Nathan, *Revitalizing America's Cities* (Albany: State University of New York Press, 1983); and "Symposium on Neighborhood Revitalization," *Journal of the American Planning Association* 45 (October 1979), 460–556.

48. Memorandum from Jack Kerry, Special Assistant, to Nancy S. Chisholm, Deputy Assistant Secretary for Assisted Housing, 3 August 1977. Also see Nathaniel Rogg, *Urban Housing Rehabilitation in the United States* (Chicago: U.S. League of Savings Associations, 1978).

49. Eric L. Stowe, "Defining a National Urban Policy: Bureaucratic Conflict and Shortfall," in Rosenthal, *Urban Revitalization*, 148.

50. James T. Barry, "The National Commission on Neighborhoods," in Rosenthal, *Urban Revitalization*, 165–87.

51. Joseph McNeely of Baltimore's Southeast Community Organization was appointed to head the Office on Neighborhoods under Baroni. On the Baltimore organization, see Matthew A. Crenson, *Neighborhood Politics* (Cambridge, Mass.: Harvard University

Press, 1983), 239ff; and Bob Kuttner, "Ethnic Renewal," in *Neighborhoods in America*, edited by Ronald H. Bayor, (Port Washington, N.Y.: Kennikat, 1982), 209–19.

52. Geno Baroni, "The Neighborhood Movement in the United States: From the 1960s to the Present," in Clay and Hollister, *Neighborhood Policy and Planning*, 188.

53. *Federal Register*, vol. 41, no. 81, 26 April 1976, 17488.

54. *Federal Register*, vol. 42, no. 20, 31 January 1977, 5918–5922. These "proposed rules" were signed on 16 January, prior to the inauguration of Carter. The term *renewal* was later dropped from the title of the program to avoid direct identification of NSA with the urban renewal program.

55. Created in 1964, by 1979 the 312 program was assuming loan obligations of $225 million a year. In that year, Congress authorized the use of up to $60 million from 312 funds for rehabilitation of multifamily structures. See *Interim Report to Congress: The Section 312 Multifamily Rehabilitation Loan Program* (Washington, D.C.: U.S. Department of Housing and Urban Development, March 1980).

56. For Embry's role in Baltimore's neighborhood politics, see Kuttner, "Ethnic Renewal."

57. These quotations from Simons come from an interview held in Washington, D.C., on 13 April 1981.

3

NATIONAL PLANNING FOR THE NSA PROGRAM

Planning for the Section 8 Neighborhood Strategy Area (NSA) Program took place within the boundaries set by the dominant subgovernments in housing and community development, but the specific terms of the design were less a product of those subgovernments than of program entrepreneurs within the Department of Housing and Urban Development (HUD).

The program set forth by HUD officials represented only the opening gambit in a process to which local governments were expected to respond. Local governments and other important participants began very early to reformulate the terms put forward by NSA program planners to meet their own needs as an implicit condition of their agreement to participate. This is not unusual in intergovernmental relations but the present study provides an exceptionally good example of the way a national program design may be forced to yield to local pressures during implementation.

Whatever the internal logic of the NSA program design, planners could not anticipate all the problems implementation efforts would encounter. That organizational failing—if that is what it is—is often attacked in discussions of "rationality" in planning.[1] Given the experimental nature of the NSA program, however, the original design allowed considerable leeway for a variety of means to be employed toward attaining the primary goal of the program: the revitalization of target neighborhoods by local governments assuming responsibility for coordinating diverse interests.

In this chapter, we review selected aspects of the steps that led to the creation of the NSA program and some of the features of the program design itself. In the last section, we shall examine the way HUD sought to organize itself for program participation. In chapter 4, we will consider HUD's efforts to mobilize local participation and how it then dealt with local plans for participation.

DESIGNING THE PROGRAM

Three significant decisions were made by Assistant Secretary Lawrence B. Simons and Deputy Assistant Secretary Nancy S. Chisholm early in the process of turning the program concept left behind by the Ford administration into an operational program. First, the NSA program would take the form of a "demonstration," thereby obviating the need to go through a formal congressional authorization process. In part, this reflected the White House's concern that legislative initiatives be discouraged until it had moved further along in its own program planning. Second, in order to avoid what was perceived to be a major error in the Model Cities experience, instead of focusing time and energy on planning, HUD officials would move as quickly as possible to generate, review, and approve local project designs.

These two considerations were tied, in turn, to a third: a determination within HUD to base the NSA program on resources from the fiscal year 1977–1978 (FY78) budget. This meant that a commitment of twenty thousand units of Section 8 Substantial Rehabilitation (Sub Rehab) subsidies would be held aside by Secretary Patricia R. Harris for the NSA program up to the end of the fiscal year. Thus, as plans for the NSA program moved through discussions within HUD in late 1977, 30 September 1978—the end of the fiscal year—came to constitute an important target date by which subsidies would need to be allocated to localities.

Organizing the Design Process

Responses to the regulations published "for comment" by the Ford administration in January 1977 were meager. Efforts were made in May 1977, therefore, to solicit additional comments from interested organizations. The principal respondents were major actors in the housing and community development subgovernments: the National Housing Rehabilitation Association (NHRA), the organization of developers involved in building subsidized housing; and, the U.S. Conference of Mayors (USCM), the major group serving larger municipal governments.

The NHRA expressed considerable reservation about the proposed program— essentially on cost grounds: "We feel that there is an overall danger whenever any neighborhood is selected for special treatment, that [acquisition] prices within the neighborhood will be driven up, thus making housing rehabilitation more expensive than it would otherwise be."[2] While claiming to support a "neighborhood oriented program" in principle, the NHRA expressed concern that such a program not detract "from other Section 8 construction and rehabilitation within the city, nor do we wish it to get involved with local politics or local government processing."

A letter jointly submitted by the USCM and the National League of Cities (which represented a greater number of smaller municipal governments), welcomed a role for local governments in the selection of neighborhoods and developers but wished to limit any HUD reviews to making sure that NSA designs were consistent with program requirements under the Community Development Block Grant (CDBG).[3]

These letters were relatively brief since there was an understanding between these interest groups and HUD that the agency would consult further with them before regulations were prepared for implementation.

Just about the time these exchanges were going on, Jack Kerry was selected as special assistant to Chisholm to head the program design effort.[4] He was provided at first with only a small inexperienced "team" of four—a faculty intern, two undergraduate interns, and a temporary HUD employee.[5] Assistant Secretary Simons later claimed the decision to keep the NSA staff small and provisional reflected a tactical choice on his part:

[I]f you start by creating a large separate office, you then antagonize everyone dealing with existing programs. You've got to overcome their reluctance to go with the new program. NSA was not a substitute program. It was something that was being interlineated into the Section 8 program. It was going to remove from the jurisdiction of certain people certain parts of that program.[6]

Several battles within HUD were fought in the course of developing the program's design. First, Kerry and his staff grappled over the issue of relocation responsibilities with personnel from the Office of Community Planning and Development (CPD) who were in charge of formulating HUD's policies on relocation. Out of that encounter emerged an understanding that local governments would be required to cover the costs of either temporary or permanent relocation from those structures rehabilitated through NSA. (Normally, Section 8 was considered to be "private" development, so that the costs of displacement did not have to be absorbed by HUD, the locality, or the developer.[7])

Second, local governments would be responsible for targeting resources (including funds from CDBG) to approved Section 8 NSAs on a scale sufficient to assure a full range of necessary support services to the area by the conclusion of a five-year period contemplated for the life of the program. This understanding locked CPD into a situation in which the Housing tail might conceivably wag the CPD dog.

Third, the fate of NSA was linked to the reversal of a major policy formulated during the Ford years. Reacting to demands for opening subsidized housing opportunities for low- and moderate-income (LMI) and minority households in the suburbs and in predominantly white outer-city neighborhoods, the Ford administration had promulgated a requirement that assisted housing opportunities for minorities be provided in "nonimpacted" areas. Residents of "impacted" neighborhoods could only be aided if "equal and comparable" opportunities were made available to them in less highly impacted areas.[8]

While members of the new HUD hierarchy recognized the desirability of such a policy in principle, they accepted the argument that the practical effect of that policy was to make housing resources available to suburban and outer-city areas at the expense of inner-city neighborhoods. The new policy approved by Secretary Harris held that improving the living conditions of minority households in central city neighborhoods was desirable in itself, whatever the speed of housing integration on a metropolitan basis. Indeed, an argument made in favor of the NSA program was that residents of neighborhoods eligible for rental subsidies would be given a wider range of choices. Substantial improvement in their current neighborhoods and in the dwelling units located there would have the effect of enhancing housing opportunities equal to moving to a nonimpacted area. At the same time, residents would still be eligible for participation in other types of Section 8 programs in nonimpacted areas should they choose to move.

Fourth, there was the expectation that intradepartmental negotiations would be successful in involving FHA in the NSA program and that FHA would review project materials for federal mortgage insurance on an expedited basis.[9]

Formal Requirements and an Operational Model

The design developed within the Office of Housing required local governments to compete for rental subsidies on the basis of preparation of formal requests to HUD. Thus, instead of setting up a block grant, HUD adopted a traditional categorical grant approach.[10] In justifying this decision, Simons argued that HUD needed to take into account the inexperience of localities in running housing programs:

One of the things that was obviously needed was to create the capacity on the local level so that cities wouldn't just be throwing the resources around, but would be concentrating it [sic] and bringing to it [sic] the other resources necessary to keep these neighborhoods vital. . . . The reason for the elaborate review process was to try to analyze what would work. Even if you are dealing with a general program, the specific needs of each city and community are going to differ. We wanted to see what would be necessary in each case.

While Simons's comments reflect an experimental or "sharing" attitude that higher-level HUD officials brought to the program, the program design also bore the insignia of a "control" approach to intergovernmental relations. HUD officials alone would be responsible for designating the localities that met the agency's criteria. After designation, localities were expected to work with local property owners to prepare building-specific applications to HUD field offices for Section 8 subsidies and, where appropriate, for mortgage insurance, thereby further involving HUD officials in making important implementation decisions.

At no time, however, did HUD attempt to define precisely the size or character of an NSA. Instead, the final regulations published on 31 January 1978 simply stated that an NSA "must be a residential area where concentrated housing and block grant-assisted physical development are being, or are to be, carried out in a coordinated manner.'' The regulations then went on to define the character of a target area as follows: "The area shall be of manageable size and condition, so that block grant and other resources to be committed to the area can reasonably be expected to meet the identified physical development and housing needs within a 5-year period.''[11]

Program regulations did specify a series of elements that local governments were expected to include in their submissions:

1. A Neighborhood Revitalization Program would involve a detailed analysis of the existing condition of the neighborhood and of the measures the local government proposed to take to correct deficiencies. Shortcomings both in physical conditions and in the range of available services were to be identified. An optimal approach would have involved providing a complete cost breakdown of neighborhood needs and a statement showing how public and private resources would meet those costs. Localities were expected to draw upon CDBG, in particular, for neighborhood improvements, but programs in addition to HUD's were expected to form part of the mix. Evidence of investor interest in the neighborhood or attractive opportunities for commercial or residential investment were also to be highlighted.

2. A Housing Rehabilitation Program would survey the condition of the entire housing stock in the neighborhood and identify the means by which all substandard units— both rental and owner-occupied—would be brought into conformity with prevailing standards. While NSA could only assure resources from the Sub Rehab Program, localities were asked to identify other HUD programs and private housing resources that they might employ to "reach" structures not treated through the provision of Sub Rehab.

3. An Administrative Plan describing the administrative capacity of the locality to carry out its NSA design required the local government to submit evidence of past performance on other HUD programs and to develop a schedule for using Section 8 resources.

4. A Relocation Statement was required that analyzed the displacement effects of the NSA design and specified the means by which the local government would assist persons displaced by the program.

5. A Participation Plan would outline how residents and property owners had been involved in the design of the NSA request and would be given subsequent opportunities for "continuing participation in the implementation, monitoring, evaluation and adjustment" of the NSA strategy.[12]

All of these items were included in the regulations published in January 1978. What was not specified were several expectations held by key program personnel within the Office of Housing. These constituted an operational model that influenced staff behaviors at the outset of the program.

First, to the extent that HUD maintained high standards of qualification for participation, requests would be approved mainly for localities which already had some experience in revitalization. Whether through participation in urban renewal or through more recent involvement in private or public investment in neighborhood upgrading, the local agency responsible for administering the NSA program would need to know a good deal about the target neighborhood and should have demonstrated some capacity to organize the various components needed to make an NSA work.

Second, a notion that target neighborhoods should be fully functioning entities within a period of no more than five years would set a constraint on the character and the size of the neighborhood selected.[13] As Chisholm was fond of telling audiences, local governments were expected to approach the task of preparing NSA proposals with the watchwords *Not too big, not too bad, and not too many*.

By this means, planners implicitly incorporated a "triage" model into the NSA program—a model widely discussed at the time.[14] This model favored concentrating resources in neighborhoods experiencing some disinvestment but still at an early enough stage of decline that infusions of limited public and private resources would have a reasonable chance of achieving a stable, self-sustaining neighborhood. In other words, this was not to be a program for the South Bronx.[15]

Third, although participation by large-scale developers was not explicitly discouraged, those most directly involved in the design of the NSA program—particularly Jack Kerry—emphasized the need to involve owners of smaller rental properties. As he and Chisholm regularly pointed out in public meetings and written communications, 73 percent of all rental units in central cities were in buildings with twenty or fewer units and most rental units were owned by persons who had only a small number of structures. Few public programs had involved these owners. Activity under Sub Rehab, for example, had been in projects that averaged seventy-five units per structure.

Where such large projects were concerned, mortgage bankers or developers were likely to serve as the "packagers" of applications for HUD mortgage insurance and for financing and would guide those projects through the complex steps required to gain private financing and HUD approvals for mortgage insurance and rental subsidies. Under NSA, the central office of HUD was proposing to make the local government the "packager" for small and inexperienced owners. This would also mean placing a greater burden on HUD field office staffs. These people had found it easier in the past to work with large developers than with small property owners since their expenditure of effort was more a function of the number of applications received than of the number of units in a project. The program design staff was hopeful that field officials could be resocialized to become more responsive to the problems of small-scale owners.

Finally, while most local plans were expected to focus on declining neighborhoods in order to arrest such decline, the NSA approach was also expected to attract local governments concerned about neighborhoods that were beginning to experience gentrification. Among policy makers at HUD, the issue of displacement due to neighborhood upgrading had become a major concern by the end of the first year of the Carter administration.[16] NSA could be used as a tool to help poorer households remain in areas where private investment was going on since rental subsidies were expected to make low-income renters competitive with others in the private rental market.

Comments from the Interest Groups

The formal design process came to a temporary halt in the fall of 1977 when the NSA staff produced a set of draft regulations that were then circulated to other units within HUD and later to the principal interest groups. With action imminent, both the USCM and the NHRA submitted detailed comments. The former expressed general satisfaction with the role assigned to local governments and with the benefits that would flow from linking community development and housing rehabilitation. USCM indicated concern, however, that the NSA program might take place within the framework of the "fair share" allocation system which would mean eating into existing allocations of Section 8 rather than being the "add-on" program it had hoped for. While obviously self-serving in that it sought to assure additional resources for central city housing, this concern fore-shadowed decisions that were to cause considerable unhappiness among local governments.

The USCM also feared that a two-track method for resource allocations—the fair share approach for the allocation of "regular" Sub Rehab, a categorical grant approach for NSA units—would complicate the administrative responsi-bilities of HUD's field staff and, perhaps, decrease the attention given to the NSA effort. As the USCM letter noted, "By carving out so broad a territory to cover, we are concerned that the Department may find itself too greatly committed to adequately staff this effort."[17]

Unlike the Conference, the NHRA had reservations about the NSA concept itself. The proposed regulations, they argued

set forth not a rehabilitation production program, but a governmental planning program that promises to get itself bogged down in unnecessary red tape, requires the expenditure of a large amount of governmental manpower and money for program design and planning purposes, establishes too many layers of governmental review, and takes a much longer time to generate rehabilitation and neighborhood revitalization activities than is desirable or possible.[18]

Like the USCM, the NHRA claimed that they wanted cities to be allowed to determine the neighborhoods they would redevelop without undergoing a major HUD review. They argued that HUD should encourage direct relations between local governments and rehabilitation developers with minimal oversight. The NHRA also found requirements for citizen participation and relocation assistance to be dampers on the activities of both developers and local governments.

While recognizing a need to make some relocation benefits available to "needy and displaced tenants," the organization found the proposed requirement that local governments provide temporary or permanent relocation benefits to all tenants displaced by the program too demanding. Although local governments might cover these costs from CDBG, the NHRA contended that the effect of that requirement would be to keep many cities from participating "or force the program to be limited to buildings which are currently vacant, and are typically not located in neighborhoods amenable to potential upgrading. . . ."[19]

Rather than being swayed by these comments, program entrepreneurs at HUD made few changes in the draft regulations. As one key informant suggested at the time, much of the interaction with interest groups had been conducted to gain their general support for the program or neutralize their opposition rather than as a real opportunity for negotiating details of the design. This reaffirms how substantially program formulation was dominated by HUD officials.

More Rules of the Game

The program regulations established general guidelines for the preparation of local requests. Other important decisions about the programs were made outside the framework of those rules, however. A number of these were announced in a HUD notice issued on 27 February 1978:

First, the program would depend on a special allocation of twenty thousand units from a secretarial "set-aside" of Section 8 Sub Rehab.[20] (A rough estimate of the value of the program was set at $160 million in federal contract authority.[21]) All funds would come from the FY78 budget.

Second, local governments would be given only ninety days (until 30 May) to prepare applications. (This deadline was expected to favor localities already well along in the development or implementation of plans for neighborhood revitalization.[22])

Third, eligible localities would include local governments of at least twenty-five thousand in population; or urban counties eligible to receive assistance under CDBG.[23] (The latter eligibility factor was seen as a concession to suburban communities that had established a stake in community development programs under CDBG.)

Fourth, of the twenty thousand units made available, half were expected to receive construction financing through state agencies. The remainder could be financed through other sources—by property owners from their own funds; by conventional lenders; or through other public or private arrangements. An expectation of state agency participation reflected a desire on the part of NSA planners to foster greater cooperation between those agencies and their own local governments in rehabilitation activity. As one HUD staff member described the situation, "Many state agencies didn't really understand their cities at the outset of the program. They dealt mainly with developers. We tried to bring the state agency and city together to pursue common goals. It has been a brokering function." The notion of the federal government brokering relations between state and local governments is an interesting commentary on the understanding that existed among HUD officials of their role in intergovernmental relations during the Carter years.

Fifth, no more than five hundred units would be made available "for any local government except where a larger proposal is clearly superior based on the applicable criteria." This principle reflected a fear that the program might easily be swamped by the demands of a few large cities. To prevent that and also to gain the political support of Congress by highlighting the program's distributive character, the notice stipulated that among the criteria to be employed in the final selection was representation of a "broad cross-section of local governments by size and geographical distribution."

Finally, the notice affirmed that it would be the responsibility of HUD field offices to review each request and send only the best ones to the central office. Field offices were empowered to reject applications, but Assistant Secretary Simons reserved to himself the final designation of localities.

Once recommended by field offices, NSA designs that met minimum standards would be reviewed by the central office on the basis of seven selection criteria identified in the regulations.[24] Assuming that the total number of requests exceeded twenty thousand units, the two criteria specified in the notice (size and geographical location) and the seven in the regulations would form the basis on which all requests would be judged.

Even as the program design and the notice were being circulated, the "purity" of the design began to encounter certain political problems. Marginal in themselves, they reflected the kinds of pressures for program change that would occur throughout the process of converting the program design into local projects.

A case in point involved HUD's response to expressions of interest by local governments with populations under twenty-five thousand, some with quite substantial records of urban renewal or other community development activities. Telephone calls from Senate or House offices expressing support for such localities in allowing them to qualify for participation became a regular part of the NSA staff's day at this time. After some internal debate, the Office of Housing adopted a procedure by which localities with populations smaller than twenty-five thousand might qualify for waivers on the basis of past performance in other HUD programs. Waivers were eventually granted to all localities that pursued the issue. However, the option was not widely publicized, so that it is impossible to estimate how many more localities might have sought program participation had they known about it.

Other elements in the notice began to disintegrate either wholly or in part as localities began to compose their applications. Thus, the 500-unit ceiling—a stipulation aimed especially at New York City, which had a great appetite for assisted-housing programs—was controlling for most communities. Indeed, in some instances the figure had an effect opposite to the one intended, because some localities treated 500 units as a target figure. Many of these applied, therefore, for more units than they could reasonably expect to use. This action was based on the premise that a local official should always request more than needed so that national cuts in requests would still leave localities where they really wanted to be. Still, since some applicants were careful in their estimation of their needs, there were anomalies in which big cities with substantial needs (e.g., Atlanta, Baltimore, and Boston) applied for about 500 units each for two or more NSAs while much smaller cities applied for as many as 500 units to be used in only one target area.

In a few instances, localities requested more units than the ceiling figure appeared to permit. New York City, in particular, exceeded the 500-unit figure by applying for NSAs in ten neighborhoods involving an aggregate request of 5,000 Section 8 units. After New York came San Francisco which sought a total allocation (for three NSAs) of 995 units. In keeping with this variability, the city that sought the second largest allocation of units for a single neighborhood (after New York City's request for one of its NSAs) was Toledo, which requested 860.

The issue then became how HUD would make its selections. We will treat that question in chapter 4 after considering the effort the agency made to prepare its field offices for participation in the program.

PROGRAMMING THE FIELD

HUD field office personnel were formally introduced to plans for the NSA program in sessions held in December 1977 and in the second week of January 1978.[25] At those meetings, some expressed skepticism about their ability to take on the responsibilities for a new program. Nevertheless, each field office was asked by the Office of Housing to designate an individual as an "NSA coordinator"—a contact person who would link NSA staff in Washington with local officials responsible for designing and ultimately for implementing project plans.

Among his/her many duties, the NSA coordinator was expected to alert eligible local governments to the program and then to work closely with them in preparing local plans. They were supposed to hold orientation sessions with each interested local government to review program regulations and procedures for submitting materials. The coordinator would then visit each prospective target neighborhood and advise the locality on the appropriateness of its choices. After 30 May, when plans were due in the field offices, the coordinator was expected to play the leading role in overseeing field office reviews. This meant working with various divisions in the field offices to satisfy informational or evaluational requirements specified in the program regulations.[26]

Unfortunately, NSA reached the field just about the time the effects of a major field reorganization were being felt. Some offices were being moved; others were experiencing major changes in personnel or in individual assignments. The result was that there were morale problems in some locations and confusion in others about specific responsibility for coordinating NSA activities.

While most field offices were prepared to name coordinators, the seriousness with which the coordinator role was undertaken varied enormously. In a few places, coordinators assumed the multidimensional role intended for them; in many others, coordinators took none of the initiatives expected of them beyond notifying localities (often only by mail) about the program and waiting for questions. There were many instances in which coordinators did not pay visits to localities which might have considered participating in the program; in a few cases, this occurred even though localities were accessible by automobile.[27]

Indicative of the quality of some field offices' program commitment, one busy office initially assigned the role of NSA coordinator to a first-year law student who was serving as a summer intern in 1978 and, then, in the fall, to an undergraduate student intern from a local college. Several local government officials within the large territory served by that office later complained that it was difficult to get important questions answered by the field office. Similar complaints were heard, however, even where more experienced persons filled the coordinator position.[28]

CONCLUSIONS

The NSA program emerged out of a policy consensus that existed in support of the provision of a limited amount of housing assistance through subsidies to the private sector. The program took several important steps forward from Model Cities and CDBG by seeking to target both community development funds and available resources from the Section 8 program to particular residential areas and did so by assigning to local governments the leading responsibility for planning and coordinating these efforts. The NSA program was expected to elicit the support of elements within both the housing and community development subgovernments—developers, financial institutions, local government officials— and working-class white and minority residents who were expected to acquire a stake in the revitalization activities targeted to their neighborhoods.

While those responsible for formulating the program were aware of the difficulties involved in promoting neighborhood revitalization among local officials in a fashion that would promote housing opportunities for LMI households, they accepted the decentralizing notions of the Nixon and Ford administrations. Thus, they were prepared to work through local governments in encouraging the development of project plans for areas selected by those governments.

NSA's centralized origins made it possible for program planners to adhere to their working model somewhat longer than might have been the case had they been forced to enter into serious negotiations with other interested parties from the outset. Rather than passing through the normal legislative process, however, the program was created largely within HUD's policy-making stratum. In that respect, it closely resembled the "technocratic" program development processes described by Samuel Beer, even though it was subsequently "sold" by program entrepreneurs as a way of placing greater responsibility and resources in the hands of general purpose local governments.[29]

Viewed from an intergovernmental perspective, what is noteworthy is the limited role played by state and local governments in program formulation, except for the tangential role of the USCM. Instead, the "in-house" nature of program development came close to resembling the control model of intergovernmental relations introduced in chapter 1.

Yet, indicative of the idealism with which the program was put together within HUD, program entrepreneurs appeared to envision the operation of a relatively frictionless world as the program passed from design to implementation. This was consistent with the Carter administration's "sharing" approach to urban policy generally. Unfortunately, this image of sharing among federal agencies, local governments, residents (including those threatened with displacement by proposed projects), developers, sources of financing, and state government agencies proved to be unrealistic.

Based as they were in the central office of HUD in Washington and having little field office experience of their own, those responsible for designing the NSA program ignored early warning signals from field officials that indicated that even HUD's own staff might be reluctant to cooperate fully both in the macro- and micro-implementation of the program. We will review certain intraorganizational problems in the following chapter along with pointing to some of the intergovernmental difficulties associated with the early stages of macro-implementation.

NOTES

1. In this connection, see Charles E. Lindblom, "The Science of 'Muddling Through'," *Public Administration Review* 19 (Spring 1959), 79–88; and Yehezkel Dror, "Muddling Through—'Science' or Inertia?" *Public Administration Review* 24 (September 1964), 153–57. For a further development of Lindblom's argument, see his, "Still Muddling, Not Yet Through," *Public Administration Review* 39 (November–December 1979), 517–26.

2. Letter from Arthur R. Hessel, National Housing Rehabilitation Association, to Deputy Assistant Secretary Nancy S. Chisholm, 13 June 1977.

3. Letter from Donald A. Slater, Office of Federal Relations, National League of Cities, and Melvin A. Mister, Assistant Executive Director, U.S. Conference of Mayors, to Nancy S. Chisholm, 23 June 1977.

4. He later became head of the office that administered the NSA program and then chief of a new rehabilitation division within the Office of Multifamily Housing which oversaw the NSA Program.

5. I observed many of the events that took place during the program development process from my position as a faculty intern at HUD.

6. Interview, Lawrence B. Simons, Washington, D.C., 13 April 1981.

7. Local governments would be responsible for providing relocation payments and services "at a level substantially comparable to the requirements of the Uniform [Relocation] Act," thus avoiding the issue of broadening the terms of that 1970 act that required relocation assistance when public projects were involved. See "Section 8 Housing Assistance Payments Program—Substantial Rehabilitation: Special Procedures for Neighborhood Strategy Areas," *Federal Register*, vol. 43, no. 21, 31 January 1978, sect.

881.309. This action was a response to complaints that the Section 8 New Construction and Sub Rehab programs had weakened government commitment to protecting those displaced by subsidized projects.

8. For an account of one attempt by HUD to force a local government to take a deconcentrated approach to the use of Section 8 subsidies, see Donald B. Rosenthal, *Sticking Points and Ploys in Federal-Local Relations* (Philadelphia: Center for the Study of Federalism, Temple University, 1979), 45–56.

9. No agreement was ever actually reached with the FHA on this "fast-tracking" approach. Delays in the approval of mortgage insurance by FHA later contributed significantly to problems in program implementation.

10. On the differences between categorical grants and block grants, see Parris N. Glendening and Mavis Mann Reeves, *Pragmatic Federalism*, 2d ed. (Pacific Palisades, Calif.: Palisades Publishers, 1984), esp. 236–48.

11. "Special Procedures for Neighborhood Strategy Areas," 4238.

12. Ibid., sect. 881.304 (a) (8).

13. The choice of five years as the period for completing the program was arbitrary, but it was one common at the time as a rule of thumb in distinguishing neighborhoods worth investing in from those too far gone in the cycle of decline to merit the concentrated use of public resources.

14. On "triage," see the work of Anthony C. Downs, including most recently his *Neighborhoods and Urban Development* (Washington, D.C.: Brookings Institution, 1981) where the term itself is not used but the concept is nonetheless present. Also see Roger Starr, "Making New York Smaller," *The New York Times*, 14 November 1976.

15. Interestingly enough, New York City originally proposed the South Bronx for the NSA program but subsequently dropped the area when it was led to believe (after a visit from Carter in October 1977) that the area would receive separate and special attention from HUD.

16. Only a few of the neighborhoods proposed as NSAs were actually experiencing gentrification. Nonetheless, the displacement issue received a good deal of attention during the period of program planning.

17. Letter from Barry Zigas, Director, Housing Assistance Staff, U.S. Conference of Mayors, to Lawrence B. Simons, 16 November 1977. The Conference also appeared to be hesitant about the proposed allocation process which might disperse Sub Rehab units even more widely than under the "fair share" system rather than concentrating units in the larger, older central cities, where they argued the need for rehabilitation was greatest and where, coincidentally, the support base of the Conference was concentrated.

18. "Comments of the National Housing Rehabilitation Association," unsigned, 16 November 1977.

19. The NHRA proved to be extremely perceptive in this assessment.

20. This was intended to relieve the concern of those who had sought assurances that resources would not come out of "fair share" allocations.

21. This figure represented a commitment only for the housing assistance subsidies for a single year when the program would be in full operation. It did not include the total expenditure over the expected fifteen-year-life of each contract, nor did it calculate costs associated with FHA mortgage insurance or the tax expenditures that developers would receive through the accelerated depreciation allowances supported by the program. The real cost of the program, even if it had been committed at only the original 20,000-unit level, would have run to several billion dollars.

22. At that time, program entrepreneurs believed that there might be a second round of competition. The second round never took place.

23. Originally, program entrepreneurs attempted to define eligibility in terms similar to CDBG—communities of fifty thousand population or more—but the department settled on the twenty-five thousand figure in response to complaints from smaller cities that their problems had been overlooked by the way CDBG and other HUD programs were administered.

24. See chapter 4 for a review of those criteria.

25. The basic unit of field organization at HUD was the area office, but in some places limited-function service or insuring offices existed mainly to handle mortgage insurance. For the sake of simplicity, I have employed the term *field office* to cover these different types.

26. These included the units normally involved in reviewing CDBG materials and the persons responsible for examining various aspects of housing projects (including financial feasibility, developer insurability, and construction standards) as well as divisions that engaged in the analysis of environmental impacts, citizen participation, and fair housing and equal opportunity requirements.

27. Some field office personnel claimed this resulted from department freezes on travel money then in place.

28. The marginality of these positions is similar to the situation of the "weak generalists" responsible for administering community development elements of the urban renewal program described by Richard Legates in "Can the Federal Welfare Bureaucracies Control Their Programs?," *The Urban Lawyer* 5 (Spring 1973), 228–63. Legates contrasts these officials with the "dominant technicians" who performed such functions as fiscal management and the review of planning and engineering designs for urban renewal projects.

29. See Samuel H. Beer, "The Modernization of American Federalism," *Publius* 3 (Fall 1973), esp. 74–80.

4

MACRO-IMPLEMENTATION I: THE NATIONAL EFFORT

In this chapter and the next, we examine the macro-implementation of the Section 8 Neighborhood Strategy Area (NSA) Program——the phase during which the program's goals were converted into local proposals subject to approval by the Department of Housing and Urban Development (HUD). In the present chapter, we view matters largely from the federal perspective. As we shall see, the working model favored by NSA program staff (described in chapter 3) suffered major setbacks during this phase, in part because of the political and administrative pressures that operated within the agency, but also because many local governments chose to deviate from the national approach.

We will have occasion toward the close of the chapter to examine examples of struggles over program definition between HUD and two cities, Detroit and New York. In both cases, the locality ultimately negotiated terms that reflected its own preferences rather than those of the program planners. In these cases, as in others, one might argue that the locality was seriously committed to revitalization of the target areas, that is, they shared general program goals with HUD. Where they differed was in their search for the means that would achieve those goals with lower local political costs. Chapter 5 examines the local efforts of other localities taking as the standard of analysis the terms of the working model introduced in the last chapter.

This chapter is organized around four specific aspects of macro-implementation: (1) mobilizing the interest of local governments; (2) reviewing the materials submitted to HUD field offices and forwarded to the central office for processing; (3) conducting the final selection reviews; and (4) dealing with examples of localities that raised issues of consistency with the national program design.

MOBILIZING LOCAL PARTICIPATION

Public attention was first drawn to what was to become the NSA program when Secretary Patricia R. Harris, in her first major speech to the U.S. Conference of Mayors (USCM) in Tucson, Arizona, in June 1977, held out the prospect of a special allocation of up to twenty thousand units of Section 8 Substantial Rehabilitation (Sub Rehab) to aid cities in ongoing efforts at neighborhood revitalization. Harris argued that such funds should be used in conjunction with the Community Development Block Grant (CDBG) "to reduce the isolation of low-income people—to promote the diversity and vitality of neighborhoods, and to revitalize your communities."[1]

It is not clear how effective HUD would have been in stimulating interest in NSA if it had relied only on its field offices. In fact, the agency turned to public interest organizations as a major vehicle for promoting participation. Not only was the USCM consulted during the development of the program, but HUD contracted with it (and the National Community Development Association) to prepare a guidebook for local governments laying out the rationale for the program and procedures for preparing a program design.[2]

Those two organizations were also funded by HUD to organize information sessions at three sites (Washington, Chicago, and San Francisco) in January 1978, to which local government officials were invited. Participants were provided with considerable detail about the NSA program by Deputy Assistant Secretary Nancy Chisholm and by Jack Kerry and his staff. The three meetings were well attended and proved to be an important vehicle for mobilizing local interest.

Some involvement was also stimulated by the Office of Neighborhoods (located under the new assistant secretary for Neighborhoods, Voluntary Associations and Consumer Protection) which circulated announcements to community organizations. In a few instances, such organizations precipitated local government initiatives; in a handful of cases, local organizations wrote the proposals which were then endorsed by their local governments. Finally, various professional media were employed as outlets for information about the program.[3]

The response to these efforts was much greater than HUD had anticipated. Since the regulations called for submission of a great variety of data that would need to be put together rapidly, program planners had expected that only larger cities with considerable past experience or substantial planning staffs would apply. Much to their surprise, by 30 May 1978, field offices were swamped with proposals from 147 local governments for 211 neighborhoods involving requests for more than 51,000 units of Section 8.

REVIEWING THE REQUESTS

Local government plans varied widely in quality. Some localities knew what they wanted and developed quite precise designs. The greater number, lacking meaningful guidance from HUD field offices, assembled a melange of materials only vaguely related to the documentation envisioned in the regulations. Important pieces of information were frequently lacking. Instead of the ninety-day planning period having served as a barrier to participation, many local government officials apparently assumed that the program's expectations about the quality of proposals and the deadline were so unrealistic that they could submit considerably less than the planning model requested.

Even cities with acknowledged planning capacity submitted weak NSA designs. Among the local officials interviewed for this study, many conceded that they were eager to bring additional Section 8 resources into their communities but they were either skeptical about the ambitious character of the program or unwilling to invest the necessary time and staff energy.[4] Citing Model Cities, in particular, they argued that HUD had frequently made promises at the outset of programs on which it had never delivered. While they were prepared to submit sufficient material to indicate an interest in the NSA program, they were unwilling to do so in a fashion that would box them into a set of resource commitments before HUD made its own allocation decisions. One of the other consequences of this uncertainty was that most localities avoided alerting residents of targeted neighborhoods at this stage, in part because they did not wish to stir up expectations on which they might not be able to deliver.

Field Office Reviews

Originally, HUD field offices were expected to complete program reviews in about thirty days so that all NSA requests would reach Washington by early July. The NSA staff (now expanded to include seven full-time persons) would then spend another month reviewing requests recommended by the field offices. Given the heavy demand, this schedule required adjustment. Since 60 percent of the requests fell within the jurisdictions of nine field offices, those offices were given an extension to July 30. In the meantime, central office staff could begin to review requests processed through the other (approximately thirty-five) field offices.

Even with the additional time available to some field offices, a number seemed to engage in only the most perfunctory reviews. They were willing to pass on poor designs to Washington even though they ultimately might be responsible for overseeing project implementation. This was an easier bureaucratic solution than having to get involved in intensive negotiations with localities. Part of the problem was that many of the persons designated as NSA coordinators in February had been moved to other responsibilities by April as a result of a HUD field reorganization and others had left the department entirely. In a few offices, it took considerable time for the original person to be replaced and a new coordinator to learn his/her duties.

Finally, some field officials shared with certain local governments the view that HUD would fund communities less on the basis of the design criteria in the

Table 4–1
Activity Levels in the Seven Most Active Field Offices

Area Office	No. of Localities	Proposed for Approval	
		Number Submitted	Recommended
Boston	16	23	22
Columbus	12	14	8
Philadelphia	12	12	12
Buffalo	11	13	12
Newark	9	14	9
Richmond	8	12	9
New York	7	23	18

regulations than on the basis of political considerations. This perspective was especially common where field staffs were faced with requests from large cities whose political influence in Washington was thought to be substantial.

Willingness to accept local materials with minimal review was by no means uniform. Some area offices took their responsibilities quite seriously. Thus, the Boston area office, which (along with the one in New York City) received the greatest number of proposals, passed almost all of them through to the central office with recommendations for approval, but only after the field staff concluded careful negotiations with each locality and conducted systematic internal reviews. All the same, the Boston staff accepted local designs with which they would feel comfortable working rather than ones that necessarily conformed to the operational model advocated by Chisholm and Kerry.[5]

The Columbus area office (which was responsible for processing all of the requests in Ohio) was equally careful in its efforts; in contrast to Boston, it turned down nearly half the requests submitted (6 of 14). For example, it rejected two proposals from Cincinnati and one from Dayton because the designs were little more than plans to do one particular building in each area rather than serious efforts at neighborhood revitalization.

Field office actions are presented in table 4–1 which provides an overview of the seven most active field offices in terms of the number of local governments that submitted proposals, the total number of NSAs they requested, and the number recommended by each field office. As a result of the attitudes HUD field personnel adopted, only 38 NSAs (involving about 8,600 units) were rejected. The remaining 173 NSAs were sent on to the central office for review and final action.

The Central Office Review Process

While the central office NSA staff made preliminary plans for reviewing NSA submissions, they had not prepared for a review process that would involve more than twice the number of units set aside for the program.[6] Still, in the months leading up to the review, much discussion went on about operationalizing the seven ''selection criteria'' listed (but not spelled out) in the program regulations and the two ''additional criteria'' of size and geographical distribution added in the notice. The first seven criteria were as follows:

1. the degree of commitment by the local government of public funds to neighborhood revitalization activities;

2. the extent of existing or proposed private financing available for housing rehabilitation or commercial revitalization;

3. the overall quality and feasibility of the local program;

4. the extent to which rehabilitation was expected to be completed without causing permanent displacement;

5. the demonstrated capacity of the local government to handle HUD programs;

6. evidence of the local government's capacity to promote fair housing and equal opportunities for minorities;

7. the likelihood of achieving speedy utilization of Section 8 program resources.[7]

There was considerable disagreement within the Office of Housing about how to operationalize these criteria and how much weight to give to each item. The list was diverse, having emerged out of a need to satisfy the concerns of particular divisions or individuals within HUD during the elaborate clearance process required by the department for approving regulations. While included in order to speed the regulations through that process, they now constituted major hurdles to developing a coherent selection process.

To further complicate matters, in the rush to get the program underway, the central office had been unable to develop a standard format that local governments could follow in preparing their submissions. Consequently, local plans followed the general outline contained in the regulations but in idiosyncratic ways. Efforts were made late in the day to organize the field office reviews by distributing forms that highlighted the selection criteria. However, field staffs treated these materials unevenly. Field letters from Assistant Secretary Simons urging greater efforts by those officials to oversee the process had little effect. As a result, the NSA staff in Washington was forced to spend a great deal of time after 1 July working back through the original submissions to reach the point where the selection criteria could be applied on a relatively comparable basis.

Initially, the central office staff attempted to develop absolute standards applicable to each submission. However, a process which began with an almost Platonic model of what an NSA should look like, and how local designs should be analyzed, began to disintegrate as the reality of reviewing requests for funding for 173 markedly different target areas dawned on the small review team.

In part, changes in approach reflected an increasing recognition by the review staff that the relatively brief planning period allowed to local governments had proven to be unrealistic. As one staff member later remarked:

One of the problems we had to struggle with was how come [proposals] were in the shape they were in. We wanted plans that made sense. The problem was whether the difficulties resulted from the neighborhood itself, from the capacity of the local government [to design a strong plan], or the role played by the area office people.

The result was that the gradual emergence of a less demanding attitude was reflected in a shift away from an emphasis on selectivity to one that sought inclusiveness. What caused the largest part of this change, however, was a political decision at the upper reaches of HUD to maximize the impact of the NSA program by treating weak submissions and absent data as potentially correctable through further negotiations. This approach minimized the number of NSAs that needed to be rejected outright. Indeed, as the review process proceeded, it became increasingly clear that HUD's political leadership expected the staff role to be less evaluative than a matter of procedural formalism which could be used to legitimate the allocational decisions made by Assistant Secretary Simons and Secretary Harris.

MAKING THE SELECTIONS

Altering the Game Plan

Two major decisions were made by senior HUD officials around Labor Day, only three weeks before the scheduled announcement of NSA awards. Those two decisions were: (1) that the program would no longer be based upon Section 8 units from the Fiscal Year 1978 (FY78) budget; and (2) that the ceiling of twenty thousand units would be breached.

As we noted in chapter 2, the commitment of twenty thousand units of Section 8 was expected to come from a reservation of funds held by Secretary Harris out of the FY78 budget. However, a number of legal and administrative objections were raised about committing Section 8 allocations to projects that might not be approved for construction for as long as five years. While a general announcement of NSA designees could be made before the end of FY78, many project details would still need to be worked out before legal and financial obligations could be finalized.

Equally important, the political leadership of HUD decided to allow the 20,000-unit ceiling to be exceeded at the last moment. They did this for several reasons. First, a decision to change the funding base for the program would make less pressing the need to limit the program to the parameters of the FY78 budget. Second, there had been some hope earlier that the 1978 competition would be the first of several. With rising concern about the federal budget and political controversy stirring over the high cost of Section 8 construction programs, there was a desire on the part of HUD to make budgetary commitments to as many localities as possible before changes were made in the budget.

Third, given the technical problems involved in identifying the best NSA proposals and the political difficulties that might result from turning down particular ones, the leadership of HUD opted for the easiest solution: promise funding to as many localities as reasonably possible and then come up with the necessary resources. Should circumstances prove some localities incapable of implementing designs, political blame could not be fixed directly on HUD. This approach also had a potential for mobilizing a larger political constituency behind NSA and other assisted housing programs should questions about future funding arise. As Assistant Secretary Simons later described the thinking at the time:

We had a number of options in July–August when the demand for NSA units was evident. One was simply to cut off the demand at the resources available. Another was to cut it off and promise them to run it again the following year. The third was to do what we did: to say to everyone that we would include them but that funding would have to come partly out of fair share beyond a certain amount. . . . If we had announced that earlier, you would have lost any attempt to get quality in the program. My experience in government is that if it is an entitlement program, the local government just doesn't worry about it as much as if it was a competitive situation.[8]

Asked about the ethics of changing the rules in the middle of the game, Simons responded:

It might have been a little unethical to do what we did, but the overall result was to give us some better quality. The one area where we were hurt was where area offices did work seriously on a review and rejected a locality because they had done their jobs too well.

Announcing the Decisions

As a result of the less demanding standards applied, the central office rejected only 18 neighborhoods in 14 localities involving a total request of 4,725 units of Sub Rehab. Even for some of these, means of meeting their particular needs were found through other HUD programs. Thus, when Secretary Harris made the announcement on 21 September that 117 neighborhoods had been designated "fully" and 38 "conditionally"[9] as NSAs with claims upon 37,688 units of Section 8, there was considerably less at stake than had been anticipated by those who designed the selection process.[10] In keeping with the Alice-in-Wonderland character of the situation, the secretary asserted at the ceremony that the fact that only 18 neighborhoods had been rejected outright was a positive sign: "It is obvious from the very few rejections that this is proving to be one of HUD's most successful programs."[11]

With respect to conditional approvals, the secretary understated the degree of difficulty involved in some of those cases when she remarked, "Those [designs] receiving conditional approval basically meet the program guidelines and are critical to ongoing revitalization endeavors taking place in their cities, but require modification before HUD can accept proposals for Section 8 commitments."

That some of these required more than "modification" is indicated, for example, by the fact that as late as the summer of 1979, several cases still had not been resolved.

It was also on 21 September that the secretary announced that awards would not be based on the FY78 budget but would depend upon annual allocations. The central office would obligate itself to a subsidy commitment out of the FY79 budget equal to the total first-year schedules that localities had developed—21,635 units. Beyond that, however, the remaining 16,053 units would come from the area offices' "fair share" allocations but "on a priority basis."[12] Even that commitment was hedged about with the disclaimer that the allocation of units would be contingent on "appropriate congressional action and the availability of funds." Those words became more significant after the presidential election of 1980.

The September announcement caused a good deal of unhappiness among those local governments that had expected the NSA program to provide project resources above their regular allocations of Section 8. Furthermore, the new funding arrangements rewarded localities which had fortuitously scheduled a large share of their Sub Rehab allocations in the first year of the program.[13] New York City benefited disproportionately from this approach because it applied for five thousand units to be obligated in the first program year on the basis of what one local informant described as the city's "take-the-money-and-run" attitude toward dealing with HUD. Reservation of units did not mean approval of project plans, however, so that subsidy funds would still be held in reserve while detailed project plans went through construction and financing reviews.

THE AFTERMATH OF SELECTION

Despite the equivocations involved in the 21 September announcement, HUD moved quickly to remind local governments about its expectations for program implementation. In October, participating local governments were invited to meet at three sites (New Haven, Atlanta, and Denver) where program obligations were spelled out by central office staff. Among the matters emphasized were procedures for financing multifamily rehabilitation, how to prepare proposals for Section 8 under the rules of the Sub Rehab Program, and relocation requirements.

It was at one of these meetings that a policy conflict that had simmered for some time between Jack Kerry and Lawrence Simons first emerged publicly. After Kerry made an often repeated statement stressing the importance of targeting the program to small structures owned by inexperienced persons, Simons intervened to make it clear that he also wished to encourage the involvement of experienced developers. As Simons later remarked (not referring to Kerry by name):

There were certain people in the department who were very anxious for the program [to be used] for small structures. . . . There are certain cities that have that kind of stock;

they certainly should be part of it. There are other cities that do not have that kind of stock. You should have a program that deals with both. Certain people felt my perspective was too much large-developer oriented.

In addition to these meetings, field office personnel were encouraged to meet with local government officials on specific issues arising out of local circumstances. While a few took seriously the additional obligation to monitor local efforts, most either ignored that recommendation or soon abandoned any effort in that regard. As a result, the small central office NSA staff became heavily engaged by the spring of 1979 in trying to spur smoother and more effective relations between field offices and local governments—"firefighting" particular issues.

Indicative of the problems encountered in gaining the support of field office personnel, a letter to the field issued on 1 November 1979 by Assistant Secretary Simons urged personnel to become more involved in the NSA process. Reviewing the previous year's activities, he wrote:

The most important lesson learned was that the area office should be involved in the NSA from the beginning. Serious problems developed when the area office began reviewing an NSA request which they had never seen or discussed with the City prior to submission. Most cities which started out on the wrong foot never recovered or required large investments of staff time from the area office and headquarters. Many problems could have been avoided if the area office had taken the time in the beginning to explain the program, and if the NSA had been given high enough priority in the office to ensure that questions from the cities were answered. Where these steps were taken in the area office, most of the cities had good programs.

DEALING WITH THE "CONDITIONALS"

Up to this point, we have not dealt with the problems associated with particular local plans. In cases involving conditional approvals, for example, the reasons varied greatly. In some instances, field offices questioned the character of the neighborhood selected, or the administrative capacity or resource commitment of the local government; at other times, the field office supported local allocations only to find reservations expressed by central office personnel. Furthermore, programs were approved without condition for some places on the basis of designs that received conditional designation elsewhere.

There does not appear to be a clear relationship between such factors as size and planning capacity, on the one hand, and conditional status, on the other. Thus, among the thirty-two localities listed in table 4–2 whose thirty-nine NSAs were conditionally approved, there were many large cities whose planning capacity might have been expected to be greater than many of the smaller jurisdictions approved outright. The situation is further complicated by the fact that for eleven of the thirty-two local jurisdictions, at least one NSA request was approved while one or more other NSAs were being given conditional approval.

Part of the problem apparently resulted from the attitudes of officials in larger municipalities who approached the planning process in a rather casual manner either because they were not ready to devote the time of their planning staffs or their program resources to NSA or because they assumed their participation was assured by their political "clout." Indeed, it might be argued that at least in some cases smaller communities "tried harder" because they expected their selection to be more problematic.

Whatever the limited generality of any particular case, it is useful to review the experiences of two cities—Detroit and New York—to illustrate the sorts of intergovernmental negotiations associated with the macro-implementation process.

Detroit

Rather than submitting an area that could be characterized as "predominantly" residential—as the NSA regulations recommended—Detroit proposed the conversion of half a dozen downtown office buildings into 610 units of elderly housing. Elsewhere in the country, notably in Massachusetts, area offices might have looked quite favorably upon such a proposal. However, the Detroit area office balked at the city's initial plan to designate one-third of its central business district (CBD) as its NSA and to create residential units in an area where almost no housing and few neighborhood facilities existed. In this case, the area office raised questions about the substantial public improvements targeted for the NSA, many of which were part of a "wish list" the city was in the process of proposing to the federal government. These included a new downtown sports complex and a shopping mall.

Despite the early expression of area office concern about this program approach, city staff submitted their plan with only minor modifications. Allegedly, this was because the city anticipated a favorable reception from Washington toward any proposal it made, given Mayor Coleman Young's access to the Carter administration. After attempts to promote negotiations with the local government failed, the area office submitted the city's proposal to the central office without a final recommendation, thus forcing the central office to handle this political "hot potato."

The Washington staff shared the area office's misgivings, but the only action they took prior to the 21 September announcement was to assign Detroit to "conditional approval" status. The central office hoped that negotiations would be held with the city that would decrease the size of the NSA (so that whatever impact the Section 8 units might have would not be dissipated by dispersion), that a lease would be secured from a competent food store retailer in order to assure at least minimal support services for the elderly residents of the NSA, and that a more substantial "assessment of the non-housing related deficiencies of the neighborhood" would be done.[14]

The city and area office then embarked on a prolonged and difficult set of

Table 4–2
Cities Receiving Conditional Approval Status
Name of Locality

Atlanta, Ga. (1/2)*
Atlantic City, N.J.
Austin, Tex.
Boston, Mass. (1/4)
Burlington, Iowa
Chester, Pa.
Dade County, Fla. (1/2)
Detroit, Mich.
Gary, Ind.
Grand Rapids, Mich.
Hartford, Conn.
Hoboken, N.J.
Indianapolis, Ind.
Jersey City, N.J. (1/3)
Los Angeles Co., Calif. (2/2)
Louisville, Ky. (1/2)
Luzerne Co., Pa.
Kansas City, Mo. (1/2)
New York City (7/10)
Philadelphia, Pa.
Pittsburgh, Pa.
Reading, Pa.
Richmond, Va. (1/2)
St. Louis, Mo. (1/4)
San Antonio, Tex.
San Francisco, Calif. (1/3)
San Juan, Puerto Rico
Seattle, Wash. (1/2)
Trenton, N.J.
Utica, N.Y.
Williamsport, Pa.
Wilmington, Del.

*Figures in parentheses indicate the number of neighborhoods of the total requested that were given conditional status. Other localities requested participation for only one neighborhood.

meetings and correspondence touching on the city's basic approach to NSA. Some of the flavor of that exchange is reflected in a five-page, single-spaced letter written by the city's director of community and economic development to the Detroit area (office) manager in response to questions about the commitment of the city to providing support services to the NSA:

The city is being recognized nationwide for the joint private and public success in creating development, much of it in the CBD. It is necessary to examine the NSA as part of the total CBD redevelopment effort. Renaissance Center, a new downtown shopping center, the people mover, and other projects as listed in the original NSA [request] are all either within the NSA, or contiguous to or lie within a 15 minute walk of the area. All of these projects are increasing the demand for high-density housing oriented to persons who wish to live near these employment and service centers.[15]

Nonetheless, the area office continued to view the plan with considerable skepticism. Thus, the area manager wrote to the central office that the design amounted to no more than converting a small number of office buildings to residential use:

[T]he area will remain predominantly commercial (10 from a potential 96 buildings are under consideration for conversion . . .); with the exception of a few taverns, services in the area are . . . closed and vacated by 7 p.m. The degree to which the completion of the malls and open area produced as part of the public works projects increase opportunities for area tenants is at this point a matter of conjecture. . . .[16]

Further on in the same letter, he argued:

The policy issues outlined above are not easy to articulate; their resolution will be no less difficult. The primary concern this decision would seem to rest upon is risk—at what level and borne by whom. Measured simply in dollar terms, the Federal risk approaches $70 million in permanent financing insurance and $17 million in public works . . . as compared to $1 million in City revenue bonds for a parking garage. Measured more importantly in social terms, the costs associated with anything short of a sustained success, particularly in Detroit, would be significantly higher for the Department.

In this case, however, political and administrative pressures were used to good effect. In one of the few instances where an official from one of HUD's ten regional offices became directly involved in an NSA case, the regional administrator based in Chicago (with responsibility for Detroit) wrote to Simons in early April rejecting area office arguments:

We as a Department have, by now, firmly established CBD environments as not only acceptable, but desirable areas for housing development. I also feel that we have firmly established that it is Departmental policy to lead, rather than follow, in center city revitalization. The City of Detroit's commitments to the NSA are not only substantial, but are firmly rooted in reality and practicality. It makes no sense to me to attempt to enforce an outmoded planner's concept of single-purpose land use on the City of Detroit.[17]

Negotiations with Detroit ended in June with approval of the city's basic design by Simons. That action followed a visit to Detroit by Deputy Assistant Secretary, Marilyn Melkonian, who wrote a lengthy memorandum to Simons in mid-June which contained a notably mixed review of the Detroit situation.[18] Although she pointed out that many of Detroit's plans for downtown redevelopment had "progressed no further than the conceptualization phase," she argued that the variety of proposed projects reflected a serious effort at downtown revitalization. Thus, while weighing the risk involved, she favored the NSA design as one vehicle for enhancing "the city's ability to achieve its development and investment objectives" including increasing "the prospect of more people living downtown."[19]

While Assistant Secretary Simons approved the proposal, he did so with reservations reflected in his letter to the area manager:

> It should be made clear that approval of the NSA concept does not mean that we reduce our standards in reviewing proposals for specific buildings that the City submits. Accordingly, the Area Office should, in the case of supporting neighborhood facilities and services, identify those that are presently lacking in the area and that are essential to supporting this residential development. . . . Your office will work with the City to assure that HUD housing approvals at each stage are given only after you are satisfied that the City has taken the actions necessary to provide supportive services and facilities by the time the housing is available. In addition, your office is requested to monitor the progress of the planning and implementation of the [projects proposed by the city].[20]

The city's plans were shaped from the outset by its desire to respond to the indicated interest of one of the largest national rehabilitation companies in undertaking work on the target office buildings. That firm was designated by the city immediately after the city's plans were accepted by HUD. The firm proceeded immediately to implement its project plans with the result that Detroit was one of the first cities in the county to request a speedup in its schedule of unit allocations so that it could complete the Section 8 element of its plan ahead of time.[21]

New York City

Initially, New York City seriously considered submitting 12 areas (including the South Bronx) as NSAs for a total of over 7,200 units of Section 8. In presubmission discussions with the area office, they were dissuaded from submitting the South Bronx and one other neighborhood in an equally devastated condition. What they did submit were proposals for 10 NSAs involving 5,000 units. This was seen, at least by some informants, both as a device for initiating bargaining with HUD and as a symbolic gesture toward responding to the demands of neighborhoods for attention during a bleak period for the city's fiscal health.

When HUD announced its awards, three of the NSAs New York proposed were accepted outright; the other seven were put in the conditional category. In most of the seven cases, the key issue was size—a measure that the central office staff used as a surrogate indicator of the capacity of the city to deliver on community improvements and to design a realistic means for treating the many rental and owner-occupied structures not reached directly by the NSA allocation. While one of the proposed NSAs contained as "few" as 11,000 people, the city and the HUD area office bargained for several months over the acceptability of areas with as many as 86,000 and 190,000 people. On the whole, the city won. The person who served as the city's NSA coordinator later conceded, "At first there was a kind of obstinacy on both sides in our relations with HUD. There were a lot of grays involved in the discussions but people in the city were strongly opposed to targeting [to smaller areas] and some at HUD were adamant for it."[22]

While other details proved to be more readily negotiable, HUD insisted that New York target smaller areas. An agreement was finally reached after prolonged negotiations under which the original NSAs were kept intact but "subareas" were identified where much of the local resource commitment would be focused. As the city's NSA coordinator argued, this still left open the possibility of putting resources into "real eyesores" outside the subareas. At the same time, the city was unwilling to give up the flexibility that went with the designation of larger areas:

There was . . . a reluctance to hone down to subareas because so many needs existed in some of these areas. In addition, if you identify an area, you will alienate others in which you are still trying to work. It becomes a problem to justify outside the areas you have selected.

Despite the seeming narrowness of the issue, it took nearly a year to work out the terms of the deal. The intergovernmental agreement was summarized in an eleven-page memorandum dated 27 August 1979, to Assistant Secretary Simons from Deputy Assistant Secretary Melkonian. Along with the compromise reached on the size issue, it contained more detailed plans for housing rehabilitation and neighborhood revitalization in the designated areas than in the original submissions.

Throughout these negotiations, the interests of the city were well served by the supportive attitudes of key persons in the area office, including the area manager who previously had been deputy mayor of the city. One area office person also noted that the city was receiving "all kinds of assurances [during the period of NSA negotiation] from Jack Watson [of the Carter White House staff] about the resources that would be made available."

Although these negotiations were intended, in part, to maintain federal control over the commitment of Section 8 resources until the conditions were removed, New York went ahead in the spring of 1979 (without central office approval) to advertise all of the five thousand units with the expectation that by one means or another the NSA projects it selected would be funded. The central office's eventual approval of the city's NSAs was regarded, therefore, with obvious cynicism by some area office personnel. As one remarked:

The city picked huge areas and couldn't really commit the kinds of development funds necessary to make those areas really change. As a result, the housing will have very little effect and the [Community Development] effect, if anything goes in there at all, will be minimal.

Nonetheless, political pressures both from within and from outside HUD had made the difference in the decision to accept the problematic NSAs.

CONCLUSIONS

This chapter has traced the steps by which the Office of Housing attempted to create a coalition behind the NSA program by manipulating both policy-related and pork barrel incentives. In the course of the program design process, HUD mobilized support both from those elements of the national progrowth coalition represented by the National Rehabilitation Association and from local governments associated with the USCM. At the same time, Kerry and other program entrepreneurs at HUD brought to the process a concern for the interests of neighborhood organizations and owners of small-scale properties who had never been effectively incorporated into federally financed housing rehabilitation and neighborhood revitalization activities.

Significantly, among the major hurdles for the program designers at that point were HUD's own field offices which failed to play a supportive role in working with local governments to develop strong program plans. Lacking this key commitment and given the reluctance of many local governments to adopt the program entrepreneurs' model for NSA, the central office staff soon came under pressure to relax any effort it might have made to exercise control over the selection process. The greatest pressure for such relaxation, however, came from the political leadership of HUD which came to see political advantages to the agency in maximizing participation.

Thus, what had begun as a relatively centralized program formulation process collapsed during macro-implementation into approval of many questionable plans. To the extent that negotiations with cities given conditional approvals might have constituted additional opportunities to exercise national influence, there were instead more instances of federal retreat from the program entrepreneurs' operational model.

A number of political and administrative considerations brought this situation about. First, HUD's own incapacity to generate sufficient internal agreement about the standards to be applied in reviewing local plans left open to question almost any decision the agency reached. Second, the agency's inability to employ its field staff effectively left the central office inundated with local plans which the review staff was unable to process effectively.

Third, and probably most important, the play of political considerations within HUD worked against maintaining a controlling national position in the macro-implementation process. As it became increasingly clear that the federal budgetary future was likely to be cloudy and that HUD's claims on that budget might shrink, political appointees at HUD saw merit in committing as many resources as quickly as possible to the NSA program even if that meant making resource commitments to localities that had submitted poorly designed plans. Under the circumstances, what may be surprising is not that the selection system went out of control but that HUD officials found some value in engaging in the time-consuming labors involved in negotiating the "conditional" awards, for by that time even full-fledged NSA designations were little more than temporary hunting licenses for properties to be rehabilitated within target areas.

By not holding to its original strategies for resource commitment and program reviews, HUD confirmed the reservations expressed by many experienced local officials that the agency was not capable of living up to its promises. The collapse of the selection process further signaled that local governments were pretty much free to do with the NSA program as they wished.

The way the selection process was conducted was also bound to reinforce the cynicism of field office personnel. To the extent that the idealism of those personnel might have been aroused at the outset of the program, the selection process did little to overcome existing skepticism about the leadership of the department. Certainly, those officials in area offices like Columbus and Detroit who invoked the program model developed by Chisholm and Kerry were not rewarded by the actions taken in Washington. Rather, the decisions of the central office justified the reluctance of field officials to invest energy in highly labor-intensive program planning activities associated with programs like NSA.

NOTES

1. HUD News Release, 13 June 1977.

2. See *Neighborhood Strategy Areas: A Guidebook for Local Government*, prepared for the Office of Policy Development and Research, U.S. Department of Housing and Urban Development, by the U.S. Conference of Mayors and the National Community Development Association, March 1978.

3. See Donald B. Rosenthal, "Neighborhood Strategy Areas," *Journal of Housing* 35 (March 1978), 120–21.

4. For more details on sources for this study, see Appendix A.

5. Thus, the Boston Area Office worked closely with the Massachusetts Housing Finance Agency, which assumed a major role in financing projects in that state, in supporting large-scale projects that deviated significantly from the designs promoted by NSA program entrepreneurs.

6. Little systematic work has been done on grant-related review and selection processes. One of the few attempts to do so in a sophisticated fashion is J. Theodore Anagnoson's work on selection procedures under the Economic Development Administration's public works program and HUD's water and sewer projects program. See his, "Equity, Efficiency and Political Feasibility in Federal Project Procedures," *Policy Sciences* 14 (August 1982), 331–45.

7. "Special Procedures for Neighborhood Strategy Areas," *Federal Register*, vol. 43, no. 21, 31 January 1978, sect. 881.304 (e).

8. Interview, Lawrence B. Simons, Washington, D.C., 13 April 1981.

9. As table 4–2 (below) indicates, there were actually thirty nine NSAs that received conditional approvals. The official list distributed on 21 September excluded Reading, Pennsylvania.

10. There continued to be shifts in numbers as some communities dropped out of the

program and, in a few cases, new NSAs were created. By the end of the second program year (30 September 1980), HUD estimated its outstanding commitment to be 36,449 units.

11. "Successful NSA Applicants Announced," *HUD News*, 21 September 1978.

12. Thus, the fears stated earlier by the U.S. Conference of Mayors were beginning to come true. A further concession was made in March 1979, however, when HUD agreed to contribute 2,150 units from a central office reserve for FY80 toward the estimated 4,150 units expected to constitute the demand for that year.

13. At the time localities applied for participation in the program, few could have anticipated how important these schedules would become in allocating program resources.

14. "Successful NSA Applicants Announced," 46.

15. Letter from Ronald J. Hewitt, Director, Community and Economic Development Department, City of Detroit, to Stephen W. Brown, Area Manager, Detroit Area Office, 9 January 1979. Within the boundaries finally developed for the NSA, the only existing residential structure was a 42-unit apartment building containing market-rate units.

16. Memorandum from Stephen W. Brown to Lawrence B. Simons and Jack Kerry, 30 March 1979.

17. Memorandum from Ron Gratton, Regional Administrator, Region V, to Lawrence B. Simons, 5 April 1979.

18. In a reorganization late in 1978, Deputy Assistant Secretary for Assisted Housing Chisholm was replaced by Melkonian who became Deputy Assistant Secretary for Multi-family Housing Programs. The latter unit included a new rehabilitation division headed by Jack Kerry in charge of NSA.

19. Memorandum from Marilyn Melkonian to Lawrence B. Simons, 18 June 1979.

20. Memorandum from Lawrence B. Simons to Stephen W. Brown, 19 June 1979.

21. On the success of the Detroit project, see William G. Rosenberg, "Downtown Adaptive Reuse Project Signals New Public/Private Partnership," *Journal of Housing* 38 (August–September 1981), 437–43. According to other sources, investment in the area continued and some of the private residential activity predicted for the areas has taken place.

22. Steven Gratwohl, New York City NSA Coordinator, Department of Housing Preservation and Development, 8 January 1980.

5

MACRO-IMPLEMENTATION II: THE LOCAL PERSPECTIVE

Many localities chose to develop proposals that differed significantly from the national model. That is not to suggest that the national model was intrinsically better than the strategies that localities pursued, but rather to indicate the extent to which local redefinitions of the national strategy occurred during macro-implementation.

THE NATIONAL MODEL

Major elements of the design preferred by NSA program entrepreneurs involved selection of a target area that would have the following characteristics:

1. it would be predominantly residential;
2. it would have a size and composition amenable to marked improvement in no more than five years given the resources available;
3. it would contain relatively small rental structures owned by inexperienced landlords who would be interested in participating in the program.

In addition, HUD wished to encourage designs that showed evidence that a local government would use the program as a vehicle for enhancing its capacity to carry out future programs of housing rehabilitation and neighborhood revitalization.

In practice, few localities' plans displayed all four of these characteristics. In this chapter, we examine deviations from features of that model in order to better understand the nature of local choices.

Creating "Neighborhoods"

As we saw in the case of Detroit in chapter 4, if one of the major premises of the NSA program was to improve declining residential neighborhoods, a large number of localities flatly rejected that goal in favor of introducing residential units into areas where they were not already present. Where it was employed, this strategy often was a way of avoiding controversy with neighborhood populations while responding to local demand for assisted housing, particularly for the elderly. A related strategy involved providing assisted housing in previously nonresidential structures in areas that did contain residential populations. In such cases, local goals included both providing housing and ridding the neighborhood of "eyesores."

Some local designs shared the NSA program entrepreneurs' goal of revitalizing declining areas (whether downtown or neighborhood); in other instances, the decision was less a product of the goal of neighborhood revitalization than of a desire to satisfy a private developer's interest in making a handsome profit on rehabilitating or converting a large structure for residential use.

Because of the ambiguity associated with defining a neighborhood, most localities did not have much difficulty satisfying HUD that they were meeting this criterion. The situation was particularly favorable for smaller communities where the lines between nonresidential and residential areas were not sharply demarcated. It was rare to encounter a case quite as clear-cut as Detroit's, though other instances might have been open to considerable debate had HUD field offices been as strict as Detroit's area office in applying a "neighborhood" standard.

Thus, localities like Fall River, Lowell, New Bedford, and Waltham in Massachusetts, Cohoes, New York, and Winooski, Vermont, were all authorized to undertake the conversion of abandoned textile mills to senior citizen housing in downtown business areas. In such cases, HUD contented itself with local arguments that the structures were of historic interest, constituted major blighting influences, or that conversion to housing fulfilled an important need in high demand housing markets.

Perhaps the least problematic of these cases involved the approach taken by the city of Lowell, which converted a large vacant mill in its central business district (CBD). This came in the wake of HUD's earlier Demonstration Rehabilitation (Demo Rehab) program commitment to convert three other nearby commercial and manufacturing structures into housing for the elderly. The latter projects had earlier aroused considerable local controversy with respect to the high concentration of such housing in an area that contained few neighborhood facilities.[1] Furthermore, the mill selected by the city for NSA was a source of local concern because of heavy traffic nearby and the presence in its immediate vicinity of a textile company that utilized suspect chemicals.

Nevertheless, Lowell's preference was endorsed by HUD's Boston area office for several reasons. Most importantly, the rehabilitation of the mill was part of a larger plan for the city's revitalization that had already received favorable national publicity as part of the city's selection by the National Park Service as the site of the first national urban park. Through skillful local government leadership and with the assistance of then-Congressman Paul Tsongas and Senator Edward Kennedy, the city had embarked on a major CBD revitalization effort.[2] The commitment of $40 million by the National Park Service and an additional $10 million under the state's own Heritage Park Program were part of a plan to restore the waterways and historic areas around the mill.

Equally important, the Massachusetts Housing Finance Agency—by far the most active state housing finance and development agency involved in the NSA program—was ready to provide construction finance to rehabilitate the mill. HUD was influenced by the vigorous participation of that agency in this and other local program efforts. The result was that projects like the mill in Lowell, vacant commercial or industrial facilities in Chicopee, New Bedford, Taunton, and Worcester, and empty school buildings in Fall River, Pittsfield, and Revere became NSA projects once the state agency indicated its financial support without much concern for the residential character of the neighborhood.[3]

"Not Too Big Nor Too Bad"

During presentations to local governments, central office program personnel stressed HUD's desire to promote the selection of areas where a reasonable concentration of effort and resources might be expected to reverse disinvestment in no more than five years. This goal was reduced to a slogan, "Not too big nor too bad." That many local officials were aware of that catchphrase was evident by the regularity with which it was quoted back to me in the course of interviews.

While the standard is difficult to operationalize, it is clear that some of the largest cities (e.g., New York, Chicago, Houston) proposed areas that were disproportionately large in relation to the resources available. In those three cases, as well as in another set of cities (including Atlanta, Baltimore, Gary, New York, and Wilmington, Delaware), the target areas were also (by many observers' standards) "too bad." In the latter cases, the probability was high that the locality would be unable to attract sufficient investment to rehabilitate a significant proportion of those dwelling units (both rental and owner-occupied) not covered by the Section 8 Substantial Rehabilitation (Sub Rehab) commitment. Nor was there much likelihood of the revitalization of critical neighborhood commercial and service infrastructure—the wherewithal to assure a self-sustaining neighborhood.

Still, there were several reasons for the choices that localities made. Among the most frequently cited was a desire to complete work in an area that had received an infusion of resources under earlier federal programs including urban renewal and the Community Development Block Grant (CDBG) Program. This approach was actually encouraged by the Carter administration's emphasis on concentrating resources from CDBG on low- and moderate-income populations through a requirement that local governments designate Community Development Neighborhood Strategy Areas (CD NSAs).

Some localities responded to that requirement by selecting neighborhoods in extremely poor condition. It followed, then, that when the Office of Housing sought proposals for the Section 8 NSA program that would focus resources in areas already designated as CD NSAs or that would be eligible for such designation, some fairly bad areas would be submitted. In a sense, it was HUD's own internal conflicts that caused the contradiction. For, while the Section 8 NSA's program entrepreneurs were pressing localities to select the best of the worst neighborhoods, those administering CDBG encouraged the same localities to select more marginal areas.

A second reason for including neighborhoods that were "too bad" was an interest in treating blighted areas close to parts of a city—most commonly the CBD but also sometimes gentrifying neighborhoods—where private investment of the kind the city sought to encourage was evident. Third, the emphasis of the NSA program on the rehabilitation of existing rental structures limited available choices in many communities to only a few neighborhoods where substandard rental units were concentrated. Fourth, the selection of areas was sometimes the result of political efforts by neighborhood residents or by other organizations concerned with neighborhood redevelopment.

In instances where the area selected might be regarded as "too big," a major reason was that the program could be used to reach a few large structures considered to be blighting influences on different portions of the NSA. This approach was particularly common where local governments did not wish to engage in efforts to rehabilitate small-scale residential stock. The selection of large areas was also premised on a desire to avoid speculation among property owners who might drive up asking prices to developers because they knew the buildings they owned were primary targets for Section 8. Indeed, the added expenses to developers associated with inflated acquisition costs became a problem that many cities experienced, sometimes with the result that projects foundered altogether.

Some of the flavor of the choices made may be suggested by providing two examples. An NSA that might be characterized as both "too big" and "too bad" was Chicago's North Lawndale; one that was simply "too bad" was Hartford's Clay Hill.

Chicago's North Lawndale

North Lawndale was one of the poorest neighborhoods in Chicago both in terms of the income level of its residents and the condition of its structures. One of the major forces in Greater Lawndale (an area of 95,000 people in 1970) was Pyramidwest, a Community Development Corporation (CDC).[4] That organization was closely attuned to the availability of federal resources. It sought to use them in promoting plans for such projects as a community bank, a community health center, and a shopping mall. These projects had met with mixed success up to 1978.

At the same time, using various nonprofit and for-profit subsidiaries, the CDC sponsored several federally assisted new construction housing projects and also managed approximately 1,400 units of rental housing that had reverted to HUD as a result of defaults under earlier federal programs. Of those units, 788 (in 91 structures) were located in the target area within Greater Lawndale identified for the Section 8 NSA program. The fact that these units were occupied did not attest to their condition, for some were in a state of disrepair that must have caused them to fall below existing housing standards if Chicago had bothered to maintain an active code enforcement program in the area.

Nevertheless, the quality of many of the structures targeted for NSA did not require the kind of ''gut rehab'' expected to be done under Sub Rehab. Therefore, the CDC was working on two problems at the same time: it wished to provide rental subsidies to as many of the low-income residents of the neighborhood as possible, including those living in the HUD-owned properties it managed; and it hoped to reach beyond those properties to improve some of the other structures in the area, including a 57-unit complex owned by the city of Chicago as the result of another default.

The city government showed little interest in Lawndale, so that when the NSA program was announced, Pyramidwest took the lead in writing the proposal for the area on behalf of the city. It also negotiated details with HUD prior to formal submission of the proposal. Indeed, when it appeared for a time that the city government might be required to make a major commitment of CDBG to support neighborhood improvements under NSA, the city considered dropping out of the program altogether; at that point, the CDC and senior area office officials convinced the government that it would not be held to such a commitment and it decided to remain involved.

Despite the effort the CDC was making, improvement in the area was in considerable doubt. Not only was Chicago unlikely to provide CDBG in substantial amounts, but there was no evidence that private investment either in residential structures or in commercial activity would be enhanced as a result of the designation of the area as an NSA. Nevertheless, as a spokesperson for Pyramidwest argued in November 1980, the CDC was committed to helping those people already living in the neighborhood with whatever resources became available—even if the NSA program failed to stimulate significant revitalization.

Hartford's Clay Hill

Like Lawndale, Hartford's Clay Hill had been the ward of federal programs for many years. As a result of urban renewal, many substandard units were demolished during the 1960s. By 1978, about 25 percent of the land area consisted of vacant lots. The availability of such land for development had failed to stimulate private investment. The residential structures that remained on the site contained 482 dwelling units; of those, 407 required some degree of rehabilitation. Fewer than 10 percent of the structures were owner-occupied.

Despite considerable doubts among central office program officials that the neighborhood would succeed as an NSA, the city's proposal was given conditional approval contingent on a greater commitment by the city to the concentration of CDBG in the area and receipt of a grant (then pending) from the state of Connecticut under a state program for financing property acquisition and site preparation. The state awarded that grant in February 1979, which triggered removal of HUD's conditions in March.

Small Structures and Inexperienced Owners

Many local officials felt that the costs of working with inexperienced owners of small structures would require too much administrative time and energy. This was the case especially since their own experience in running such programs was limited. Instead of using NSA as a means of enhancing their administrative capacity, therefore, they turned major responsibility for project planning and implementation over to professional developers. These local governments still took seriously their responsibilities in coordinating physical improvements in the target area, but once developers were selected, they often assumed roles as interested bystanders while their developers negotiated project plans with HUD. Local officials stepped back into the rehabilitation process only when major problems arose such as the inability of a developer to move forward with the speed that HUD, the neighborhood, or the city government thought appropriate.

While that was the dominant approach of local governments, there were some instances when local officials attempted to pursue a "small structure–inexperienced owner" approach. Only rarely did that strategy meet with any great success. In some places, having pursued such a strategy for a while, localities reversed field and used their allocations in the more common manner; elsewhere, localities withdrew from the program when they realized how demanding that strategy was. Finally, there were localities which sought to combine the two strategies by focusing resources on large structures in the early years of the program with the expectation that this would enhance their capacity to work with smaller-scale owners at a later point in program implementation.

We shall reserve to later chapters more detailed descriptions of the experiences of those local governments which attempted to carry out the "small structure–inexperienced owner" strategy. We should note here, however, two variants of that approach that were tried in a number of places. The first involved combining professional developers with some small-scale landlord participation; the second used experienced developers to rehabilitate small structures.

WHOSE CAPACITY IS IT, ANYWAY?

Program entrepreneurs expected that the involvement of local governments in allocating Section 8 units and coordinating a range of other activities in NSAs would contribute to a significant increase in local capacity to administer similar programs in the future, particularly if HUD moved toward a housing block grant. On balance, capacity building may have occurred, though such learning as local officials acquired should be weighed against the painful experiences that many had to go through in order to acquire it. In many cases, local governments sought to minimize their administrative and political costs from the outset.

One consideration that influenced this attitude was the absence of a front-end grant from HUD (unlike the procedure under urban renewal or Model Cities) that would have reimbursed the locality for program planning costs. Instead, HUD made it clear that any administrative costs incurred by a locality would have to be defrayed out of local program resources, including CDBG. For many localities this was a major concern since they were reluctant to devote staff time to engaging in a program design process when they were not guaranteed program participation. They were also concerned about committing resources to a "demonstration" program that might prove to have no future. A major result of this HUD decision, according to some informants, was the poor quality of many applications.

It was particularly unreasonable for small cities with limited staffs or even larger cities with NSA programs that involved rehabilitating only a few large structures to undertake programs that required major staff investment. Consequently, in a substantial number of instances the NSA program was, in effect, "contracted out"—using that term in its broadest sense—not only to private developers but also to other types of nongovernmental organizations.[5]

"Contracting out" took a variety of forms. In a few instances, local governments became little more than "pass through" agencies for the program—hiring private consultants to develop the original request for participation; selecting development organizations to prepare applications, to negotiate project details with HUD and with financing agencies, and to deal with antagonistic groups in the target neighborhood. In other instances, governments turned to locally based nongovernmental and quasi-governmental entities to play such roles. The second approach may have contributed to enhancing local expertise and the understanding of federal programs more than the first by increasing technical capacity within the community even though it did not directly expand the capacity of the local bureaucracy.

Thus, in a number of places neighborhood-based organizations (NBOs) (or those we shall identify as advocacy planning organizations [APOs]) assumed major roles in local program design processes. While some of these groups had been created earlier to oppose particular redevelopment projects, others were developed as organizational means for delivering social services to a neighborhood or providing an ongoing voice for neighborhood concerns. In some instances, neighborhood interests were institutionalized as CDCs: multifunctional development organizations with bases in particular neighborhoods operated as entities with independent claims to technical skills.[6]

CDCs may be viewed as one among several types of NBOs that lay along a continuum from those organizations claiming to represent largely unmobilized residential populations to neighborhoods where a large number of residents regularly take part in local decisions through such organizations. On that continuum, one would also need to place groupings of episodically mobilized citizens.[7] Obviously, only the more formalized NBOs would have been in a position to play a leading role in the deisgn of NSA programs, though others were capable of influencing project implementation, as we shall see in chapter 6.

Along with the activation of many NBOs, the 1960s gave birth to APOs that came to perform important programmatic functions within lower-income neighborhoods even though they were not necessarily run by residents of the neighborhood nor did they always claim to "represent" residents' interests except in a transcendental sense. Of particular relevance to the present study are those planning or social service organizations whose creation or purpose reflected the social commitments of the 1960s. Some of these were sparked by the debate within the planning profession over whose interests that profession should serve in urban project planning. Advocacy planning, as it came to be known, argued that trained planners should treat the residents of neighborhoods targeted for redevelopment as their "clients" and should put their skills in service to those residents.[8]

In addition to Pyramidwest, NBOs or APOs in such places as New Haven, Savannah, St. Louis, Pittsfield, Massachusetts, and Troy, New York, as well as in several of New York City's NSAs, became the developers of either part or all of the NSA units. In other places, such organizations took on major roles as consultants to the local government in expediting negotiations among developers, property owners, and HUD.

For the most part, these organizations had permanent staffs with considerable experience in dealing with federal programs. Groups varied in the depth of their connections with the target neighborhoods. They included some that had long-term commitments to particular neighborhoods like Pyramidwest in North Lawndale, the Bedford-Stuyvesant Restoration Corporation in Brooklyn, and the Union-Sarah Economic Development Corporation in St. Louis. In other cases, organizations had general expertise but were not neighborhood specific; rather, they had chosen to focus on a particular neighborhood in planning for and implementing NSA. It was rare to find a totally inexperienced organization attempting to assume major responsibility for operating an NSA program. Where one did, as in San Antonio, both it and the city soon discovered that they were trying to undertake an effort considerably beyond their capacity; they dropped out of the program.

In some cases where nongovernmental entities ran NSA programs, city officials were only marginally involved in program oversight. At other times, there emerged a functional division of labor in which the nongovernmental entity assumed much of the responsibility for housing rehabilitation while the city government focused on implementing other important elements of the design.

It may be useful to illustrate this kind of relationship using the Troy Rehabilitation Improvement Program (TRIP), an APO based in Troy, New York. Organized in 1968 as a tenant and home owner counseling organization, by 1977 it had grown into an organization that sought to provide "home ownership opportunities to low and moderate income families through housing rehabilitation" by helping to "rehabilitate homes, arrange bank financing and obtain assistance from the city and other levels of government."[9] It was put together as a nonprofit organization of volunteers, half of whose board was made up of individuals from the four Community Development (CD) NSAs that the city had designated. Working with that board, the organization claimed (by 1980) that its technical staff had "brought about the rehabilitation of over 300 units through assistance such as finance packaging, preparation of construction documents, and job supervision."

TRIP acted as the city's consultant in developing the local proposal for the Section 8 NSA program for one of the city's CD NSAs; eventually it was designated as the developer for the neighborhood. The area involved was one that had been adversely affected by highway project proposals (one built; another terminated before construction) and by heavy disinvestment resulting partly from the threat of construction but also from the ills commonly found in older urban neighborhoods. As the executive director of TRIP admitted, the area might have been considered "too bad" by some standards, but this had served as an advantage to the organization, for the city had allowed it a freedom of operation that might not otherwise have been available. As she commented, "If it had been a gentrifying neighborhood, the situation would have been very different politically."[10]

The experience of a small number of other communities indicated that NSA provided them with an opportunity to shift existing capacity among government agencies without necessarily resulting in expanded capacity. Earlier housing and community development programs had required localities to develop a set of relatively autonomous specialized administrative structures like public housing and urban renewal agencies. When CDBG came along, part of its appeal to local government officials was the expectation that program responsibilities would shift back to generalist control. In practice, the shift in responsibilities varied with local political situations, including the political power that existing agencies had.[11]

For example, in Akron, Ohio, the Akron Metropolitan Housing Authority (AMHA) under two aggressive executive directors had come to play a significant role in operating a variety of assisted housing programs, including the Existing and Moderate Rehabilitation (Mod Rehab) elements of Section 8. It also was one of the leaders among local housing agencies in the issuance of bonds to

finance private-developer, assisted-housing projects. Initially, the AMHA expected to play a major role in the development and implementation of Akron's
NSA program. As discussions about the program proceeded, however, the municipal Department of Planning and Development became more assertive. The
result was that the AMHA eventually withdrew from a leading role in program
development except in helping to provide financing for some of the projects.

While we have highlighted difficulties in the way of enhancing technical
capacity within localities for doing rental rehabilitation or in shifting organizational capacity among local government structures, other cases illustrate a growth
in such capacity that should not be minimized. Interestingly enough, one of the
localities where this occurred most clearly was New York City.

New York City

In 1973, New York designated five neighborhoods for participation in an
experimental Neighborhood Preservation Program (NPP) intended to decentralize
administration of a number of housing programs to neighborhood offices run by
city staff. At the same time, the city created a network of community planning
boards which constituted neighborhood advisory bodies on project planning;
however, their effective control over both programmatic and administrative resources was limited.[12] However, When CDBG was introduced in 1974, the city
was reluctant to designate any of the five NPPs or other areas as target areas for
the purpose of concentrating resources from CDBG.[13]

With the advent of the Section 8 NSA program, this resistance became even
more pronounced. In chapter 4, we mentioned the lengthy negotiations that went
on between the city and HUD over the designation and delimitation of neighborhoods for NSA. What was partially at issue was the matter of targeting CDBG
resources selectively. Thus, at the same time that New York was negotiating its
ten Section 8 NSAs, it was reluctantly agreeing to designate fourteen CD NSAs,
including all ten of those areas chosen for participation in the Section 8 NSA
program. At the time, too, NPPs were being created for six additional areas,
three of which were coterminus with proposed Section 8 NSAs.

As community groups which had pressed for designation of their areas either
as CD NSAs or as participants in NPPs (or both) soon discovered, the resources
the city was actually willing to give to areas in excess of what had been provided
formerly under CDBG were minimal. Nevertheless, such focusing of administrative attention as did take place served as a stimulus to more integrated efforts
at neighborhood revitalization.

While the resulting Section 8 NSAs varied enormously in their needs, and in
the mechanisms through which they were administered (as well as in the level
of administrative capacity displayed by intermediate institutions), the process of
political dialogue generated by designation was impressive. This is far from
asserting that the plans eventually implemented succeeded in reversing deterioration in all of the areas involved or that improvements in the more ''successful''

NSAs were simply a function of public programs. On the contrary, in several areas, notably the three NSAs on the west side of Manhattan (Manhattan Valley, Hamilton Heights, and Washington Heights), such upgrading as took place during the period from 1978 to 1983 may have been mainly the result of private investment decisions, given the heated residential market in the city. Government programs appear to have played a more significant role in the improvement or stabilization of three Brooklyn NSAs (Flatbush, Crown Heights, and Sunset Park), but even there other forces were at work.

Nonetheless, the negotiations that went on in connection with the designation of Section 8 NSAs in New York City coincided with other program activities that required regular administrative interactions among various combinations of NPP officials, CDCs (where present), community planning boards, property owners, tenant organizations, developers, and state and local government actors. In a curious fashion, then, the mechanisms set in place in some of New York City's NSAs came to resemble more closely the participatory processes the program's entrepreneurs originally had in mind than in many other localities.

New Haven

In a number of other communities, however, NSA may actually have been part of a process of taking a step backwards from the kinds of planning and implementation responsibilities performed by specialized agencies of local government in the past. The city of New Haven is interesting example. For, as early as the 1950s, New Haven had developed a highly centralized and professional bureaucracy to design and administer the city's urban renewal programs. When CDBG came along, municipal operations began to run in a direction different from conventional notions of capacity building, particularly as the city government decentralized and "deprofessionalized" some aspects of its program.[14]

New Haven selected as its Section 8 NSA an area that had been targeted for CDBG funds since 1975. Under the city's Neighborhood Preservation Program, participation in planning for the neighborhood involved employing a "planning team" made up of both residents and planners. The neighborhood in the target area found itself wrestling in particular with the problems of a residential street that was described by one informant as having "some very nice architecture but a lot of houses are vacant, vandalized."[15] After two years of struggle with these problems, the team turned for help to Neighborhood Housing, Inc. (NHI), a local APO.

NHI was formed in 1971 as an outgrowth of the local antipoverty agency's activities. It bought, rehabilitated, and sold houses on a small scale and provided technical assistance to neighborhoods throughout the New Haven area. As part of the NSA plan, NHI proposed working with small owners to submit individual structures for program participation.[16] However, the Hartford area office of HUD discouraged this small-scale approach. NHI then turned to the National Corporation for Housing Partnerships (a federally created development organization) to assist them in playing the role of developer for a set of small structures.[17]

At the same time, the city of New Haven had contracted out some of its neighborhood planning programs to a quasi-governmental organization, the Housing Rehabilitation Institute. The institute performed consultant work for neighborhoods both inside and outside the city.[18] At some points in the NSA process, therefore, the two nongovernmental organizations found themselves conducting negotiations over such matters as community improvements on the street where NSA work was being done—one on behalf of the city government, the other acting for the neighborhood.

Capacity building is even more difficult to assess when the issue is raised with respect to a few cases where complex political and governmental relationships were involved in the design and implementation of local plans. Two such cases—those of Erie County, New York, and Greenbelt, Maryland—illustrate the issues involved.

Erie County, New York

Erie County acted as the initiating agency for the NSA application for the use of Sub Rehab units in the community of Cedargrove Heights in the white working-class suburban town of Cheektowaga. Under New York State law, counties have no direct responsibility for housing programs.[19] Erie County's involvement in NSA, therefore, was based on its role in administering a consortium of localities (towns and villages) that received CDBG under urban county entitlement procedures. To further complicate matters, Cheektowaga was in the process of withdrawing from the consortium even as local plans for NSA were being developed.

The administrative situation was made more problematic by a county decision to contract out responsibilities for providing technical assistance to owners and administering the relocation element of the design to a local private consulting organization which had considerable experience in operating Section 8 Existing and Mod Rehab programs in the city of Buffalo as well as in the county.[20] This decision made sense in terms of the county's inexperience in the administration of housing programs but provided limited potential for either the county or the town to develop capacity for administering revitalization programs in the future.

Greenbelt, Maryland

An equally anomalous situation arose in Greenbelt, Maryland, a ''new town'' created by the federal government in 1937. Located on what was then the outer perimeter of the District of Columbia, by the 1970s it had become a central location in the metropolitan area and one in great demand as a residential community. During the 1950s, Greenbelt had been converted into a housing cooperative with its own resident board operating through a corporate entity, Greenbelt

Homes, Inc. (GHI).[21] Governmentally, however, GHI housing constituted only a portion of the municipality of Greenbelt, which in turn fell within the jurisdiction of Prince Georges County.

By the 1970s it was apparent to the board of GHI that their 1,548 single-family units were in need of rehabilitation. The community initially applied for a multiunit Section 312 loan. Up to that time, 312 had been used primarily for rehabilitating small (1–4 unit) owner-occupied structures. While, in principle, housing cooperatives were eligible for participation in the 312 program, the application of GHI on behalf of the entire community represented a novel step. Through much effort, GHI managed to qualify for the largest residential 312 loan on record up to that time, $5.7 million. However, members of the cooperative sought to assure that upgrading would not undermine the mixed-class character of the community.[22]

GHI sought participation in the NSA program as a means of assuring that low- and moderate-income residents would not be displaced under the pressures of the middle-class market interested in buying into the community. It went about the complex process of putting the pieces together for an NSA request that was shepherded through the municipal government, through the county, and through various agencies of the state and national governments. These negotiations were made even more difficult by a series of issues raised by the Maryland State Historic Preservation Office concerning the preservation of the special features of Greenbelt as a community of historical significance. Unfortunately, preservation of some of those features conflicted at critical points with the FHA's standards for providing mortgage insurance.

Viewed only from the narrow perspective of capacity building, the considerable effort expended by GHI to ford a series of administrative rapids on its way toward revitalization was nonsustaining. For once its plans for the community were completed, few of the lessons so painfully learned were likely to carry over to the administrative operations of either the municipality of Greenbelt or to Prince Georges County.

CONCLUSIONS

In this chapter, we have examined how local governments acted on the four principal operational standards promoted by NSA program entrepreneurs. Those standards involved: (1) predominantly residential neighborhoods; (2) neighborhoods capable of marked improvement in no more than five years; (3) small structures owned by relatively inexperienced landlords; and (4) administrative plans that would enhance the technical capacity of local government agencies to carry out future housing rehabilitation and neighborhood revitalization projects.

While we shall have occasion to review the experiences of localities that attempted (at least at the outset of the program) to implement these program principles, a considerable number of local governments submitted plans that deviated from the model: nonresidential areas were targeted; large areas or areas containing high percentages of substandard dwelling units were selected; many local plans focused on rehabilitating only one or two large structures using professional developers; and a number of local governments sought to minimize their administrative commitments by assigning major program responsibilities to others.

One possible result of these deviations from the program entrepreneurs' model could have been to provide an opportunity to HUD either to reject errant NSA designs outright or to assign them "conditional approval" status. As we saw in chapter 4, in fact, the principal outcome of the review process was the acceptance of a wide array of local designs by HUD, many of which deviated in significant measure from the operational model.

From the materials presented in this chapter, it might well be argued that the federal government succeeded in "selling" the NSA program to local political interests but those local interests only "bought" those features of the program that reflected their own political preferences. Clearly, this was not an instance of local progrowth coalitions serving simply as subordinates of the national government. To achieve such programmatic understandings as were struck, the federal agency had to pay a relatively high price in accepting local diversity. In terms of the intergovernmental models introduced in chapter 1, what was intended to be a "sharing" approach to program formulation was rapidly taking on bargaining and pork barrel qualities.

If the study had concluded at this point, one might well have argued that this was merely another case in which an initial semblance of federal direction or coordination gave way to a purely pork barrel approach to the distribution of public resources. As we shall see in the following chapters, the permissiveness apparent at the outset was followed by a tightening of federal control as the program moved into micro-implementation—but that control came from a direction not presaged by the national model.

NOTES

1. One way Demo Rehab was significantly different from NSA was that HUD selected projects rather than leaving those decisions to local officials. That led to a good deal of acrimony in Lowell about the former program when the choice of structures by HUD (based on developer submissions) were markedly different from those preferred by the local government. See *The Sun* (Lowell, Mass.), 26 September 1977.

2. See Neil R. Pierce, "New Life in Spindle City," *Washington Post*, 29 December 1977; and Lewis T. Karabatsos, "Lowell Reborn," *National Parks and Conservation Magazine* 54 (January 1980), 4–9.

3. In a few cases (e.g., New Bedford and Waltham) the target structures were not in CBDs but in relatively isolated sections of those cities—a strategy that might have been even more debatable than the selection of CBD sites.

4. For an introduction to various nongovernmental participants in the NSA program, including CDCs, see the final section of this chapter.

5. On the theory and practice of "contracting out," see E. S. Savas, *Privatizing the Public Sector* (Chatham, N.J.: Chatham House, 1982).

6. On CDCs, see Milton Kotler, *Neighborhood Government* (Indianapolis: Bobbs-Merrill, 1969), esp. 39–61.

7. On issues of neighborhood organization and activation, see Jeffrey R. Henig, *Neighborhood Mobilization* (New Brunswick, N.J.: Rutgers University Press, 1982); and Sandra Perlman Schoenberg and Patricia L. Rosenbaum, *Neighborhoods That Work* (New Brunswick, N.J.: Rutgers University Press, 1980).

8. See, in particular, Jane Jacobs, *The Death and Life of Great American Cities* (New York: Vintage, 1963); and Paul Davidoff, "Advocacy and Pluralism in Planning," *Journal of the American Institute of Planners* 31 (November 1965), 331–38. For a critique of that perspective, see Rosalie G. Genovese, "Issues in Combining Social Action with Planning: The Case of Advocacy Planning," in *Research in Social Problems and Public Policy*, edited by Michael Lewis, vol. 1, 195–224 (Greenwich, Conn.: JAI Press, 1979).

9. This and the following quotation come from "TRIP Profile," an undated statement distributed by the organization.

10. Interview, Barbara Jones, Executive Director, TRIP, Troy, New York, 24 June 1980.

11. For the adaptations that special-function agencies made to generalist efforts to gain control over the distribution of CDBG, see Paul R. Dommel et al., *Decentralizing Urban Policy* (Washington, D.C.: Brookings Institution, 1982); and Donald F. Kettl, *Managing Community Development in the New Federalism* (New York: Praeger, 1980).

12. See, Allen H. Barton, et al., *Decentralizing City Government* (Lexington, Mass.: Lexington Books, 1977); and Ira Katznelson, *City Trenches* (Chicago: University of Chicago Press, 1981), esp. chap. 7.

13. Informants suggested that neighborhood groups put a much greater weight on gaining designation as CD NSAs than as Section 8 NSAs, so that it might be argued that the former was a more important trigger for coordinated planning and program activities than the latter. Nevertheless, the resource commitments the city was asked to make in the course of Section 8 NSA negotiations provided an important additional element in efforts to develop and implement plans for particular neighborhoods.

14. For the earlier period, see Raymond E. Wolfinger, *The Politics of Progress* (Englewood Cliffs, N.J.: Prentice-Hall, 1974); for the later, see Kettl, *Managing Community Development*, esp. 37–49; and Norman L. Fainstein and Susan S. Fainstein, "New Haven: The Limits of the Local State," in *Restructuring the City* edited by Susan S. Fainstein et al., 27–79 (New York: Longman, 1983).

15. Interview, Stephen Darley, Neighborhood Housing, Inc., New Haven, Connecticut, 19 January 1981.

16. The city had been negotiating with a Boston-based developer to convert a large light manufacturing structure in the area to elderly housing prior to NSA. When New Haven decided to participate in the program, 144 units of the city's 300-unit allocation were dedicated to the large project; the remainder were targeted to small-property rehabilitation.

17. New Haven's NSA program was one of several assisted by that corporation. For a brief consideration of that organization's role in other NSAs, see chapter 8.

18. The institute can also be characterized as an APO, since its orientations were as much toward neighborhood services as were those of NHI. Indeed, the attitudes and styles of the heads of the two organizations were similar.

19. Erie County was the only county in New York State that participated in the NSA program. Several counties in other states took on program responsibilities.

20. The town also employed a consultant to administer its CDBG programs.

21. While Section 8 NSA regulations explicitly qualified housing cooperatives for program participation, few made use of the opportunity.

22. HUD was opposed from the outset of the NSA program to using a "double subsidy" which would have combined 312 loans and Section 8 subsidies in the same units. Therefore, GHI proposed that its allocation of Section 8 would go into structures whose rehabilitation would be financed by a bond issue while the 312 resources would be used in other structures.

6

MICRO-IMPLEMENTATION I: ORGANIZING FOR PROJECT IMPLEMENTATION

Once a program design was approved by HUD, the local government or its designated agent assumed the primary responsibility for converting that design into local projects. This chapter and the two that follow deal with different aspects of this micro-implementation process. The present chapter extends the discussion begun in chapter 5 by focusing on the perspectives of those who sought to accommodate project plans to local political circumstances; in chapter 7, we examine intergovernmental issues in implementation. Chapter 8 then considers the principal factors that accounted for getting Section 8 Neighborhood Strategy Area (NSA) projects underway.

Based on an examination of case materials, three sets of behavioral principles appear to have shaped the projects that local program implementers pursued. Those principles were:

1. *Minimize displacement* either: (a) because substantial displacement is likely to arouse political opposition within the target neighborhood; or (b) because large-scale displacement will require the local government to divert resources from other purposes to relocation benefits.[1]

2. *Minimize political opposition from target area(s)* by selecting as NSAs: (a) nonneighborhoods (of the kind identified in chapter 5); or (b) areas where a preponderance of residents are likely to be either eligible for Section 8 subsidies or apathetic, rather than neighborhoods undergoing gentrification or ones where strong social networks exist.

3. *Minimize the costs of administration* either: (a) by concentrating program resources in the hands of experienced developers who will undertake conversion projects or the rehabilitation of vacant structures; or (b) by relying on neighborhood-based organizations or local housing development groups to assume much of the administrative responsibility.

The elements of this local program agenda were rarely verbalized but the sum of their operation reflected decisions by local governments to bring as many resources as possible from the Section 8 program into the locality while minimizing local conflict, even at the occasional cost of enhancing intergovernmental conflict. As a result, most local program designs moved into project implementation without much rancor but also without significant local participation or even much local awareness that a federal program was underway. Such an approach did not guarantee program "success," since factors exogenous to local control frequently intervened. Indeed, certain programs were born quietly, lived lives of quiet desperation, and then died quietly while others were successful even when they appeared to be doomed at various stages because of heated local conflicts.

While only a few programs attracted much public attention, a number of them merit review because they reveal the potential for community conflict that existed within the NSA program and why most local governments avoided several of the options available to them.

THE DISPLACEMENT ISSUE

Aside from locating projects in nonresidential areas in order to minimize displacement, localities supported project plans in predominantly residential areas that targeted resources to nonresidential structures or vacant residential buildings. Where such a strategy was not adopted, serious opposition could arise. The cases of Hayes Valley in San Francisco and Hoboken, New Jersey, illustrate such opposition.

San Francisco's Hayes Valley

The immediate problems of the Hayes Valley NSA grew out of San Francisco's attempt to carry forward its own Rehabilitation Assistance Program (RAP). That program resulted from the city's participation in a state program created in 1973 which authorized cities and counties to establish rehabilitation programs and issue revenue bonds to finance those activities.

RAP called for systematic code enforcement based on mandatory inspections and made available low-interest loans to owners to upgrade units. It also involved a major commitment of public funds to community revitalization activities, was supposed to have a strong citizen participation component, and was expected to be associated with a systematic effort to assist those displaced by rehabilitation activities. As the city's 1979 Community Development Program report described the approach, it was to be a "continuation and modification" of the Federally Assisted Code Enforcement (FACE) program completed in the city in 1978.[2] This program had focused on seven areas of the city; the city government claimed that over the course of its eleven years, the FACE program had helped bring ten thousand dwelling units up to code.

While loans under RAP were available to owners on favorable terms, according to one informant only about one-third of the owners who participated used government-related loans. These were the only ones who were required to cover the costs of displacement, whereas those who financed improvements out of their own pockets were not. The result was that there was growing opposition to RAP because of its displacement effects, even though RAP itself was not the principal cause of the worst displacement effects.

At the time NSA was under discussion, Hayes Valley was a predominantly depressed residential area with an estimated 60 percent minority population. According to city estimates, 5,220 of its 7,277 dwelling units required some degree of rehabilitation. Its housing consisted mainly of single-family homes and small multifamily structures containing no more than 20 dwelling units each. Despite its deficiencies, the area was becoming increasingly important for speculative investment. A HUD official described the situation in 1979 in the following terms.

[There is] a good code enforcement program in the area adjoining on one side and the Western Addition urban renewal area on the other. 476 units in condominiums are going in close by and old Victorian houses in the area are rapidly being converted through private investment to offices or private use. It is a ripe area for private development. No doubt, there is a lot of crap in the area but private financing is going on.[3]

Given a heated housing market elsewhere in the city and beginning to feel the threat of movement in their direction, home owners and tenants in Hayes Valley were nervous about the implications of programs like RAP and NSA. Thus, efforts to bring RAP into the area met with stiff resistance. A local activist recalled the situation:

I remember a meeting on a Saturday morning where 225 people attended and made their opposition to the RAP program known. They [hadn't liked] the implications of the FACE program, which by 1976 was already encouraging calls [from speculators] to people at 11:30 at night about selling their Victorians.[4]

Because of the antagonism of both low-income home owners and organized renters in the neighborhood, plans for RAP seemed to be reaching a dead end when the city submitted its NSA request for 245 units of Section 8 to be used in Hayes Valley. The city's design contained only ambiguous references to plans to implement RAP in the neighborhood.

Both that question and the weak commitment of resources from programs like CDBG to neighborhood improvements caused concern at HUD, but the design was unconditionally approved by the central office. Still, the NSA review urged the city to proceed with its efforts to establish a RAP area and to submit a detailed five-year plan ''which identifies the neighborhood deficiencies, how they are to be remedied and their source of funding.''[5]

In order to pacify opposition, in early 1979 the city government recommended changes in the RAP program which took the form of a new Housing Improvement Program. It was described, in part, in a letter prepared by the Department of City Planning in March 1979. The critical issues were laid out as follows:

The large number of lower income residents, who tend to be renters, together with the relatively high estimates for the average rehabilitation cost per unit, indicate that displacement and/or dispossession of such residents could occur on a wide enough scale that the program would be disruptive to the existing community. . . . It is on these grounds that community residents object to [RAP]; yet the community does recognize the need for a rehabilitation program to bring existing structures up to housing code standards.[6]

The new program would involve mandatory code enforcement and loan availability similar to RAP for all structures containing three or more dwelling units but would merely encourage a program of voluntary rehabilitation for smaller structures. Under the latter arrangement, inspections would occur "only at the request of the building owner, and the results of the inspection [would] be for the owner's information only. No record of code violations [would] be made against the property and . . . [the city] will not require correction of code violations."[7]

When matters reached the city's board of supervisors, they began to hear from neighborhood opposition; according to a central office staff member who monitored the progress of the city's program for HUD, "The black woman who represents [the area] on the Board of Supervisors has been opposed to any government programs going into the area." The result was a request from the city to cancel the NSA which HUD accepted.

Hoboken, New Jersey

The threat of displacement also stirred considerable controversy in Hoboken, a small city (42,500) across the Hudson River from New York. It had experienced considerable decay in its residential stock by the 1960s. The area targeted by the city for 500 units under NSA constituted about half the residential portion of Hoboken; it was an area that contained an almost equal number of whites and nonwhites (principally Hispanics).

Since the 1960s, the city had been pursuing a mixed strategy of promoting the use of assisted housing resources to its poorer population while encouraging private investment in its substantial stock of brownstones. As a result of success in the latter regard, there was much talk of a "renaissance" in Hoboken and of the arrival of the "gentrifiers."[8] Vacancy rates in existing rental units were extremely low.

A professional development organization, Applied Housing, had become the leading developer of assisted housing in Hoboken by the 1970s. It had moved into the city to participate in Project Rehab and was developing projects under the Demonstration Rehabilitation (Demo Rehab) Program when NSA arrived.[9] By that time, it was managing or in the process of developing upwards of one thousand units of assisted housing. What particularly upset many tenants and observers was that the firm approached rehabilitation through "gut rehab" of units (which resulted in tenants being forced to move out permanently) rather than undertaking more modest rehabilitation that might have accommodated itself to temporary displacement. Furthermore, prior to NSA, Applied Housing refused to assume any financial responsibility for relocation costs.

That issue had been joined with plans for Demo Rehab when the Hudson County Legal Services Corporation (LSC) was approached for help by Hispanic residents of buildings targeted by Applied Housing. The company was planning to develop one- and two-bedroom units in buildings where 129 families then resided. The LSC estimated that 42 percent of those families required three- and four-bedroom apartments.[10] If left to its own devices, Applied Housing would have assumed no responsibility for the displacement caused. Neither would the New Jersey Housing Finance Agency which was financing the project have done so, nor would the state's Department of Community Affairs (DCA), which had oversight responsibility because of the location of the project in an urban renewal area. Only under pressure from the tenants and from the LSC was an agreement reached under which relocation costs were split (in thirds) among the city, the developer, and the DCA.

Relocation benefits were only part of the answer to the displacement problem. Given the low vacancy rate in the city, what tenants also wanted was assurance of suitable units elsewhere or a right to return to the rehabilitated structures. That was something Applied Housing opposed, in part because they insisted upon exercising maximum control over the selection of households permitted to rent their units.[11]

While this controversy was going on, the city submitted plans to HUD for an Urban Development Action Grant (UDAG) which would have involved the construction of three hundred market-rate condominiums by Applied Housing on the city's waterfront. This plan would have resulted in considerable displacement of low-income households. An already tense situation was exacerbated by a comment included in the city's UDAG application that the project would reduce "the image of Hoboken as primarily a working class community with an increasingly Spanish-speaking population."[12] Regarded among Hispanics as racist, this remark served to reinforce their fear that the city's "renaissance" was being carried out at their expense.

The NSA proposal added yet another log to the fire. It anticipated that as many as four hundred more households would be displaced. This came on the heels of a formal complaint submitted by the LSC to HUD on 28 July 1978, which highlighted the displacement problems they associated with Demo Rehab and with the proposed UDAG. That complaint and visits from tenant representatives to the HUD central office reinforced the thorniness of the displacement issue in Hoboken and led to a decision on HUD's part to grant the city's NSA application only conditional status subject to the submission of evidence by the city that citizens had participated in the development of an appropriate relocation strategy for the NSA.

In order to reassure HUD on that point, the city allegedly promised to provide eighty "buffer units" of Section 8 existing housing to assist in relocation. Furthermore, according to a memorandum supporting removal of the conditions, Hoboken promised to create an NSA task force to represent "all major neighborhood organizations and interests." The memorandum described the task force's purposes in the following terms:

The Task Force will be responsible for disseminating information on relocation assistance, serve as a mechanism for obtaining citizen views and support, participate in the selection of developer proposals, and make recommendations on the relocation aspects of developer agreements and the provision of relocation assistance. The Task Force will be required to meet at least quarterly and will convene more frequently if necessary.[13]

On that basis, Assistant Secretary Simons lifted the conditions. The promises made about the creation of a task force were apparently never kept.[14]

As developed by Applied Housing, phase 1 of the NSA program was expected to involve eighty-two units in eleven structures. The developer did not receive approval for this project from HUD until November 1980. In the interim, the organization ran into problems with acquisition because the properties were owned by seven or eight different persons, several of whom had abandoned them. Furthermore, while the city argued that relocation responsibilities ran only from the time of formal obligation of HUD resources to particular projects, the poor condition of two of the buildings reached the point where the city felt obligated to step in and provide interim services to residents pending HUD approval of the project.[15]

The city's relocation officer reported in 1981 that thirty-nine families had been relocated with city assistance from the targeted structures with twelve going into assisted housing units (including public housing), two buying homes, and the remainder getting full relocation benefits (of up to $4,000 over a four-year period).[16] Whether accurate or not, a spokesperson for the LSC claimed that Applied Housing encouraged owners to abandon their properties during the period of HUD processing and before formal acquisition of properties, thus reducing the relocation obligation that would be borne by the city because benefits would accrue only to those still in place at the time the project was approved.[17]

During the course of implementation, Legal Services tried various maneuvers to hold the developer to relocation responsibilities, including taking the firm to court. In a hearing that took place on 9 October 1980, the issue of the timing of federally required relocation payments was raised by the plaintiffs but sidestepped by the state court judge, who ruled, nonetheless, that New Jersey state law required both payments and relocation assistance in finding "safe, sanitary and decent" housing. The court also held that the developer was required to provide such assistance. As a result, by April 1981, the LSC informant conceded that Applied Housing was undertaking "Herculean efforts to find places" by relocating some of the displaced to their other projects. The city also came up with relocation funds. However, at this point, Applied Housing had apparently had enough and was no longer interested in doing additional NSA projects in the city unless it could be assured of vacant structures. By that time, too, the city's plans for the UDAG had fallen through, thus relieving some of the displacement pressure.

MANAGING CITIZEN PARTICIPATION

Local governments that targeted nonresidential areas or previously nonresidential structures in residential neighborhoods justified those strategies in terms of such considerations as: (1) preserving historic structures; (2) the adaptive reuse of essentially sound structures; (3) the promotion of mixed uses in previously nonresidential areas; and (4) the desirability of avoiding displacement.

These approaches not only reduced citizen involvement but also tended to be linked to limited involvement by the local government in project design and implementation. Private developers were left largely on their own to develop plans for rehabilitation and to negotiate "technical details" and financing arrangements with HUD and lending institutions.

On the whole, developers' relations with residents of target areas were cordial, although in only a few places did neighborhoods have a meaningful voice in the selection of a developer. In some cases, amity resulted from the fact that cities selected such deteriorated areas that anything that could be done to improve the standard of housing and other neighborhood services was regarded as a gain by residents.

The style of accommodation varied. In New York City, Washington, D.C., and Atlanta, where participatory mechanisms in neighborhood planning were institutionalized, neighborhood residents demanded and received certain forms of recognition from developers. Thus, in New York, the city government formalized a requirement that developers enter into agreements with bona fide neighborhood groups under which those groups would receive a share of the developer's profits.[18]

In Atlanta, "neighborhood participation units" had been created in the 1970s in connection with the city's annual Community Development Block Grant (CDBG) reviews. These units took an active interest in other programmatic activities affecting their areas. Thus, in one of the city's two NSAs, according to a city planner, the neighborhood contained "a very vocal citizens group—very cohesive and well organized. The women, especially, were very knowledgeable about programs and they want their neighborhood redeveloped."[19] In that case, neighborhood residents worked closely with the developer chosen by the city to redesign and upgrade a public housing project constructed immediately after World War II that had become a major blighting influence.

In some instances, resident populations reacted strongly against the designs proposed by local planners or developers. A few of these reactions reflected fears among home owners that minorities would move into "their" neighborhood. On occasion, those fears were verbalized in terms of undesirable increases in residential densities; at other times, conflicts took the form of battles over such issues as the number of parking spaces that would be available after the proposed project was completed. However, conflicts over parking took on a life of their own in some places, independent of class or racial issues.

In this section, we shall deal with two examples of the effects of neighborhood opposition to NSA designs—proposals for Jersey City, New Jersey, and Somerville, Massachusetts.

Jersey City's Hamilton Park

Public participation was absent from the development of the original designs for three NSA proposals Jersey City submitted to HUD. The municipal staff played the major role in selecting the areas and in preparing the documentation in support of those designs.

The proposal for the Hamilton Park neighborhood included an area of historic interest that had attracted a population of gentrifiers to its smaller residential structures. There were also a few large, multifamily structures in the area which provided rental opportunities for a substantial proportion of the neighborhood's minority population (25 percent Hispanic; 8 percent black). The city had put considerable public money into upgrading the area's infrastructure prior to NSA in order to encourage private investment. The city thought that Section 8 would deal with the multifamily buildings. However, the NSA proposal was caught in the cross fire between the gentrifiers and the developer when the latter proposed rehabilitating some multifamily structures into market-rate condominiums while converting a former Wells Fargo warehouse into 153 units of Section 8 housing for families.[20]

In a publication that reviewed the emerging conflict, the city's director of development attributed the opposition to project plans to various factors, including the density of the project, parking problems, and questions about whether the project "would flood the neighborhood with people." Ultimately, he argued, "under it all were aspects of social and economic racism." That point was reinforced by comments attributed to a man identified as one of the first "brownstoners" in the area: "People who spent upwards of $50–60,000 on these places didn't want it turned into a zoo, and that was what was feared."[21]

The conflict crystallized at a public hearing in the summer of 1979 held to review the developer's proposal. Opposition surfaced from the Hamilton Park Neighborhood Association, which represented the interests of the gentrifying home owners. As a result, the developer abandoned plans not only for the warehouse conversion but also for the condominiums. By 1980, city officials conceded that assisted housing would never be built in the area, and they sought to transfer NSA units to other parts of the city. They also admitted that the situation would leave low-income residents of Hamilton Park at the mercy of a private housing market that was beginning to displace residents.[22]

Somerville, Massachusetts

Not all opposition from neighborhood residents was generated by whites against blacks or Hispanics. For example, in Somerville, a working-class suburb of Boston, city planners designated an area where owner occupancy was high (estimated at 82 percent in 1978) and vacancy rates low (2.2 percent). NSA participation was intended partly to protect the moderate-income rental market against further incursions from higher priced rental markets in adjacent Cambridge and Boston.

The original program design for the NSA would have involved using 100 of the city's 325-unit allocation for the construction of a new elderly housing project while preparations got underway to work with small owners in using the remaining units.[23] When the project came before the city's zoning board of appeals for a permit, neighborhood residents organized for action. They complained, in particular, about the refusal of the developer to discuss their concerns about the placement of the proposed structure on a 1.4-acre site which would dwarf their homes, exceeding both the allowable densities of the community and its height limitations. As a leader of the opposition argued in a letter to the local newspaper, "This neighborhood is already fragile, and it needs encouragement to grow uphill, not to deteriorate further." He feared that if the project were not carefully designed and managed it would turn into little more than "a depressing warehouse for low-income people."[24]

Nonetheless, the zoning board voted 3 to 2 for the project on the ground that the need for elderly housing was too great to postpone action. The neighborhood association then brought suit against the developer to enjoin the project. That action forced the developer to enter negotiations which resulted in an agreement that permitted no more than sixty-five units to be built on the site. In this case, as one local government official conceded, it made a considerable difference in limiting the scope of the conflict that the project was for the elderly—an issue that was more open to compromise than a proposal for family units might have been.

PARTICIPATION BY NONGOVERNMENTAL ORGANIZATIONS

As we indicated in chapter 5, many local governments limited their investment in administrative commitment to the NSA program, contracting out responsibilities to nongovernmental organizations. In the greater number of cases, that meant relying on private developers; in a smaller number of instances, localities turned to neighborhood-based and advocacy planning organizations (APOs) to implement part of their projects.

Most of the APOs that played a role in NSA implementation included persons professionally trained in some aspect of neighborhood revitalization, but that category might well be extended to include Legal Services units that made their expertise available to neighborhood residents in influencing implementation.[25] A number of organizations with religious affiliations also participated in mobilizing resident participation in program implementation. Most are readily classified as APOs. For example, the Catholic Church's Campaign for Human Development had ties to neighborhood groups in several NSAs. In Cleveland, for instance, several nonsectarian, neighborhood-based housing development corporations operated as affiliates of a housing rehabilitation network promoted, in part, through the leadership of Famicos, a church-related organization. In Wilmington, Delaware, one of the two designated nonprofit developers was the St. Anthony's Community Center, an organization based in one of the city's parishes.[26] While the technical skills of some of these organizations may have been limited at the outset of program implementation, they provided important resources to neighborhood residents in the form of organizational skill and political entrée.

It is necessary to exercise some caution in taking at face value the claims of representativeness that some neighborhood-based organizations (NBOs) and APOs made. For, along with private developers who occasionally needed to negotiate relations with neighborhood groups, NBOs and APOs frequently had to work hard to define their relationships with neighborhood residents—particularly with those who resided in the buildings targeted for rehabilitation.

In this section, we briefly examine four such cases. We are more concerned with illustrating the range of project design arrangements that were developed locally than with the specific modes of participation of NBOs and residents, though we shall touch on those matters. The cases proceed in order of the degree to which the designated nongovernmental organization appeared to dominate the local project planning and implementation process. Thus, the first two saw efforts made by different types of development corporations in St. Louis to use the NSA program as part of their plans to redevelop ''their'' neighborhoods. In the third case, we examine the TRIP organization's efforts to mobilize and work with neighborhood residents in Troy, New York. Finally, we look at Providence's Elmwood neighborhood, where a variety of neighborhood groups came together to negotiate the terms on which a developer was permitted to undertake an NSA project.

St. Louis's Midtown Medical Center

A state law was operative in Missouri in 1978 that permitted local governments to designate corporate entities which would assume condemnation and acquisition powers akin to those available to redevelopment authorities under urban renewal. Qualification for such status allowed those corporations to employ special tax abatements to promote revitalization. Several NBOs in St. Louis acted as prime developers for their respective areas under this arrangement.[27]

One of these was the Midtown Medical Center Redevelopment Corporation (MMCRC), whose actions, its critics charged, resembled the worst behaviors of past urban renewal agencies. In large part, that behavior reflected the origins of the organization in a consortium of hospitals centered around St. Louis University Hospital which sought in the mid–1970s to upgrade the area. After its creation, the corporation moved to clear the predominantly black low-income residential population from the area—an area plagued by a high crime rate and transiency. The corporation developed project plans with an estimated value of $73 million for redevelopment of the 273-acre site. As the executive director of MMCRC explained, the corporation saw itself assuming "an entrepreneurial role in the major development projects in the area."[28]

The MMCRC required the approval of the city's board of aldermen for its special powers. That approval was given in April 1978, in the face of vocal opposition described by the executive director in the following terms:

The issue was that low-income tenants were afraid of being displaced. That issue was aided by a local political boss who felt we were getting too much power and used his skill to fragment the neighborhood group. Then the middle-class residents—mostly black—coalesced around the Corporation and asked for our assistance and we started another neighborhood association which is now becoming very broadly based.

The corporation was capitalized by the contributions of the member institutions it served and by interested banks. They dominated its thirteen-member board, which also included four neighborhood residents. Despite sharp criticisms of the MMCRC from black residents and activist organizations in the city with respect to the quality of neighborhood participation, the executive director insisted that the redevelopment plan had gone through multiple drafts in response to neighborhood comments.

Nonetheless, other informants charged that the MMCRC operated in an authoritarian fashion. In particular, they claimed the corporation made every effort to encourage those segments of the population the organization viewed as undesirable to leave the area either by not renting units to them when such units became available or by evicting them.

By mid–1981, the corporation's role in the neighborhood had taken on particular importance because it owned 50–60 percent of the housing stock and was establishing strict standards for residential eligibility in those units. Indeed, those standards and the procedures for eviction and rentals had caused some concern on the part of the local LSC unit which forced the corporation to enter negotiations over assuring full procedural rights to tenants. In contrast to the Hoboken case, however, those negotiations slowed down the developer only temporarily. Project activity proceeded apace once legal procedures for displacement had been agreed upon.[29]

St. Louis's Union-Sarah

While the Union-Sarah neighborhood in St. Louis suffered from many of the same disabilities as Chicago's North Lawndale, the neighborhood was more centrally located in respect to redevelopment areas and included prime urban real estate. A leading role in neighborhood revitalization efforts was assumed by a Community Development Corporation (CDC), the Union-Sarah Economic Development Corporation (USEDC). The organization influenced the city to commit local and federal funds to the neighborhood prior to NSA and assured itself a major role in housing and commercial rehabilitation that increasingly moved the CDC away from the social service emphasis that characterized its initial operations in the 1960s.

Like Chicago's Pyramidwest, USEDC played a multifunctional proprietary role in the neighborhood. In both cases, one may question the degree to which the CDC sought to "represent" residents of the area in which it was based. In the USEDC case, in particular, questions arose about the corporation's efforts to promote upgrading within its "turf," in addition to providing services to persons already living in the area. Indeed, the question of representativeness was raised by the HUD area office in the course of its review of the CDC's proposal.[30]

Given the neighborhood's promising location in the city—near an area that was undergoing gentrification—USEDC sought to encourage middle-income housing as well as housing for low-income residents in what the president of the USEDC characterized as previously a "very marginal disinvested area." In his view, "any community that is going to survive has to bring those sorts of normal market forces to bear."[31] To achieve its purposes in the NSA, USEDC entered a joint venture with a private developer, but the head of the CDC did not see it becoming dependent on that corporate partner because the CDC had developed its own technical capacity to "package" projects.

Characteristically, he did not recoil from exercising the political clout available to the USEDC, "so that no one wants to mess with us." In fact, he insisted:

Another developer can't simply come in and do whatever he wants to do in the neighborhood. He has to knock on our doors, and if we don't like a project, we just won't let it go ahead. A lot of people don't like that, but I think control is very important. That is in keeping with our desire to maintain the community for the people who live here.

Troy, New York

In the last chapter, we mentioned the role played by TRIP as an APO in attempting to revitalize a badly deteriorated neighborhhod in Troy. At the organization's recommendation, the city initially applied for only forty units of Section 8 with the expectation that TRIP would be the developer. As project planning proceeded in 1979, however, it became apparent that there were more structures worth doing in the target area than originally anticipated. As a result, TRIP applied for and received an additional eighty units of Section 8 for NSA projects.

Even before it received approval of projects from HUD, TRIP took a financial risk by setting to work on the small structures targeted by employing neighborhood youths to gut some of them under a contract with the local Comprehensive Employment and Training Act Program. At that point, TRIP was operating on a grant from a local foundation and a private bank loan. This was done, according to its executive director, because of the organization's fears that HUD's typical delays in processing projects would frustrate the neighborhood. In her opinion

People in the neighborhood need the assurance that something is actually happening. . . . At least they [saw] the kids coming in and working for the last six months. It is interesting that there have been no fires or other disasters in the neighborhood during the period. . . . It was [also] important for us to establish credibility in the neighborhood for being in the forefront of the project.[32]

From the outset, TRIP sought to work with residents of the target neighborhood in developing project plans. Later, after construction was completed, they attempted to involve residents in the tenant selection process. Relations were not always harmonious on this issue as neighborhood residents attempted to maintain fairly tight control over the character of the tenants permitted to live in the rehabilitated units, whereas TRIP tried to follow HUD's formal guidelines—guidelines that limited inquiries into such matters as tenants' previous rental histories and credit-worthiness. The result was the selection of a population which was "unbalanced" according to some residents. As a leading white activist in the neighborhood (and city) argued:

We had a neighborhood [before] with blacks and whites and some Puerto Ricans . . . but one that was able to cope with it. . . . Then, all of a sudden, that is the major problem with this whole project: all black. . . . I know you can't discriminate but you also are discriminating against the people who live there by just renting to blacks.[33]

Nonetheless, older residents seemed pleased with the effort TRIP had made to revitalize the neighborhood.

Providence's Elmwood

As part of its procedure for developing proposals for four NSAs, Providence designated a lead NBO or APO in each neighborhood to coordinate program efforts.[34] In the case of the Elmwood neighborhood, they selected the Neighborhood Housing Services (NHS) unit serving the area.[35]

Elmwood was a wedge-shaped area segmented into three sectors: an area near downtown containing large Victorian homes, many of which had been subdivided; a middle zone of deteriorated single-family and small multifamily structures; and an outer zone of smaller single-family homes built in the 1930s that were in reasonably sound condition. After the designation of the neighborhood by HUD, the NHS took the lead in selecting a private developer, but that firm struggled for over a year to come up with suitable structures for inclusion in the program. By the spring of 1980, that effort had failed and the firm withdrew.

This created a dilemma for neighborhood residents and for the NHS. Shortly after World War II, a family in the neighborhood had begun to acquire a number of properties and eventually had become one of the leading property management firms and developers in the state. During the period of their expansion they had held on to rental properties in Elmwood, particularly a set of 11 2-to-4-unit Victorian structures along a tree-lined boulevard. By the 1970s, those properties had fallen into decay and were being abandoned. As a leading developer of Section 8 projects in the state, the company sought to qualify their Elmwood structures for Section 8 but they ran up against the neighborhood's well-organized opposition. This bitterness flowed, in part, from a feeling among residents that the firm had mishandled earlier displacement of about 40 families from the properties in anticipation of failed efforts to rehabilitate those structures.

Opposition to the selection of the developer was led by PACE (People Acting Through Community Effort), an NBO that one informant described as a "Gail Cincotta-type group," which drew support from the diverse ethnic base of the neighborhood (including racial minorities).[36] Another organization that participated in the opposition coalition was the Elmwood Foundation for Architectural and Historical Preservation which objected to the approach to preservation that the family firm had taken on past projects.

When the initial developer withdrew, city planners argued with neighborhood organizations that the only alternative available (short of losing the NSA allocation) was to reach an agreement with the second firm. Given the desire of residents to secure the Section 8 subsidies and to promote rehabilitation of the neighborhood, they agreed to seek a compromise. The first step was to negotiate among the various neighborhood groups to establish a unified bargaining position. These negotiations were carefully orchestrated by the NHS. Only then did the neighborhood enter into formal negotiations early in 1981 with the developer over a variety of issues including exterior designs and preservation of wooden clapboards (rather than permitting vinyl siding), as well as assurances that minorities from the neighborhood would be included among those employed on the project. The result was a 42-unit project for families in the 11 structures owned by the developer.

CONCLUSIONS

In this chapter we have dealt with some of the circumstances under which conflicts were generated locally over NSA plans and how local arrangements were made to deal with those problems or, in some cases, to defeat program implementation. Again, it is necessary to stress that most NSAs stirred little neighborhood reaction. Since many local governments used NSA as a vehicle for converting large nonresidential structures to housing or for rehabilitating vacant residential structures, potential conflicts with neighborhoods were preempted.

Elsewhere, neighborhoods were chosen where the introduction of Section 8 housing, particularly if it was aimed at the elderly, gained the support of both renters and home owners. It is difficult to identify all the factors that led local governments to select such a strategy but a major consideration was the availability of blighting structures (often vacant) worthy of rehabilitation which would be attractive to private developers.

In a distinct minority of places, local planners were unable or unwilling to anticipate adverse reactions from neighborhood residents or from organizations which claimed to speak for those residents. This happened in Hoboken, Jersey City, and Somerville. Elsewhere, neighborhood opposition emerged in response to NSA proposals when projects aimed at families were involved. Even where projects for the elderly were proposed, opposition could arise occasionally if home owners perceived a threat to property values.

Those we have identified as local government planners varied, of course, in their sympathies toward neighborhood residents. As a result, in some places little more participation occurred than holding symbolic hearings before turning program responsibilities over to professional developers. Only in a few communities was the "ethos" of participation such that citizens were seen from the outset as having an important role to play in shaping designs for projects. That did not guarantee participation even in those cases, since many projects were unexceptionable to local residents. Where such a right was acknowledged from the outset, as in the Elmwood neighborhood in Providence, it provided neighborhood groups with considerable leverage in program implementation.

At the same time, the presence of formal organizations affecting neighborhood life added an important layer of complexity to implementation efforts. While NBOs like Pyramidwest and USEDC adopted the style of private developers— if not their predominantly market-oriented values—some APOs were concerned about giving equal weight to promoting participation and technical competence. Indeed, in some ways, the APOs were even more variable than the NBOs. Falling somewhere between traditional private development organizations and ideologically generated organizations, APOs were sometimes affiliated with religious organizations; sometimes they had academic connections (TRIP, for example, had ties to planning programs at Rensselaer Polytechnic Institute). What was most significant about these groups was that they assumed responsibility not only for developing and using technical skills on behalf of neighborhoods but for mobilizing public support on behalf of the projects they designed and implemented. Furthermore, like the CDCs, in a few places APOs competed with or effectively replaced local governments that had proven ineffective or uninterested in assuming responsibility for neighborhood revitalization.

In sum, most local governments shared program implementation responsibil-

ities with professional developers. A minority of localities engaged in participatory activities which (sometimes reluctantly) recognized existing neighborhood
interests. In a small number of cases, neighborhood-related organizations either
were given or demanded the responsibility for program design and project implementation, sometimes acting as the developers, but more commonly working
with an experienced developer to reflect the concerns of the neighborhood about
projects.

NOTES

1. In response to local complaints about these pressures, late in 1979 HUD revised
its rules to permit negotiations between the local government and the developer over who
would be responsible for relocation costs. Still, as Assistant Secretary Simons wrote to
field officials on 1 February 1980, "While the city is no longer legally responsible for
relocation, it is essential that the city remain involved in the process . . . and if relocation
problems arise, the city will undoubtedly be forced to become involved if the NSA is to
be successful."

2. Office of the Mayor, San Francisco, "Public Display on the Performance of San
Francisco Community Development," April 1979, 4.

3. Interview, Harriman Thatcher, NSA Coordinator, San Francisco HUD Area Office,
25 July 1979.

4. Interview, Calvin Welch, San Francisco Information Clearinghouse, 25 July 1979.

5. That phraseology appears in the summary analysis prepared by the central office
staff and signed by Jack Kerry on 17 September 1978.

6. Letter from Rai Y. Okomoto, Director of Planning, to the Board of Supervisors,
City and County of San Francisco, n.d., 2. The letter accompanied a document prepared
by the Department of City Planning, "Feasibility of a Rehabilitation Assistance Program
and Recommended Alternative Program for Hayes Valley," March 1979.

7. "Feasibility," 28.

8. For a skeptical view of that "renaissance," see Ralph Seligman, "Hoboken Rediscovered Yet Again," *New York Affairs* 5 (Summer–Fall 1979), 26–38.

9. See Martin A. Bierbaum, "The Applied Housing Program," in *Housing Rehabilitation*, edited by David Listokin (New Brunswick, N.J.: Center for Urban Policy
Research, Rutgers University, 1983), 225–34. Bierbaum reports that the firm was created
in reaction to problems in Newark following the riots in that city. It came into Hoboken
in 1971 at the behest of that city's Model Cities director.

10. Interview, Stephen St. Hilaire, Hudson County Legal Services Corporation, Jersey
City, New Jersey, 8 April 1981. According to St. Hilaire and other informants, Hispanics
in the city saw Applied's approach to rehabilitation as part of a calculated effort (allegedly
reflecting the preferences of the city government) to reduce minority presence in the city.

11. The LSC was greatly concerned about the considerable freedom permitted by HUD
to private developers to control the tenant selection process. The same issue was raised
in other NSAs, including the Midtown Medical Center NSA in St. Louis discussed later
in this chapter.

12. The statement was cited on page 16 of a document submitted to Secretary Patricia
Harris and Walter Johnson, Area Manager for the Newark Area Office, on 28 July 1978,

by José Espinosa, Chairperson, Washington and Bloomfield Streets Tenants Association, on behalf of a coalition of Hispanic organizations.

13. Memorandum from Marilyn Melkonian, Deputy Assistant Secretary for Multi-Family Housing, to Lawrence B. Simons, 10 April 1979.

14. Neither of the two city officials interviewed on this point, both of whom had been involved in the earlier program negotiations, claimed any knowledge of an agreement to form a task force or of the eighty "buffer" units.

15. Confusion existed throughout the early administration of the NSA program among field offices and local governments about the timing of relocation benefits so that some interpreted HUD rules to mean benefits ran only from the time a project received final approval for Section 8 rather than from the time of submission of a project to HUD for review. Since there might be a gap of a year or more between those events, the choice of triggering dates had major consequences for tenants. Instead of making a clear and consistent ruling on this issue, the central office allowed field offices discretion in determining the date of each project "start."

16. Interview, Lena Milan, Relocation Officer, City of Hoboken, 4 March 1981.

17. Interview, St. Hilaire.

18. A similar arrangement between a developer and a neighborhood organization was reached in Washington, D.C. In other places, organizations became junior partners in rehabilitation projects or took on responsibility for some aspects of program implementation, most commonly management of the structures after rehabilitation.

19. Interview, Debra Renner, Community Development Planner, Bureau of Planning, City of Atlanta, 25 June 1981.

20. The developer was, again, Applied Housing, but in this case the organization planned to use a vacant structure.

21. "Class Conflict in Jersey City: The Rich Get Brownstones," *New Jersey Monthly*, December 1979, reprint.

22. See "Jersey City's Revival Raising Hopes, and Some Eyebrows," *New York Times*, 8 January 1981.

23. NSA regulations permitted up to 20 percent of a city's Section 8 allocation to be used for new construction in conjunction with rehabilitation. Field offices varied considerably in how broadly or narrowly they interpreted this rule.

24. Letter to the editor from David Wagenknecht, *Somerville Journal*, 25 October 1979.

25. In addition to Hoboken and Jersey City (which were both served by the Hudson County LSC) LSCs were involved in controversies in St. Louis's Midtown Medical Center NSA (see below), and in NSAs in Bucks and Montgomery Counties in Pennsylvania, and Lewiston, Maine.

26. While St. Anthony's experience as a developer was limited, it worked with a "consultant," Leon Weiner, who was one of the major developers of assisted housing in the country.

27. The city designated five NSAs initially and then turned over responsibility for implementation to an NBO or APO for each.

28. Interview, John Abramson, Executive Director, MMCRC, St. Louis, Missouri, 7 July 1981.

29. The continuation of conflict in the area is indicated in a later newspaper story, "Power Struggle Grips Renewal Area in St. Louis," *New York Times*, 12 December 1983. After reviewing the history of difficulties between the corporation and black work-

ing-class residents of the area, the writer noted, the local situation had been marked by "protest marches, public debates, rallies and court actions."

30. In response to HUD questioning, the CDC argued that fifteen of the twenty-eight members of the corporation's board were residents of the neighborhood and that twenty-four of them were black. The CDC pointed out that thirteen nonresidents were "selected by the original fifteen from the professional and business communities to provide additional representation and technical assistance."

31. Interview, Nesby Moore, President, USEDC, St. Louis, Missouri, 6 July 1981.

32. Interview, Barbara Jones, Executive Director, TRIP, Troy, New York, 24 June 1980.

33. Interview, Marian Hernberg, Executive Director, N-Act, Troy, New York, 4 March 1983.

34. Only three of the four NSAs were approved by HUD. One of these, Federal Hill, was a classic example of a strong ethnic neighborhood opposed to Section 8 housing. The neighborhood dropped out of the program early when no owners or developers took an interest in participating.

35. This was one of the few instances where an NHS played a major role in NSA implementation. Normally, the emphasis of that program on home ownership rather than on improving rental stock accounted for its absence from NSA entrepreneurship.

36. Interview, Arthur Hanson, Elmwood Neighborhood Housing Services, Providence, Rhode Island, 21 June 1983. On Cincotta, see Harry G. Boyte, *The Backyard Revolution* (Philadelphia: Temple University Press, 1980), esp. 54–56.

7

MICRO-IMPLEMENTATION II: BUREAUCRATIC AND INTERGOVERNMENTAL HURDLES

Those who created the Neighborhood Strategy Area (NSA) Program assumed that it would be relatively easy to achieve cooperation among actors both within the national administration and within the intergovernmental system. Furthermore, they believed that program implementation would occur along the lines they preferred by assigning major responsibilities to HUD field offices and local governments.

According to this theory, the responsible local agency would bring together: (1) residents and property owners in the target neighborhood; (2) the financial institutions that would provide the funds necessary to rehabilitate not only those structures targeted for Section 8 but other rental and owner-occupied properties that required upgrading; (3) other business and institutional interests that would need to invest both money and energy to make the neighborhood a more attractive place in which to live and work; and (4) those governmental agencies involved in important aspects of project implementation.

In previous chapters, we identified some of the considerations that local governments or their organizational surrogates took into account or that local actors forced them to take into account in designing programs that were locally implementable. In chapter 8, we shall review in greater detail some of the successful financial and administrative solutions to the implementation problem. Here our focus is on obstacles to rapid implementation created by federal or state agencies. For, contrary to the sharing model present at the inception of NSA, interagency and intergovernmental noncooperation or indifference characterized program implementation at many points.

What is probably most interesting is that many localities worked extremely hard to overcome those obstacles, at least fulfilling the expectations of program entrepreneurs on that score. Prominent among those obstacles was a credit market marked by rapidly increasing interest rates and rapidly rising costs of construction. We will deal with those financial aspects in chapter 8; here we emphasize the behaviors of a nonsupportive set of federal and state officials.

In particular, we shall consider: (1) the lack of control by the HUD central office over field personnel in respect to expediting assistance to localities and their developers in implementing project plans; and (2) the difficulties localities experienced in dealing with other federal and state agencies, particularly those involved in historic preservation. Another important set of state agencies were Housing Finance and Development Agencies (HFDAs), which were expected in the original program design to play a major role in financing projects. We shall touch on their role in the next chapter.

HUD'S BUREAUCRATIC PROBLEM

As Aaron Wildavsky has pointed out, coordination is a slippery concept that may range in meaning from mutual adjustments among parties to domination of one set of actors by another.[1] In the case of NSA, coordination was a notion that was extolled from the outset of the program, yet not translated sufficiently into institutional agreements.

Thus, HUD field staffs played no part in the program design process and were skeptical of aspects of the program from its inception, especially the capacity of local governments to assume the responsibilities assigned to them, and the ability of their own offices to provide the technical assistance necessary for successful implementation. Despite these reservations, the central office proceeded from the outset as if those offices would eventually come to terms with the program. However, save for a handful of NSA coordinators, most field office personnel were either apathetic or hostile to the program. The latter attitude was particularly notable among those we characterize, following Legates, as "technicians"—persons responsible for evaluating the project applications submitted by owners and developers for technical feasibility, for FHA mortgage insurance, and for Section 8 subsidies.[2]

These attitudes were apparent in the lack of speed with which technicians proceeded in reviewing project-related materials. Even where experienced developers were involved, many complained bitterly about the time HUD took to process their applications—this despite a notion originally promoted by Jack Kerry that NSA projects would receive special attention within field offices. Instead, even minor details delayed action on some projects for months and major issues took years to resolve.

No doubt, some of the concerns typical of HUD technicians were warranted: initial project designs were sometimes inadequate with respect to important matters such as fire protection or the environmental setting of the proposed project; local governments were sometimes too hasty and selected developers with questionable performance records. Thus, claims of financial soundness on the part of a firm might be found to be misplaced on closer scrutiny by a HUD technician familiar with a firm's past performance.

Warranted as such caution might have been, each detail reviewed added to project delays and attendant increases in costs as developers acquired and renewed options on properties or held on to properties they owned in anticipation of project approvals.[3] Problems were further compounded by HUD office routines: developers and local government officials recounted numerous anecdotes about materials lost or misplaced by HUD personnel for long periods, sometimes inadvertently but also allegedly as a reflection of the feeling among technicians that the complexities of rehabilitation were much less worthy of their attention than proposals for new construction.[4]

If delays were commonplace when professional developers proposed large-structure conversions—and they were—they were even more common for owners of smaller structures, many of whom were inexperienced in dealing with HUD (including filling out HUD's complex forms) and among developers of projects that involved a mix of large and small structures scattered over a targeted neighborhood. The common understanding was that HUD technicians did not favor the smaller so-called "Mom-and-Pop" projects with the result that they placed them at the bottom of any pile of project proposals. NSA proposals, furthermore, were simply one among many types of project proposals contending for the attention of these technicians during a period of high federal activity.

Part of the difficulty was that HUD procedures for allocating field office personnel and related housing resources favored those offices that generated greater numbers of units. There were fewer rewards in personnel and budgets to those offices that worked on small projects involving fewer total units. Since the review procedures used for processing small projects were essentially the same as those for larger ones, there were disincentives for pursuing smaller, more complex rehabilitation projects.

The problems of the financial market and the hesitancy of HFDAs to involve themselves in NSA projects also overloaded HUD technicians in unanticipated ways. Originally, HUD expected state HFDAs to finance at least half the units allocated under the program through mechanisms that would not require FHA insurance; in a normal credit market, some of the projects—particularly the smaller ones—might have been financed through conventional lenders without federal mortgage insurance. Both events did not occur. Furthermore, the increase in the initial program commitment from twenty thousand to over thirty-seven thousand units of Section 8 simply added to the potential workload of HUD technicians without augmenting field office personnel.

From 1981 on, the Reagan administration moved to limit expenditures on NSA even more. The new administration's efforts took three forms. First, it sought to terminate commitments of Section 8 for projects that developers submitted to field offices for formal review before the end of Fiscal Year (FY)81, thus leaving out in the cold some communities with schedules that had called for project allocations in the fourth and fifth years of the program. The effect of this policy was reflected in the drop in new project units authorized from 4,070 units in FY81 to 346 in FY82 and none in FY83.[5]

Second, HUD undertook a major effort to get those projects for which units had already been reserved either into production or terminated by threatening to withdraw units not already in construction. This campaign to "shake out the pipeline" succeeded in moving some projects ahead that had been stalled for one reason or another, usually related to financing. Under this pressure, as well as in reaction to a more favorable credit market, a few HFDAs which had been hesitant earlier about involvement in NSA became more responsive.

In "shaking out the pipeline," HUD also clamped down on procedures for amendments and exemptions to local designs which had been accepted under the Carter administration. This resulted in an arcane bureaucratic battle over the project number assigned to each project when a proposal was submitted to HUD for preliminary approval and reservation of Section 8 resources. That number would remain in the HUD Management Information System even though the developer would still have to satisfy technicians' concerns to finalize financial commitments before submitting projects for final approval.

In the course of technical reviews, developer accommodations to a changing financial market or to problems as varied as local topography or arson might lead to alterations in the original project. These changes might still be covered under the initial project number. If localities found it necessary to change developers or to drop some buildings and add others to a project, or to give up on plans for rehabilitating some of the structures originally targeted, so long as the "project" retained its original number, it was possible to treat it as the same project without requiring it to qualify for a new reservation of units.

During the Carter administration, project alterations were generally allowed after some bureaucratic delay; under Reagan, HUD attempted to tighten procedures. Even as late as 1983, however, in order to hold on to as many of their earlier reservations of units as possible, localities maneuvered to alter project activities while keeping approved project numbers—a wonderfully contorted process but reflective of a situation that resulted from local fears that HUD might withdraw resources.

Third, the Reagan administration sought to reduce the subsidies involved. In addition to attempting to decrease the size of tenant subsidies from 75 to 70 percent of income, HUD did away with a Financial Adjustment Factor (FAF) that had been added to the program during the Carter years to keep up with increases in interest rates and inflation in construction costs. The new administration also put a lid on program costs by recalculating the number of Section 8 units associated with the dollar figure appropriated for the program. The result was that the size of later projects had to be reduced in order to accommodate a smaller number of subsidies.[6]

THE CASE OF HISTORIC PRESERVATION

To this point, we have not taken account of many important participants in the implementation process. In this section, we shall attempt to rectify this

situation by examining the role played by agencies responsible for historic preservation reviews. These were by no means the only agencies that merit special
attention in addition to HUD and local governments but interviews with local
officials and developers revealed that after HUD itself, their greatest complaints
about program implementation involved historic preservation agencies.

The reviews done by such agencies were part of a bureaucratic system involving a distinct set of local, state, and federal entities whose concerns had to
be reconciled with those of HUD in order to permit a commitment of Section 8
resources to a project. The leverage of such agencies was assured by federal
regulations that mandated reviews where buildings were located in recognized
historic districts or where the structures themselves were either listed or eligible
for listing on the National Register of Historic Places. Developers eagerly sought
the latter designation because of tax benefits provided by the Tax Reform Act
of 1976.[7]

While most local historic preservation agencies supported the efforts made by
developers to rehabilitate structures in NSAs and accepted proposed modifications
in original structural features (particularly where only interiors were concerned),
State Historic Preservation Offices (SHPOs) were more cautious in authorizing
such changes. Matters were further complicated by the required participation in
the approval process of the Department of the Interior's Heritage Conservation
and Recreation Service. To complicate matters, that agency's regional offices
appeared to differ in the stringency of their interpretations of preservation rules,
so that developers working in different parts of the country found themselves
dealing with varying interpretations of the same rules in similar project situations.
Even if developers received a certificate of "no adverse impact" for their projects
from preservation agencies, that did not assure them that their structures would
qualify for inclusion on the National Register once work was completed. That
might leave the question of tax benefits in abeyance until late in the process,
thus placing the developer in an uncertain position with respect to the project's
profitability.

Some SHPOs approached the plans submitted by NSA developers with notable
caution. That caution and their requests for historic versimilitude caused much
unhappiness among developers and local program officials. The complaints of
a former employee of a development firm based in Ohio were commonplace:

There are two areas that really bother developers—the areas of historic preservation and
environmental control. In both cases, the same interest groups that created the legislation
went in and staffed the agencies. So you have fanatics—in Eric Hoffer's sense of the
word—they are fanatically devoted to their cause. . . . What happens in appealing upwards
on matters of historical preservation is that at each level you have a higher level of
fanaticism. So it is very difficult to negotiate a deal at the local level because then you
have to wait for a response from the higher levels or run the risk . . . of [not] being able
to straighten out any mess at the end.

Another informant highlighted differences among Interior's field offices in handling issues. Thus, he had found the Detroit regional office generally co-operative, while he had serious reservations about the one in Atlanta with which his company had also worked. Of the latter, he commented that it was "tougher because they expound the words from Washington inflexibly, whereas Detroit is more willing to permit discussion."[8] It was Interior's national policies on which he laid the greatest blame, however, for adding to the firm's costs in doing rehabilitation of historically significant structures:

They are totally removed [from the local scene] and are totally inflexible in their attitudes. You go into a multifamily structure that was built in the 1920s and it has been housing barely adequately low-income people for the last twenty-five years. There is nothing left to save, but they want us to save the window sashes; they want us to save the woodwork. We tell them that there is no woodwork left to save. The window sashes are rotten and would cost five times [normal replacement costs] to restore. We wouldn't repair them but put in brand-new, old-looking sashes. There just isn't the money available to do what the preservationists want or we would be spending $30,000 rather than $20,000 per unit. . . .

If problems were at least negotiable with some offices, there were others that were extremely difficult to work with. Thus, in respect to a (non-NSA) project undertaken in a Georgia city, the first informant (quoted above) remarked:

All the buildings [we were doing] were historical. . . . There we did some old mill housing—some very nice historical stuff. I would get together with the lady from [the local historic preservation group] and go through the neighborhood and agree on what we would do—what was reasonable and suitable. The trouble there was that the state people then would not either back or even accept recommendations from the local level. So they would take their own ninety days to go look at the thing. In turn, the Atlanta regional office was horrible to deal with. They are very nasty and arrogant.

Difficulties in dealing with the SHPO in New York will be considered later in this chapter when we review the Utica case, but first we shall briefly examine local efforts to deal with intergovernmental obstacles.

OVERCOMING THE INTERGOVERNMENTAL SYSTEM

Despite stumbling blocks placed in the way of implementation, some local governments made enormous efforts to see their projects realized. Some localities were still struggling as late as 1983 and 1984 to wrest resources from a reluctant national government. For example, New York City gained permission from a sympathetic area office to publish a request in late 1983 for project proposals that would make use of program resources from the original allocation of FY79 not already committed to specific projects. Under pressure from Washington, the area office then sought to recapture the funds. A senior city official described events:

The only way we were able to talk our way out of it was to say, "Look, the area [manager] and the [area office] director for housing said, 'Go ahead.' If you had told us that you were going to recapture it, we would have stopped it, but now we are on the line, so you have to do something for us." So they said, "Okay, since this is the last time, but no more." And we did a fast-track processing . . . and I think the project will go into construction very shortly.[9]

In a different vein, a number of communities engaged in moving projects ahead when they had been stalled at various points in their convoluted histories. In the case of a project in Lewiston, Maine, for example, the original developer had dropped out because of delays by both HUD and the state HFDA in respect to a project that at various times numbered between 96 and 106 units in 13 to 15 structures. A new developer was designated in March 1980. In June, the HFDA agreed to finance the project in principle but it withdrew when interest rates made it financially unfeasible. The new developer then struggled to hold the package of properties together until financing became available.

To assure project construction, the developer needed to keep up with the rising costs of construction and to be sure that HUD contract authority for the project was adequate to cover the mortgage commitment. To do this, the city agreed to trade in units from projects originally proposed for later in the city's schedule that were stalled at the time. That trade-in allowed additional contract authority to be given to the first project. The developer also needed to negotiate a FAF with HUD in the spring of 1982 which would add to the allowable costs covered by FHA insurance.

To expedite the federal commitment, the city and developer turned for assistance to Senator William Cohen and Representative Olympia Snowe, both Republicans. The critical action, according to one local informant, involved hiring the law firm of the Republican state committeeman to lobby with the administration. The result was a HUD commitment that made the project financially feasible.

Similarly, Hartford's hope of revitalizing its NSA ran into a number of problems by the end of the Carter administration. The most important was that the city had selected a developer who failed to produce viable projects by late 1981. When a new mayor took over in early 1982, the original developer was decertified and a new one selected. HUD, which had been willing in the past to "roll over" the 199 units targeted to the NSA now demanded that the new developer come up with a proposal by no later than June. The one submitted involved 156 units in 26 structures and was accepted by HUD as feasible. (As in the Lewiston case, the number of units was cut back to cover new cost calculations.) One critical aspect of an eleventh-hour agreement reached on this project was a commitment by Connecticut's Department of Housing to support a bond issue to cover construction costs.[10] As a result of these efforts, a project which looked dead in 1981 received HUD approval in December 1982, and was in construction by early 1983.

To gain a greater sense of the range of intergovernmental problems with which particular localities had to deal, we consider cases from Utica, New York, and Savannah, Georgia. These cases highlight the diverse implementation experiences that local governments had, differing only in degree from the experiences of many localities.

Utica, New York

Utica's NSA proposal was hastily written for a large area—one that contained 13,500 people out of a total city population (in 1970) of 79,400. It was vague on many important issues, including the commitment of sufficient resources from the city's Community Development Block Grant (CDBG) to justify the 250 units of Section 8 requested. There were also doubts about the city's capacity to pursue the small structure–inexperienced owner strategy outlined in the plan. As a result, the proposal received only conditional approval.

Even while negotiations went on to remove those conditions, it became clear to city officials that a small-structure approach would not work. As one local official conceded, "HUD wanted the city to take on management of the process, but we were not really in a position to do it, which is why we looked for a developer once we saw how much red tape was involved."[11]

Matters got particularly complicated when a HUD field office employee mistakenly notified the city that it would lose its scheduled first-year allocation of 110 units because it had not received a firm commitment of units for approved projects by the end of the fiscal year. This was done by the employee without consulting the area manager, who was working directly with the mayor and the city's staff to resolve many of the outstanding issues on the conditional approval. One central office staff member remarked that "the mayor went crazy" when this happened. Tempers cooled when the units were carried over to FY80.

In the meantime, the city responded to HUD's concerns about the original size of the target area by making major boundary changes. Those changes were approved by HUD in February 1980. The city then advertised in March for developers to use 150 units; 8 proposals were received. On that basis, a local firm was selected to do two structures: Genesee Towers, a former bank building; and a vacant nursing home, which was burned shortly after proposal approval. HUD then allowed the developer a waiver of NSA rules so that the nursing home site might be used for 84 units of new construction. Once that agreement was reached—on the condition that the city not submit additional requests for new construction under NSA—the project was financed under a bond issue floated by the local housing authority. The structure was occupied by early 1982.

The Genesee Towers project was more troublesome. It involved converting the bank building to sixty-six units of elderly housing. The structure was located within a historic district, although the building itself was not on the National Register at the time of the project review. Among the concerns of the SHPO were the replacements planned for existing windows and what the developer proposed to do within the building in regard to the bank vault—the vault was ultimately removed from the structure—and the impressive staircase leading down to it. The latter was eventually preserved for display purposes.

More difficult to resolve was a dispute over an outbuilding behind the structure. A small section of the latter building went back to the nineteenth century while a larger wing had been added in the 1940s. The presence of this structure complicated the project's implementation because HUD approval of the project depended on the developer's gaining control of sufficient land on the site to provide adequate parking space and to deal with a sewage problem. Any action the city took to deal with those two problems ran up against the opposition of the SHPO to removal of the outbuilding. While the SHPO was ultimately willing to support demolition of the newer section of the outbuilding, they insisted that the older part be retained. To make matters worse, the developer did not own the structure, so that she was required as part of the deal for the bank building to obtain and preserve it for no particular purpose.[12]

Local officials blamed the SHPO for contributing to lengthy delays in working out these issues. As a senior city administrator remarked, choosing—interestingly enough—the same term employed by the developer in Ohio:

We would send them a set of plans and would not hear from them and then it would turn out that the plans had been lost, so we would have to send them another set of plans. We ran into a bunch of fanatics. . . . The historic people seem unable to recognize that there is a time line on developer costs and it is not as if we were talking about preserving a Bonwit-Teller for posterity.[13]

While the developer proceeded to qualify for Section 8 and financing, negotiations for qualification of the structure for the National Register dragged on. The result was that the project was completed and rented by 1982, but qualification for the National Register was still in dispute as late as May 1983.[14]

Another major problem encountered by the project involved the environmental condition of the city, for Utica had gotten into a controversy with both the state's Department of Environmental Conservation (DEC) and the federal Environmental Protection Agency (EPA) over the dumping of raw sewage into the Mohawk River. Indeed, the DEC had filed a suit against the city. Until that controversy was resolved, it was possible for the developer to proceed on the Genesee Towers project only with the understanding that an on-site sewage treatment facility would need to be provided. That would add at least $1,000 per unit to construction costs.

The city and Oneida County responded to this situation by hiring a consultant who was charged with developing a plan to deal with the sewage problem. In the meantime, the city argued in favor of proceeding with the NSA project on the grounds that it had lost substantial population in the two previous decades and it was hesitant about sinking funds into a sewage system that might have excess capacity once completed.

A meeting on the issue was held at the HUD Buffalo area office in June 1980, involving the city's representatives, relevant HUD field staff, and a DEC representative. According to one participant, the DEC spokesperson expressed a willingness to allow the city to proceed with the Genesee Towers project based on the city's good faith as well as acceptance of the city's position that the project would simply involve moving the existing population into better housing (rather than adding to the population of the city). However, HUD was not prepared to proceed until the EPA agreed.

To add to the city's difficulties, Utica was the only locality in this study that experienced a problem with its A–95 review.[15] Such reviews normally encountered no opposition to NSA projects. In the Utica case, however, questions were raised about the Genesee Towers project because of its location in a central business district where grocery stores and other conveniences for the elderly were not readily available. The city responded by arguing that the needs of the elderly would be met through a proposal then underway to develop nearby property into a shopping center under a recently awarded Urban Development Action Grant.[16] The A–95 review agency also expressed concern about crime rates in the NSA, although the city claimed the area had never had a major problem. While such complaints were irritants, they did not constitute major problems like the environmental and historic preservation reviews.

HUD finally approved the project in mid-August 1980, but the start of construction was delayed until early 1981 because of the unfavorable bond market. The city then pursued completion of additional structures, including the conversion of two more downtown nonresidential structures into forty-eight and sixty-eight units of elderly housing, respectively.

By.the time the Reagan administration came into office, however, the DEC had reimposed a moratorium on all construction in the county sewer district. As a city official noted, the DEC had been trying to get all the municipalities in the district to sign consent orders agreeing to resolve the sewer problems of the area. One village had been holding out. At that point, the city discovered that a federally assisted senior citizen project planned for the dissenting village had been granted preliminary feasibility status by HUD at the same time that the city's projects were being held up. Relations with HUD, according to that informant, then got "a little testy." By this time, however, HUD was less the source of the problem than the DEC.

In September–October 1981, HUD finally agreed to allow the designated developer for the last 68-unit project to submit a proposal for project feasibility. At that point, the local program ran into the problem of construction costs which needed to be resolved through the authorization of a FAF. Despite these problems, the last project was approved in September 1982, with the inflation factor included. Allegedly, this approval required the intervention of the Republican senator from New York, Alfonse D'Amato.[17] The project was under construction by February 1983. Thus, despite what at some points appeared to be an insurmountable series of difficulties, by the end of the NSA process Utica had approximately 263 units of elderly housing to show for its efforts.

In the course of these events, Utica shared with Troy's TRIP organization regular recourse to the HUD central office to complain about some of the intergovernmental problems that arose from their contacts with the Buffalo area office. As a result, the central office became concerned with the quality of the field office's performance. Of that situation, the executive director of TRIP commented:

I know that we did not create a lot of problems and we had to be very careful in our dealings because . . . it wasn't really proper for us to know how exasperated HUD Washington was with Buffalo. . . . I wasn't personally mad at any of them. It wasn't anybody's fault. . . . It was just sort of a system problem. . . . We are causing a lot of problems for Buffalo and there isn't anybody out of Buffalo who doesn't know me and doesn't know that if things don't go right—if TRIP is going to get hurt—that I am by God going to do something about it.[18]

Informants in Utica echoed these feelings, but a senior official in that city went on to sympathize with the field office people:

[The area office has] only limited manpower. I have more people working on programs here than they have in some parts of the field office. However, they seem to use that limited staff mainly for crisis intervention and have problems handling routine matters. It is certainly not a matter of incompetence because they have some good people but they need a better system of program management.[19]

Matters came to a head when the director of the Office of Multifamily Housing Development in Washington wrote to the Buffalo area manager to complain about the difficulties that various cities, most notably Troy and Utica, had experienced in working with the office. The manager wrote back claiming that his ᴜffice had experienced "frustration" similar to that of the cities "not because of any indifference or lack of knowledge of NSA policies on our part but because of the forceful personalities involved in the projects located in these cities."[20]

In regard to Utica's problems with the Genesee Towers project, the area manager insisted that they arose from trying to coordinate a variety of reviews through several agencies, including the SHPO, as well as those involved in the sewage problem. He noted that the latter issue had bogged down, in part, because EPA did not respond to a request for comments for over a month. He went on to note:

The area office has been as eager as the sponsor to see the project move ahead. However, the sponsor has not always been reasonable in understanding area office responsibility in meeting all program requirements and has attempted to exert outside pressure to dissuade the office from meeting these responsibilities.

By the end of 1980, officials in Utica were much happier with the situation after the central office intervention. As a local official stated, "Working with the area office has gotten a *lot* better. We've always had good cooperation with——, but the problems [have existed further up]. I think—— [a new official in charge of the housing division] has really gotten the reins in his hands. . . . There has been a considerable improvement."[21]

This experience suggests that, at least under certain circumstances, localities were able to convert their dissatisfaction with HUD field office operations into changes in behavior, but central office interventions of this kind were rare.[22] Instead, most localities and developers endeavored to work with the offices they had or to find methods for end-running them in order to achieve their developmental goals.

The struggles of the principal development organization in Savannah with the Atlanta area office provide another example of the difficulties that could arise between a field office and a locality.

Savannah, Georgia

The leading role in Savannah's NSA program was played by Leopold ("Lee") Adler, II, an investment banker who had been involved in earlier rehabilitation efforts in the city. Adler had worked previously with the Historic Savannah Foundation, which had done much to promote middle-class reinvestment in the Savannah historic district. When he attempted to interest that foundation in rehabilitating structures in the adjacent low-income Victorian district, however, there was little support. Consequently, he and some associates formed the Savannah Landmark Rehabilitation Project whose initial focus was the Victorian district.

That district was an area where absentee landlords had packed predominantly black households into frame Victorian row houses of one to four units. Although few repairs had been made over the years, the vacancy rate was low. According to a story by Neil R. Pierce, the situation had inspired Adler to set goals for Landmark which included

[efforts] to drive out of the slumlords, to purchase and restore 600 of the 1200 structures in the Victorian District, and then—with the help of federal subsidy programs—to rent the homes back to the poor tenants at rents they could afford.[23]

Although incorporated in 1974, Landmark was not fully in operation until 1977 when the organization began to draw upon federal and foundation grants. One of its first successes was a grant from the National Endowment for the Arts to survey the neighborhood; another grant from HUD's Office of Neighborhoods was used to restore a structure for Landmark's own offices.

Landmark's first residential rehabilitation project involved restoring three townhouses using twelve employees under the Comprehensive Employment and Training Act (CETA). Later, the organization received an "innovative grant" from HUD to redo sixty-four units in approximately twenty-five more structures. The latter effort combined Section 8 Substantial Rehabilitation (Sub Rehab) subsidies with $6 million in 312 financing—an approach that HUD later ruled out for NSA projects. To save on out-of-pocket costs, Landmark again relied on CETA employees working under a Landmark supervisor.[24]

Questions were raised within HUD about the wisdom of making such commitments to an organization whose economic viability—whatever the reputation of its head—remained uncertain. A memorandum circulated within the HUD central office, for example, cited a lack of support for the project within the city's urban renewal agency. The memorandum also expressed doubt that private investment in the Victorian district would be spurred by the commitment of federal resources.[25] Nonetheless, Landmark managed to purchase the project structures with the help of a $50,000 loan from the National Trust for Historic Preservation and seed money from one of two minority-owned banks in Georgia. They also acquired the services of an architect from the Department of the Interior under an Intergovernmental Personnel Act agreement. This individual worked on developing rehabilitation designs that would meet historic preservation standards. Finally, Landmark prevailed on local firms to donate materials and labor to the project.

Thus, by the time Savannah was ready to consider participation in the NSA program, Landmark had assumed the lead role in revitalizing the Victorian district. It influenced the city to apply for five hundred units of Section 8, half of which would be used by Landmark. The remainder would be available for other purposes, including involving the owners of smaller properties. Despite the evident concern of HUD's central office about the capacity of Landmark and the city to make use of an allocation of that size, the request was approved without conditions.

The city advertised a portion of its own allocation in the spring of 1979 and managed to elicit twenty-one proposals from small owners for seventy-five units, but progress in financing projects and doing the requisite paperwork was exceedingly slow. No commitments to those smaller properties had been made by April 1981; by that time, there seemed to be increasing evidence that eligible owners preferred to make use of the city's own interest-subsidy rehabilitation program (financed through CDBG) rather than wait for a satisfactory market situation for Section 8 financing. Under the circumstances, the city was in the process of making a commitment to an Atlanta-based developer to convert a small vacant hospital into forty-five units of elderly housing.

The fate of Landmark projects was equally uncertain at the time. Essentially, Landmark had put together three packages of properties for consideration: Savannah Neighborhood Action Project (SNAP) I—100 units in approximately 47 structures; SNAP II (89 more units of rehabilitation); and SNAP III (44 units of new construction). SNAP I was submitted for preliminary HUD approval in June 1980, the other two in November of that year.

In anticipation of qualification for NSA, Landmark had purchased structures containing 261 units with the assistance of a $1.6 million loan from the city. That loan was underwritten, in part, with a $750,000 grant from the Ford Foundation. Most of these purchases were in the NSA, although some were in an adjacent neighborhood. These debts put pressure on Landmark to get the project underway rapidly, a concern that was reinforced by a decision to hold units that fell vacant off the rental market so that the organization and the city would not be under the pressure of bearing relocation costs.

The Landmark projects experienced one delay after another. How much that was related to the personal antipathy of officials in the Atlanta area office to Adler's style is difficult to say, but there was evidence of such unhappiness in the comments of a key area office official who complained that Adler "had a straight line to Carter and when he ran into problems getting what he wanted out of us, he simply hopped a plane to Washington."

The Atlanta office argued that Landmark was attempting to "over rehab" the target structures and to get HUD to pick up as much of the resulting cost as possible. This concern resulted in a debate that went on for many months over what came to be known as the "costs attributable" issue. That term referred to how much of what Landmark was doing needed to be done to make the units decent, safe, and sanitary, and how much was being done as a reflection of the historic preservation orientation of its founder. Area office officials argued that Landmark's approach inflated the costs of rehabilitation beyond the point insurable under a HUD mortgage. As one HUD official in Atlanta remarked, "Landmark pressed [the cost] issue at every turn and wanted to play it to an extreme. We are agreeable to making adjustments where they can be clearly demonstrated but there is only so far you can move on such an issue."[26]

In order to secure acceptance of the higher costs, Landmark prevailed on Savannah's congressman to write to Assistant Secretary Simons. In response, Simons questioned whether the high costs were valid:

While the developer's position may have some merit, it appears that many of the costs he proposes to be considered as costs not attributable to dwelling use are [not] normal rehabilitation costs. We are, however, conducting an in-depth review of the request and will make every effort to work with the developer towards a successful project.[27]

In the months that followed, the technical debate over costs became enmeshed with Landmark's intense feelings that they were being treated shabbily by personnel in the Atlanta area office. Landmark brought part of the problem on itself. For, in order to draw upon outside technical assistance in packaging their proposals and to benefit from tax syndication possibilities, the nonprofit group turned in June 1980, to the Cranston Mortgage Company of Columbus, Ohio. Instead of merely relying on Cranston to provide technical assistance, however, an agreement was reached under which Adler became president of a Cranston subsidiary in Savannah. This forced him to step down from the formal leadership of Landmark, thus raising again the issue of the stability of that organization. At the same time, Cranston took on responsibility for negotiating financial issues with the Atlanta area office.

Initially, this appeared to present no particular problem for HUD, which encouraged Landmark and Cranston to put together the required financial documentation. During this preparatory phase, a senior officer of Cranston wrote to the area manager alerting him to the cost problems involved in bringing the target structures up to national and state historic preservation standards. While the total replacement cost for the project would run about $4.04 million, an amount that would require a mortgage of at least $3.6 million, under HUD's normal calculation methods the mortgage ceiling for Savannah would be only $2.9 million. A FAF would have to be provided to make the project feasible.[28]

Matters reached an impasse in late 1980. Approaches were made to the central office but the latter postponed a decision until the new administration took over. In early 1981, a former NSA coordinator for the Indianapolis area office, Marc Lancaster, joined Cranston and assumed responsibility for moving Landmark's NSA projects to implementation. After much effort on his part, the cost issue and most of the other technical issues were successfully negotiated only to find HUD reviving an older issue and raising a new one: the financial soundness of both the developer (Landmark) and of the general contractor, who was one of the leading minority contractors in the region. In regard to the former issue, the area office insisted that Cranston's senior officer assume personal financial liability for the project. This was done, even though it meant restructuring the project's paperwork. The new package of materials was then submitted on 16 February 1981, only to have them sit at HUD Atlanta for more than a month, at which time the application was rejected because it had not met a February 13 deadline which would have qualified the project for consideration in a special program for financing assisted-housing projects.

Cranston responded to that news by arguing that a careful reading of a field letter issued by former Assistant Secretary Simons would have shown that their project qualified since it had been in processing since June 1980. As Lancaster remembered, ''We called the central office which was caught up in the transition and fought and argued with them. The area office still insisted against approving it. . . . We threatened them; at the same time, we submitted everything we could.''[29]

Cranston then drew on the services of another former HUD employee to act as an intermediary in expediting the project. The result was that Lancaster and the company's new consultant visited Georgia in the spring. They engaged in the following sequence of events, according to Lancaster:

[We] went to Savannah and talked to the people there and then went to Atlanta. First, [the consultant] went in to talk to the area office people and played up my former connections with HUD and . . . greased the way. Then I went in and everything was hunky-dory. . . . All of a sudden [the financing issue] was resolved and, guess what, we were eligible. This was late April or May. But they still had questions.

Cranston later sent Lancaster to Atlanta once more to see that the project was moving ahead, only to discover that some of the questions the area office had raised and were continuing to raise resulted from the fact that no one in the office had actually reviewed all of the submissions. As Lancaster remarked:

The [area manager] wasn't there. I talked to the deputy. He acted shocked. He was very responsive. . . . He said he wanted the project out just as much as everybody else. . . . I indicated that if there were any more problems, we might use the Freedom of Information Act to show that information had all been flowing one way. At that point, they assured me that there were no more problems but I asked where the project actually was and nobody knew.

Allegedly, the materials had gone astray while waiting for people to return from vacation.

Whatever the merits of the positions taken by HUD, the feeling at Cranston by April 1981, was one of disgust with the administrative procedures followed by the agency:

We are thinking seriously of bringing a lawsuit on this thing, raising issues about the specific competence and credibility of the people down there. It has nothing to do with the program guidelines which we have worked and we have tried to be responsive in every instance and things are still sitting there. My boss is a very competent individual, but he has said that it has just gotten to the point where it is silly. It has cost us a lot of money.

The situation was further complicated by the fact that city officials had undertaken relocation in anticipation of Landmark projects being reviewed expeditiously by HUD. As of April 1981, they had spent $151,000 to relocate forty-four households permanently and another $10,000 on what was supposed to be temporary relocation for another thirty-four households.

In the meantime, the city was continuing to work with small owners on cost estimates and to do write-ups while carrying out such obligations as historic reviews. They also undertook neighborhood improvements, including work on a series of parks that formed the hub of the neighborhood and rehabilitation loan programs to home owners. Even as these public investments went forward and HUD delayed in making a commitment to the Landmark units, private investors were beginning to take a greater interest in the neighborhood. Indeed, a point had been reached by 1980 when the private market was beginning to improve markedly in the NSA. The fear of one local official was that "unless we can shake loose some action from HUD . . . we will not be able to achieve our goals for limiting displacement." Instead, the neighborhood was beginning to see "a lot of young professionals moving in, particularly young lawyers.''[30] The irony was that if HUD continued to find ways to delay action on Landmark projects, the NSA might be upgraded but in a way that resulted in considerable displacement—one of the situations the NSA program had been originally designed to prevent.

CONCLUSIONS

In this chapter, we have identified a range of intergovernmental problems that local governments or their surrogates encountered in attempting to implement NSA projects. For many localities the issues addressed were irrelevant: the structures selected were of no historic interest; they raised no issues of technical or financial feasibility; they were located in environments which raised no governmental concerns; the HUD field offices carried out their project reviews with reasonable speed or generally treated projects with sympathy.

However, it was rare for all of these "nonissues" to be operative at one time. One or more were likely to raise difficulties which local project implementers found trying. Faced with the formidable intergovernmental hurdles placed in their way, localities or designated developers might easily have withdrawn from the program. Instead, most attempted to mobilize their political resources to achieve what they had come to identify as "their" project goals.

In pursuing these goals, there was little evidence that the central office of HUD was any longer in control of the process except in a negative fashion. Thus, HUD behavior was marked essentially by its ability to delay or deny local project initiatives. Here, we must stress the distinction between central office–local relations, on the one hand, and field office–local relations, on the other. The NSA central office staff had attempted to guide and support, as well as to monitor, local program efforts at least through the end of 1979 while Jack Kerry was still in charge of the program. After early 1980, the actions of the central office became more problematic. Efforts were made on occasion to urge field offices to move projects ahead and to work with localities as particular problems were brought to the NSA staff's attention, but the earlier enthusiasm for resolving intra-agency and interagency battles were less evident, the outcome of the Buffalo area office conflict with Utica and Troy to the contrary notwithstanding.

This tendency toward indifference or passivity was reinforced by the Reagan administration, despite the fact that many of the same HUD staff members who had worked on the program in the latter days of the Carter administration remained. Given the lack of enthusiasm of the new administration, NSA staff were only willing to take limited risks on behalf of the program. To some extent, there was a quiet holding action on their part on behalf of localities that were still attempting to realize their project goals for the program, but the staff now refrained from promoting program momentum.

Under the circumstances, HUD field staffs which had never been enthusiastic were reinforced in that disposition. That is not to say that this indifference was universal. Some field offices, notably those in Boston and New York City, continued to support local project efforts, thus making possible a situation of the kind found in New York in 1983 where project commitments were still being made.

What was most notable about the course of events was that so much of the responsibility for project implementation had come to rest on the shoulders of local governments or developers even before 1981. To invoke the models of intergovernmental relations introduced in chapter 1, neither federal control nor intergovernmental sharing prevailed. Instead, implementation efforts reflected a nonsynchronization process in which serious program commitments were held by major federal and local actors but at different times in the process, so that by the later stages of implementation the federal government had lost much of its earlier interest while local governments and their associates continued to pursue program participation.

Viewed from a slightly different perspective, localities that had initially been attracted to NSA by pork barrel benefits continued to try to make the program work, but those efforts were beset by various forms of intergovernmental resistance. Some of these could be resolved through interventions by politically well-placed actors like senators and members of the House, or by "fixers" with political connections and the knowledge necessary to "work" the intergovernmental system.[31] The resulting bargaining processes were complicated by the necessity of involving not only HUD but, on occasion, other federal bureaucratic actors such as the Department of the Interior, the EPA, and state-level agencies like the SHPOs (and, as in the Utica case, New York's DEC).

In the end, the model that appeared to apply best to the situation was one of bargaining. In this case, however, a set of local project entrepreneurs—developers or local government officials who had a stake in completing particular projects—strove to devise ways to get the federal bureaucracy to bargain with them and to respond to their demands. That did not mean that localities always got their way in negotiations but they occasionally managed to make up in commitment to projects what they lacked in intergovernmental authority.

What is equally important about these findings is how much micro-implementation processes deviated from the models of coalition building discussed in chapter 2. The macro-implementation process worked fairly well because of the existence of national and local progrowth program coalitions. Those local governments or other lead organizations that adapted the program to local circumstances—including responding to pressures from within the targeted neighborhoods—were then prepared to implement at least the residential construction component of the program wholeheartedly.

What became more evident as micro-implementation efforts proceeded, however, was that the national program coalition had inadequately tapped into the support of significant actors in the intergovernmental system, most notably HUD's own field office staff and state and federal officials concerned with their own program "games," including those involved in historic preservation. To the extent that the program began to run into difficulties before 1981, then, it was less a matter of ideology or conflicting socioeconomic interests than a reflection of procedural inertia and divergent approaches to bureaucratic priorities among program participants from different government agencies.

NOTES

1. Aaron Wildavsky, "A Bias Toward Federalism: Confronting the Conventional Wisdom on the Delivery of Governmental Services," *Publius* 6 (Spring 1976), 95–120.

2. Richard Legates, "Can the Federal Welfare Bureaucracies Control Their Programs?: The Case of HUD and Urban Renewal," *The Urban Lawyer* 5 (Spring 1973), 228–63.

3. Many developers negotiated options to purchase properties from owners in target areas contingent on HUD approval of their projects. Some found themselves renewing options several times at considerable expense.

4. On the baneful consequences for implementation of multiple decision points, see Jeffrey L. Pressman and Aaron Wildavsky, *Implementation*, 2d ed. (Berkeley, Calif.: University of California Press, 1979), esp. 113–24.

5. These figures are taken from an information sheet dated 30 November 1983, provided by HUD's Management Information Systems Division. The notable exception in FY82 was Stamford, Connecticut, which engaged in a major political campaign to obligate Section 8 drawing on the services of the city's Republican Congressman, Stewart McKinney.

6. The original allocation for NSA projects was stated in dollars, although we have used a shorthand "unit count" throughout this study. At the outset, HUD anticipated that costs per unit of subsidy would be covered adequately by the budget authority available. As inflation escalated toward the end of the Carter Administration and, then, as the Reagan administration sought to limit expenditures, a decision was made to hold tighter to the dollar commitment, thereby cutting the number of rental units that could be subsidized.

7. For an introduction to the subject, see David Listokin, "Historic Preservation: Background and Issues," in *Housing Rehabilitation*, edited by David Listokin (New Brunswick, N.J.:Center for Urban Policy Research, Rutgers University, 1983), 82–87.

8. Interview, David W. Houze, Vice President, Sandefur Companies, Columbus, Ohio, 28 July 1981.

9. Interview, Manuel Mirabal, Assistant Commissioner, City of New York, Department of Housing Preservation and Development, 18 January 1984.

10. The project also drew on a $792,000 housing development grant from the state government that was used to help bridge the gap in project costs.

11. Interview, Frank Pryzbycien, Former Head, City of Utica, Bureau of Housing and Neighborhood Revitalization, Department of Urban and Economic Development, 20 June 1980.

12. By 1983, the newer section of the structure had been torn down, but the older portion remained. As a local informant remarked, "The shed is still there and it if falls down, it falls down."

13. Interview, Joseph Zilvinkis, City of Utica, Director of Housing, 20 June 1980.

14. Allegedly, the issue was the kind of paint used on the structure.

15. For the literature on A–95 and the role of Councils of Government in reviewing local plans for the use of federal resources, see the bibliography listed in Deil S. Wright, *Understanding Intergovernmental Relations*, 2d ed. (Monterey, Calif.: Brooks-Cole, 1982), 437–38.

16. Although awarded in July 1980, the project had still not reached implementation by the spring of 1983.

17. In addition to seeking help from Senator D'Amato's office, the city retained a Washington-based "consultant" who had served as an official at HUD in the Ford administration.

18. Interview, Barbara Jones, Executive Director, TRIP, Troy, New York, 11 December 1980.

19. Interview, Michael Housknecht, Commissioner, City of Utica, Department of Urban and Economic Development, 20 June 1980.

20. Letter from James F. Anderson, HUD Buffalo Area Manager, to George O. Hipps, Director, Office of Multifamily Housing Development, 18 July 1980.

21. Interview, Joseph Zilvinskis, 10 December 1980.

22. Buffalo was not the only area office of major concern to the central office. In the case of the Philadelphia area office, for example, the central office found it necessary to make extensive reassignments in order to deal with local governments' complaints about bureaucratic lethargy.

23. Neil R. Pierce, "Savannah's Human-Scale Renewal Plan," *Washington Post*, 22 November 1977; also see Ann E. Petty, "Historic Preservation Without Relocation," *Journal of Housing* 35 (September 1978), 422–23.

24. This approach proved to be inefficient. Landmark then hired a general contractor who used his own work crew.

25. Memorandum, Robert I. Dodge, III, Director, Relocation and Development Services Division, to Richard C. D. Fleming, Deputy Assistant Director for Community Planning and Development, 16 November 1977. Of the effort to apply techniques employed in the historic district to the new area, Dodge wrote, "The ability of a white, patrician, community leader like Lee Adler to apply similar procedures to hundreds of individual properties in a predominantly minority community is somewhat questionable."

26. Interview, Tim Runyan, Chief of Housing Programs, HUD Atlanta Area Office, 24 April 1981.

27. Letter, Lawrence B. Simons to Congressman Bo Ginn, 4 August 1980.

28. Letter, William E. Roberts, Vice President and Secretary, Cranston Mortgage Company, to William A. Hartman, Manager, HUD Atlanta Area Office, 14 July 1980.

29. Interview, Marc Lancaster, Assistant Vice President, Cranston Corporation, Columbus, Ohio, 15 July 1981.

30. Interview, Idella Jones, Director of Housing, Savannah, 22 April 1981.

31. On the "fixer" role in accommodating interests in intergovernmental relations, see Eugene Bardach, *The Implementation Game* (Cambridge, Mass.: MIT Press, 1977).

8

MICRO-IMPLEMENTATION III: MAKING PROJECTS GO

What accounted for the success of some local projects and the failure of others? In chapters 6 and 7, local and intergovernmental preconditions to successful project implementation were highlighted. Specifically, the presence of favorable or politically neutral neighborhoods to which units might be targeted from the Section 8 Substantial Rehabilitation (Sub Rehab) Program and the establishment of effective working relationships with state and federal agencies might contribute to implementation, but these were not sufficient conditions to assure favorable outcomes. For particular projects to succeed, they required the presence of three other factors:(1) receptive owners; (2) appropriate financing; and (3) committed agents of development.

We have touched on these factors in earlier chapters, but here we deal with each in greater detail. Particularly where the three factors were present in combination, projects were effectively implemented. Where the two preconditions of a favorable neighborhood and a supportive intergovernmental environment were present, outcomes were likely to be achieved with expedition. Still, as we saw in the Utica case in chapter 7, difficulties set in the way of implementation by state or federal agencies did not preclude successful efforts at implementation.

Where HUD area offices supported local efforts (as in New York City and Boston) or state housing finance and development agencies (HFDAs) were prominent in working with localities in selecting and financing projects, the chances of project success were greatly enhanced. Indeed, the combination of a supportive area office and an active state financing vehicle in Massachusetts, the Massachusetts Housing Finance Agency (MHFA), virtually guaranteed the successful implementation of MHFA-backed projects.

The realization of project designs for particular structures was only one of the principal goals of the NSA program, of course. The second, more comprehensive goal—revitalizing neighborhoods—is the subject of chapter 10.

RECEPTIVE OWNERS

In conformity with the efforts made by NSA program entrepreneurs, some localities submitted designs that sought to focus program resources on small structures owned by relatively inexperienced individuals—a population that had not been reached by earlier federal rehabilitation programs. As it became apparent that such a strategy would be extremely difficult to carry forward, plans were modified either to move toward the rehabilitation or conversion of large structures or to engage professional developers in "packaging" a number of smaller structures into one or more projects that could be submitted for financing to an appropriate lending agency and processed through HUD. We review these alternate approaches in the present section using case materials drawn from several cities.

The Failure of the Pure Strategy

Among those localities that attempted to implement a strategy of small owner participation in the NSA program there was a high and early casualty rate: Upper Ashbury in San Francisco; the Near West Side in Cleveland; Federal Hill in Providence; Beloit, Wisconsin; and Round Lake Park in Lake County, Illinois.[1]

Despite its earlier reputation as a low-rent "hippie" area—or perhaps because of it—by 1978, Upper Ashbury had become an area of considerable reinvestment by middle-income home buyers, as well as by landlords of middle-income rental units and speculators. Opportunities for property owners on the private market were so attractive that the availability of government subsidies to support low- and moderate-income households was an insufficient incentive to owners. As a result, even though the city advertised twice for participants, on neither occasion were project proposals received.

Working in less attractive housing markets, Beloit and Lake County experienced similar problems in stimulating small owner interest. In the latter case, the county selected as its NSA a section of the community of Round Lake Park, a village of 3,817. The village consisted almost entirely of single-family structures, although the target area was predominantly rental. The Lake County staff (like the one in Beloit) made a considerable effort to interest landlords in NSA. When that proved unsuccessful, they attempted to attract investors—individuals who might purchase the properties and consolidate them in a package that would be of interest to an experienced developer. That approach was also unsuccessful.

Informants in both communities (as well as in many other NSAs) attributed the failure of this strategy to the reluctance of owners to commit their investment properties to government programs, particularly when, as in the case of NSA, the owner would have to assume long-term obligations both for keeping the contracted tenant in place (subject to complex procedures for eviction) and for paying off any federally assisted mortgage.

Equally important, these landlords were not under strong local pressures for code enforcement. Hope had existed among federal program entrepreneurs that vigorous code enforcement would be a central feature of local NSA efforts. This would have put pressure on owners to participate in the Section 8 program or in other available loan or grant programs financed by the federal or local governments. Instead, code enforcement efforts that were minimal in many places prior to NSA rarely changed with the coming of the program. Without that sort of pressure, absentee landlords were able to make a considerable profit without bearing substantial costs.

Furthermore, for many of them, using the investment in rehabilitation as a vehicle for sheltering taxable income through syndication procedures was unrealistic. Such benefits were not readily available to owners of a small number of units; they had to rely primarily on the rental income itself for their profits. This resulted, in part, from the high "front-end" costs involved in syndicating a rehabilitation project. Informants' estimates of the break-even point for undertaking syndication varied but generally projects with fewer than thirty to forty units were not likely to employ such an approach fruitfully. As an informant in Beloit commented:

What it finally boiled down to was that the mechanics and the economic incentives do not work for a small landlord unless he is a very wealthy individual. . . . Most of the small landlords are not. You talk about sheltering income and they smile. They need cash flow, not income shelters.[2]

Alternate Strategies

When the "pure" strategy failed, only a small number of local governments dropped out of the program. Instead, most employed "mixed" strategies to make use of Section 8 resources. Two approaches involved either designating an experienced developer to acquire and "package" a number of smaller structures, or shifting resources from small structures to large ones. The first approach will be illustrated with materials from New Britain, Connecticut, and Pittsfield, Massachusetts.

New Britain was one of those communities that approached the "pure" strategy cautiously by initially targeting its 198-unit allocation to two projects: a portion for converting a vacant school to housing for the elderly; the remaining units to a street where a number of moderate-sized rental structures were located. For a time, the city attempted to interest a group of eight landlords who owned seventeen different structures on the target street (containing from one to nine units) in participating in the program. The landlords had little interest in doing so on an individual basis and the Connecticut HFDA had no desire to get involved in supporting the small mortgages that would have been required. The city then tried to interest the owners in a joint venture. That effort was also unsuccessful.

After struggling with these options for some time, the responsible city agency moved to acquire the properties under urban renewal procedures and turn them

over to a private developer. At first, the city council was reluctant to support
that approach, given negative experiences with urban renewal in the 1960s, but
it was finally convinced that the program would benefit neighborhood residents.
They also supported an application for $612,000 to a state program that would
be used (in conjunction with local funds) to acquire the properties. The city then
selected a Boston-area developer in September 1980, who was expected to
reimburse the city for its outlays for acquisition and to use the city's remaining
allocation of NSA units in the structures.[3]

The city of Pittsfield assigned 101 of its 150-unit allocation of Section 8 Sub
Rehab to 3 larger structures at the outset: a landmark educational institution
located in a residential setting near the city's central business district; and 2
smaller structures on the main commercial street, one of which had served as a
hotel for transients. The remaining units were to be used in small structures in
the neighborhood adjacent to the school.

The city pursued these goals by designating a development organization that
combined the skills of a Cambridge-based developer with the sensitivities to
local circumstances of a local advocacy planning organization (APO)—the Berkshire Housing Development Corporation (BHDC).[4] The latter had extensive
experience in housing programs. The two groups came together for the purpose
of creating Pittsfield Neighborhood Associates (PNA).

Although implementation of plans for the larger structures encountered difficulties of their own, the three structures were submitted as a single package to
the MHFA and to HUD and approved by November 1979.[5] These projects were
completed and occupied by late 1980. In contrast, efforts to involve owners of
smaller structures were ineffective.

Initially, PNA identified about twenty buildings that seemed appropriate for
participation. They approached owners but not more than three were interested
in even considering participation. The organization itself then sought to acquire
options on eighteen small structures containing fifty-two units. That package
was submitted to HUD for preliminary review. Final action required completion
of arrangements for financing which was not readily available from the MHFA
because of the negative attitude that agency took toward financing scattered-site
projects. Funding was also unavailable from private lenders, who required that
the developer qualify for FHA insurance. Along with FHA insurance would
come a series of structural requirements that PNA felt would drive up the costs
of rehabilitation for the frame structures to a point PNA felt would be financially
infeasible given the size of the rental subsidies permitted by HUD in Pittsfield.
As a respresentative of BHDC commented in mid–1980: "In effect, FHA insurance had to be ruled out. Thus, we had to go back to the city in May and
tell them that we could not work out a satisfactory financing mechanism."[6]

By that time, some of the original owners on whose properties options had
been taken had begun to back away. Ultimately, BHDC and its partner in PNA
withdrew from participation in the project. The city then selected a private
developer who began the optioning and design process once again.

One of the more interesting aspects of this case and of similar ones was that localities continued to honor their commitments to physical improvements in designated neighborhoods even while construction projects were in abeyance. One result was that such improvements enhanced the value of the properties even among particularly notorious landlords. Informants in Pittsfield highlighted a situation in which one such owner chose not to participate in NSA since his structures either had no mortgages or only small obligations and they were bringing in substantial rents by local standards. Critical to the situation was the absence of a strong code enforcement effort. The result was that there was overall improvement in the neighborhood even as his properties remained in poor condition.

New Britain and Pittsfield were not alone in attempting to include small structures in their programs by assigning the responsibility and the profits to experienced developers. In most cases, the organizations taking on that responsibility were private developers; in other instances, localities turned to nonprofit organizations.

Another tactic adopted by several localities was to expand their original NSA boundaries to include areas where larger structures were available for developer-run rehabilitation. Where relatively minor boundary adjustments were involved, HUD was generally accommodating during the Carter administration. As time went on—especially under the Reagan administration—even minor boundary adjustments became increasingly difficult to achieve.[7]

None of these strategic adaptations guaranteed success. The difficult financing problems of the period from 1979–1981—a time during which interest rates rose to extraordinary levels—made projects that might have proceeded expeditiously under more ordinary circumstances infeasible.

FINANCING NSA PROJECTS

NSA program entrepreneurs expected that both developers and small owners would be financed principally by conventional lenders or by state HFDAs. For the most part, such sources were reluctant to participate in the program, especially where small owners or small structures were involved, both because of the nature of the risks (particularly where uninsured loans were at issue) and the character of some of the structures. To make the program work, owners and developers then turned to the FHA for mortgage insurance, to bonds issued by local housing authorities under the relatively untried 11(b) program or to the so-called "tandem plan" operated by the Governmental National Mortgage Association (GNMA) which subsidized mortgages at below-market interest rates for projects intended to serve low- and moderate-income households.[8] Given the condition of the financial market, the latter became a particularly important source of financing for larger NSA projects.

Thus, a GNMA issue in November 1980, of approximately $300 million barely began to meet the demand for financing of assisted-housing projects (only a portion of which were under NSA) that were ready to go into construction. At the very end of the Carter administration, in January 1981, GNMA released another $1.3 billion in tandem funds—its allocation for the remainder of the fiscal year. In doing so, the agency established three priority categories with top priority going to NSA projects.[9]

Limitations on federally subsidized financing might have been expected to put additional pressure on HFDAs to participate in the program; instead, it reinforced their caution or encouraged them to insist upon designs that carried minimal risks. Thus, while the MHFA was unusually active, others were reluctant to accept the interest rates prevailing during the initial period of the program.[10]

Access to the credit market was assisted in several instances by other governmental or quasi-governmental entities. Thus, the National Corporation for Housing Partnerships (NHP), a federally chartered corporation created in 1969 to build federally assisted housing, was sought out by a number of localities to assist them in preparing NSA project proposals or in gaining access to the credit market. NHP provided assistance to neighborhood-based organizations (NBOs), APOs, and local governments in putting together financing packages for projects and also helped them place project management systems into operation, sometimes assuming management responsibility through a management subsidiary. What is surprising, in fact, is that relatively few localities and their development groups turned to the organization for assistance in the course of trying to work out some of the problems associated with NSA. Among NSAs that benefited from the involvement of NHP in projects were ones in New Haven, Pittsfield, Pittsburgh, Washington, D.C., Toledo, Taunton, Massachusetts, and Flatbush in New York City.[11]

Even where financing was available in principle, procedures for negotiating the financial feasibility of projects with FHA could be trying. As a spokesperson for the BHDC in Pittsfield remarked in regard to the local small-structure projects:

The situation was rather strange because, on the one hand, HUD's Housing section was prepared to support rehabbing in principle but FHA was not. A resolution of that issue finally came in April [1980] when we got the [Boston] area office to accept the notion that if we found [comparable costs for recent projects] in the area from Albany to Springfield, we would qualify for mortgage insurance. [We were] able to show that costs of work going on in Albany were comparable. Arguments were presented to HUD and the area office relented.[12]

Difficulties in arranging financing were compounded when developers undertook projects involving small structures of different design configurations on scattered sites. In Baltimore, for example, developers were selected to do two- to three-storied vacant rowhouses in two areas which contained many such properties as a result of tax defaults or abandonments. Rehabilitation costs were expected to be well over $55,000 per unit. This raised serious difficulties for the Maryland HFDA; initially committed to financing the Baltimore program, it eventually withdrew.

At the outset, the Baltimore area office was also supportive of the city's plans. However, to make the projects financially feasible, it was necessary to bring the Fair Market Rents (FMRs) established by HUD for the area into line with what the developers insisted were higher costs of construction than the FMRs permitted. The developers tried various approaches to the issue. At one point, one of them threatened to sue HUD for public disclosure of how the field office computed local FMRs. When that effort was unsuccessful, the leading developer entered into lengthy negotiations with HUD over qualifying two or more units within a rowhouse that used the same entrance as separate townhouses, which would have qualified the units for a higher FMR; for the same reason, that developer sought to treat row structures as detached units.

The conflicts between HUD and developers over these matters were reflected in a round of communications that escalated exasperation on all sides. Thus, in the Baltimore case, Assistant Secretary Simons wrote to the area manager that he was not unsympathetic to the problems of the developer, but that he was not prepared to change the definition of *walkup*, *row*, and *detached structures* in order to maximize the financial feasibility of a project. Still, he conceded, "[i]f your office can demonstrate that units such as you describe . . . are accepted in the market place as townhouse units, we could accept the modified procedures you propose. Under no circumstances, however, would we approve a rowhouse as a detached unit."[13]

COMMITTED VEHICLES OF IMPLEMENTATION

One of the critical factors in overcoming these problems was the presence of a committed development organization. In chapter 6, we identified a range of NBOs and APOs that took part in implementing NSA projects. Along with those organizations, developers and local governments played important roles in project implementation. What was most important, however, appeared to be less the level of expertise with which they began than their persistence.

One administrative form that several local governments adopted was the neighborhood-level corporation. Los Angeles's only NSA (in Hollywood), several of the NSAs in New York City, and the one in Niagara Falls, New York, benefited from such an approach. Here we review only the situations in Burlington, Vermont, and New York City's Sunset Park. In the former case, a city-sponsored neighborhood corporation backed by a committed HFDA made even small-structure projects feasible.

Burlington, Vermont

The city government of Burlington initially sought a developer who would rehabilitate a few large structures and serve as a consultant in working with small property owners, a strategy akin to the one pursued by Pittsfield. The area selected as the city's NSA was an attractive residential neighborhood close to the city's waterfront, which was itself being considered for revitalization.[14] Next to the campus of the University of Vermont, the NSA contained a high percentage of low- and moderate-income renters (in addition to students); only about 35 percent of its units were owner-occupied.

Shortly after receiving its requested NSA allocation of 350 units, the city advertised for a developer and received favorable responses from more than a dozen. The one selected in March 1979, began almost immediately to retreat from the concept of working on the rehabilitation of smaller structures. For other reasons, however, that developer cancelled its participation in June 1979.

The city responded to this situation by using funds from its Community Development Block Grant (CDBG) to create a nonprofit organization—the King Street Neighborhood Revitalization Corporation. Even while a second professional developer was being chosen to work on the conversion of two larger nonresidential structures to housing—one into a building with thirty-seven units, the other into one of sixty units—the corporation assumed primary responsibility for dealing with the other revitalization problems of the neighborhood,including working with small owners. It also acquired a structure within the NSA which it used as a prototype for local rehabilitation efforts and as a relocation resource for persons displaced from other structures. As the executive director of the corporation explained:

There are a lot of advantages to the nonprofit. The most important is the greater credibility in the neighborhood. The owners are terribly concerned about having anyone look inside their buildings because they are old buildings and don't meet codes. It is not rational, but they think the corporation is less threatening in that regard [than the city government].[15]

The corporation was also intended to provide a place for neighborhood participation by including residents on its board. At the same time, it was responsible for negotiating with landlords who owned substandard structures eligible for program participation. According to the executive director, these two different sets of concerns were reconcilable:

The whole process is one of changing attitudes among the landlords. . . . Their attitude has to change from short-term—get a buck and get out—to long-term depreciation of property, good cash flow and good maintenance. That is what revitalizing a neighborhood means in the rental sector.

The corporation was able to work with individual owners on 9 small projects involving 15 structures for a total of 111 units. Individual projects ranged in size from 5 to 27 apartments. The corporation coordinated financial arrangements for these projects with local banks and the Vermont HFDA; the latter assumed responsibility not only for financing the projects but for overseeing the architectural reviews associated with them—something not federally mandated for structures smaller than 8 units but which the Vermont HFDA required.

What was so impressive in this case was how hard the lead agency worked to realize project goals. Similarly, in some New York City NSAs, various combinations of development organizations and local government units worked together to implement project plans.

New York's Sunset Park

Unlike many New York City neighborhoods, the residential structures of Sunset Park in Brooklyn were small-scale with half the area's 10,000 dwelling units located in 1–4-unit structures. Sunset Park had experienced a series of disinvestments, but it was especially hurt during the 1960s by its reputation for being a center of gang violence, by a general decay in its support structures, and by redlining.[16]

The immediate stimulus for upgrading the area was a zoning battle that began in 1968 betweeen a hospital and a meat marketing cooperative, both of which sought to develop projects for adjacent waterfront sites. Residents and local institutional interests—merchants, church leaders, and banks—demanded a role in the planning process for the area and started a nonprofit organization, the Sunset Park Redevelopment Corporation (SPRC). As a spokesperson for that organization described the situation at the time:

The group worked with an urban planner that the city paid and . . . was sort of the neighborhood's voice in the whole process. The group developed a plan for that part of the neighborhood and really for the neighborhood as a whole in terms of traffic patterns, housing, social services. . . . They recognized that they had a role to play in the implementation of the thing—that it just wasn't going to happen because of the proposal.[17]

Even as these plans were being developed, the area was hit by the FHA scandals of the early 1970s which led to a considerable number of foreclosures on one- and two-unit structures and numerous abandonments. It was this problem that led SPRC to get directly involved in housing acquisition and renovation. However, such work as they had accomplished by the time NSA came along was on a modest scale: about twenty houses had been acquired, rehabilitated, and sold to neighborhood residents. The development costs of these ventures were prohibitive: two-family houses appraised for $40,000 might cost up to $80,000 to rehabilitate, a differential made up through subsidies.

Although the achievements of SPRC in housing production were modest, they had become an important institutional force in the neighborhood, perhaps more representative of neighborhood elites than the general population. Still, in the late 1970s, SPRC was active in pressing the city and HUD to commit subsidized units to the neighborhood. Specifically, they worked for the commitment to the neighborhood of sixty-five units under the Demonstration Rehabilitation Program and were involved in carrying out two Section 8 Sub Rehab projects (for a total of seventy-three units) in 1977 under the city's regular allocation.

The organization urged the city's inclusion of the neighborhood in NSA and Sunset Park was 1 of only 3 neighborhoods (out of the 10 the city submitted) to receive unconditional approval from HUD. Although there were some doubts among the city's NSA planners about the capacity of the neighborhood to absorb more than 100 units of Sub Rehab, the city provisionally allocated 500 units to the NSA.

When the city advertised the availability of units for Sunset Park and the other NSAs, only SPRC and its development partner—an experienced private firm—applied.[18] They were able to make use of approximately 335 units spread over 23 structures. These units were put into two financial packages—one financed by GNMA; the other by the city through its own bonding instrumentality. In contrast to many other NSAs, almost all of the units were for families.

Gaining approval for specific proposals had not come easily. The city and developers haggled with HUD over such issues as allowable costs for nonelevator buildings and the demand by HUD for a change in SPRC's general partner.[19] A long delay in financing also forced a cutback in the number of units from 388 initially planned to 335 completed. Nonetheless, because of the persistence of the city, SPRC, its new general partner, and the Neighborhood Preservation Office (which had been opened in June 1980 to promote the revitalization of the neighborhood), the first phase of the rehabilitation program went into construction in October 1982, and the second in January 1983.[20]

CONCLUSIONS

In this chapter, we have examined factors related to the successful implementation of Section 8 projects, particularly: (1) the presence of receptive owners (or of developers willing to acquire properties in order to undertake conversions of nonresidential structures or substantial rehabilitation of dilapidated residential buildings); (2) the availability of appropriate financing; and (3) the participation of an organization committed to project implementation.

In the order of priority, probably the most critical factor was the third, since problems with the others could be overcome, assuming sufficient commitment of a local government or its agent. Where buildings of an appropriate nature were lacking or ownership patterns militated against interest in the NSA program, nothing short of shifting NSA resources to another neighborhood or changing the boundaries of the original neighborhood (to include structures more amenable to rehabilitation) was possible. Both of those options were available to a politically skillful lead agency willing to invest the time and energy. Financing issues, of course, were important constraints, but again ones that such agents were capable of dealing with, particularly if they were able to ride out the worst period of interest rate increases (1979–1981).

These preconditions could be met without creating major conflicts between the local political arena and the intergovernmental system, but on occasion those two sectors did come into conflict. When that happened, agents of implementation preferred to risk conflict with federal officials in order to maintain peace within the local political arena, even if that meant losing some of the promised federal resources.

NOTES

1. See Appendix B.

2. Interview, Robert Lamb, Director, City of Beloit, Department of Community Development, 10 November 1980.

3. For the outcome of that effort, see chapter 10.

4. For a brief description of BHDC, see John R. Nolan, "Innovative Joint Ventures: The Role of Residential Development Agencies," *Journal of Housing* 40 (January–February 1983), esp. 14–15.

5. In 1983 PNA was still engaged in a conflict with the Department of the Interior over the certification of the school for historic preservation-related tax benefits. Questions had been raised about the removal of part of the roof to create an exterior courtyard in order to meet HUD and MHFA light and ventilation standards. Personnel at Interior had refused to certify the project for the Historic Register because of the effects the reconstruction had on the structure's exterior.

6. Interview, Peter J. Lafayette, President, BHDC, Pittsfield, Massachusetts, 21 August 1980.

7. Negotiations also occurred over shifting resources from failed NSAs to other ones or creating entirely new ones based on resources from NSAs that had not been able to use their allocations completely. These sometimes required difficult and lengthy bargaining with HUD field offices and with the central office but major adjustments did take place in several localities.

8. On the 11(b) program, see Gregory Schuler, "Financing Section 8 Projects: A Section 11(b) Funding Guide," *Journal of Housing* 40 (March–April 1983), 44–46.

9. For one report on that highly competitive event, see Andre F. Shashaty, "Dial-a-Mortgage System Changed to a Priority-Lottery Plan," *New York Times*, 11 January 1981, sect. 8, 1. On GNMA, see Roger Starr, *Housing and the Money Market* (New York: Basic Books, 1975), 198–208.

10. This attitude was held by the New York State HFDA, in particular, but New York City had a major advantage in its own bonding agency, the New York Housing Development Corporation, which expedited financing for NSA projects in that city.

11. On the NHP approach, see William D. Comings, Jr., "Advice to Developers: Multifamily Rental Housing Can be Built," *Journal of Housing* 37 (May 1980), 258–61.

12. Interview, Lafayette. The debate over "comparables" caused difficulties in many localities. For example, an owner-developer in Dade County, Florida, proposed putting NSA units into a deteriorated housing project located in a low-income pocket of blight in Coral Gables which had been designated as one of the county's two NSAs. There followed a battle between the developer and HUD's Jacksonville Area Office which led ultimately to the developer dropping out of the NSA program when his price was not met. He then sold the project to a firm that planned to convert the units into market-rate condominiums.

13. Assistant Secretary Lawrence B. Simons, to Thomas R. Hobbs, Area Manager, Baltimore HUD Area Office, 26 August 1980.

14. At the time the city submitted its NSA proposal, it was in the process of developing an Urban Development Action Grant (UDAG) proposal that would have affected both the city's waterfront and the nearby commercial and residential parts of the city. The pending UDAG plan increased real estate speculation with the result that acquisition costs for NSA structures went up independent of the impact of the NSA proposal itself.

15. Interview, Michael Richardson, Executive Director, King Street Neighborhood Revitalization Corporation, Burlington, Vermont, 24 September 1980.

16. For a brief treatment of the problems caused in the neighborhood as early as the 1950s by Robert Moses, see Robert A. Caro, *The Power Broker* (New York: Alfred A. Knopf, 1974), 520–25.

17. Interview, Bryan Winston, Director of Management, Sunset Park Redevelopment Corporation, Brooklyn, New York, 20 January 1984.

18. According to the director of the Neighborhood Preservation Office for Sunset Park, this was due to the lack of interest among professional developers. As she remarked:

I took a couple of prospective developers around the area. They were very polite and everything, but they were looking at Flatbush and Crown Heights, where they have much bigger buildings. The kinds of situation we were looking at here were small 20-unit buildings, 2 blocks away from another 20-unit building, 10 blocks away [from] a 16-unit building. They're hard to work with. They don't provide enough economies of scale.

(Interview, Karen Burkhardt, Director, City of New York, Sunset Park Neighborhood Preservation Office, 9 January 1981.)

19. This change resulted from complaints against the developer that his firm had handled relocation badly in other projects the firm had done elsewhere in the city.

20. One of the major benefits of the program to SPRC and to similarly placed organizations was that its developmental role and its role in the management of the project, would assure it about $185,000 a year in management fees alone. The organization planned to use the money to leverage additional housing activities. SPRC was also the recipient of funds generated under a city requirement that designated NBOs or APOs receive 2.75 percent of the income from syndication agreements to be used on neighborhood improvements. How well this program worked is open to question, however, for on 26 December 1984, a major story in the *New York Times* charged that of 89 projects authorized under this procedure—only a small portion of which were NSA projects—only two had actually completed work. Most funds remained in escrow at that date, though in some instances organization leaders allegedly had diverted funds for personal use.

9

MACRO-EVALUATION: PERSPECTIVES ON PROGRAM PERFORMANCE

The design for the Section 8 Neighborhood Strategy Area (NSA) Program anticipated that implementation would involve monitoring and adjustment of implementation processes over the five-year period of the program. In the longer run, such activity would provide the basis for developing other programs in assisted housing production and neighborhood revitalization.

Systematic monitoring of the NSA program had a poor record even during the Carter administration, and program evaluation came to function in a realm independent of action. In respect to monitoring, the HUD central office NSA staff established procedures only for keeping records on construction activity. Data was limited exclusively to such matters as the number of Section 8 units reserved for each project and how reservations were being used as projects neared completion.

Efforts to collect more varied quantitative and qualitative data on the progress of revitalization activities (including the public and private investment that went into neighborhood facilities and meeting non-Section 8 housing needs) were much less successful. A few NSA coordinators, notably those in Boston and Columbus, Ohio, initially called upon localities to submit quarterly progress reports, but most coordinators did not. Efforts at monitoring NSA progress had largely dissipated by the end of Fiscal Year (FY)80.

Similarly, expectations that intermediate evaluations would be used to make program adjustments were displaced in favor of "firefighting" project-related problems. Thus, while a preliminary formal evaluation was undertaken early, both the way it was conducted and the use of its results—or, more correctly, the lack of use—reflected its irrelevance to program operations. A second formal evaluation, undertaken in the second year of the Reagan administration, had even less impact.

While these evaluation exercises did not have programmatic impact, along with the present study, they constitute the basis for certain conclusions about the successes and failures of the program. In this chapter and the next, we shall attempt to understand the achievements of NSA using these sources. We approach the question of program outcomes in aggregate terms; the resulting macro-evaluation reaches a mixed set of conclusions. Yet, in some places, NSA clearly fulfilled many of the expectations of the program's entrepreneurs.

In order to recognize those achievements, in chapter 10 we draw upon the extensive set of case study materials collected for this report. We deal there not only with the outcomes of project activities, but also with evidence of program impact on the life of target neighborhoods. The latter is a more subtle question, obviously, than simply collecting data on the rehabilitation of structures. Indeed, as several informants stressed, there were circumstances under which more was not necessarily better if it meant creating housing that exacerbated neighborhood problems.

A SENSE OF ACCOMPLISHMENT

Measured by the number of Section 8 units completed, the NSA program was regarded by both its creators at HUD and others knowledgeable about it as reasonably successful. Former Assistant Secretary Simons, for example, recognized that the program had run into some unanticipated problems, but his comments were generally positive:

A[n] . . . issue to be addressed is whether we have created a greater capacity on the part of local communities and a greater interest in their housing strategies? We have brought into play the one element that made everyone feel that this [was] not a federal program but a local program. We gave the communities a feeling of participation, so they will deliver these programs in a more intelligent fashion in the future.[1]

Given opposition to the program's financial and administrative arrangements by the Reagan administration, it is impressive that by 30 November 1983, a total of 24,368 units had been reserved over the life of the program as against the more than 37,000 units of Section 8 awarded in September 1978. It should be recalled that the latter figure was inflated by the inclusion of many program designs that overstated the capacity of target neighborhoods to absorb NSA units and the ability of some local plans to withstand local opposition. As of late 1983, 23,421 of the units reserved were estimated to be in some stage of construction; 16,218 of those were already completed.[2]

In contrast to other studies of program implementation that have argued that little of a tangible nature resulted from the expenditure of considerable federal resources, it is possible to point to the great variety of projects that were completed in many different cities—projects that had some impact in stabilizing if not actually "turning around" selected neighborhoods. Furthermore, interviews with local officials and other leading program participants suggest that the NSA experience contributed significantly to enhancing administrative capacity in those localities that chose to center program responsibilities in local government agencies or in ongoing neighborhood-based organizations (NBOs) or local advocacy planning organizations (APOs).

At the same time, the problematic character of the program was reflected in the response patterns of local officials who were asked two distinct questions as the program began to wind down from mid–1981 onwards. First, they were asked whether they thought the program effort had been worth their efforts; even in those localities where enormous energy had been invested in achieving project outcomes, a clear majority responded that the program had been well worth the effort.[3] However, when they were asked whether the program was a wise investment of federal resources, almost all agreed with criticisms made by the Reagan administration that NSA was an extraordinarily expensive approach. Nonetheless, many of these respondents disagreed with the administration's conclusion that it was not, therefore, worth investing federal resources in pursuing the twin goals of providing assisted housing and doing so in revitalized neighborhoods. While most respondents agreed that other subsidy mechanisms should have been employed instead of Section 8, few were able to suggest concrete alternatives.

There were only a few exceptions to positive agreement among local program officials about the program concept and the effort that HUD had made, at least initially, to carry it out. One of those responses came from a professionally respected individual in charge of Pittsburgh's program. The city had taken a cautious approach toward NSA by applying for only 75 units. Nonetheless, looking at the city's experience up to the summer of 1981, he remarked:

I have been continually disappointed with the HUD management of this particular program. The whole program is a farce. They told us they were going to give us 75 extra units [above the city's fair share allocation]. It turns out that a year later, they weren't extra units after all; they were going to come out of our regular allocation. They said they would speed up processing and then they said they wouldn't. They said the city would have an expanded role in putting the application together. In a technical sense, that is true. We send over the pieces of paper, but the decision making on rents, the decision making on values is no different than it was before. It goes through the same process. I have yet to find an advantage.[4]

A senior New York City official stated a view more common to local program officials:

NSA definitely helped. There is no way the city could have dealt with some of the major problems in those [neighborhoods] without the 5,000 units. It allowed us to work on those buildings which were whole block fronts as major anchors from which to build outwards. We could then get private owners to put money into their buildings and use city-owned buildings [through various programs] so that whole neighborhoods have been changed literally.[5]

While recognizing that NSA was a costly program, he went on to remark:

The real question . . . is whether you can get people to put their time and effort into rehabilitating housing for low- and moderate-income people without assuring them a large profit. . . . The truth of the matter is that in order to build housing for low-income people these days, you are going to have to spend a lot of money. . . . The only aspect of the Section 8 program that I could see that might be worth changing is the overall cost of producing the unit which we can't do very much about because of federal regulations and [prevailing] wage rates. . . .

Despite generally positive views, when the U.S. Conference of Mayors (USCM) attempted to rally localities in March 1982, to bring pressure on Congress and HUD to fulfill the earlier commitment of units to the program in order to meet local schedules for the last two years of the program, those efforts proved unsuccessful.[6] One HUD official suggested that the USCM had hoped that a successful effort made by Stamford, Connecticut, to capture those promised resources would be a major boost to the mobilization of other communities, but as he remarked, "It didn't happen, despite the Conference's best efforts to get the word out, including sending to each of the cities copies of the letter to Stamford from HUD approving units. . . . That was pretty much the last gasp."[7]

The inability to wrest additional units from HUD for FYs82 and 83 did not mean an end to efforts to deliver on units which had been reserved earlier for projects. Thus, a staff member of the USCM wrote to the House Subcommittee on Housing in April 1982, suggesting an addition to the pending Rental Rehabilitation and Production Act of 1982 that would have given priority in resources to localities still in the process of completing work on their NSAs. He made the following argument:

This amendment will permit local governments which entered into NSA agreements with HUD to complete their programs. In most cases, these communities . . . have made commitments to local citizens to complete the housing rehabilitation portion of their programs. . . . HUD has taken the position that these communities deserve no consideration. We heard the HUD Secretary [say] that HUD's commitments are not real commitments. These communities entered into their NSA agreements in good faith. They depend on the U.S. Government to live up to its obligations. . . .[8]

Despite this plea, the administration's decision to halt new project commitments remained firm. Still, given the flexibility in the original allocation process and devices (including playing with the project number) available to local interests, scattered efforts were being made as late as 1984 to hold HUD to past reservations of units and to move those units into production. The same central office informant cited earlier described the situation:

What you have are the units that were reserved in Fiscal Years 79–80 and a small number in 1981 that got stalled for one reason or another, took a long time to process, the financing was hard to find. Some of them languished for three years or more, before they could find an alternative means of financing. . . . Area offices and regional offices were told about a year ago that reservations over two years old were to be cancelled immediately unless field offices specifically requested in writing that an exception be made, and provided there was a solid reason for doing so. Lack of financing and an anticipation that financing was still possible was considered an acceptable reason. So a number of offices came in with projects that they wanted to keep alive and, so far as I know, with very few exceptions, those requests were granted.[9]

Thus, despite expectations that the program would be terminated in all but name by 1982, officials at HUD (both in its central and field offices) quietly assisted localities in using as much of their initial allocations as they could get financing for. In a curious fashion, some of the same field offices that had stood in the way of rapid project implementation earlier now worked with localities to salvage what they could from the NSA program while not directly confronting the White House and the Office of Management and Budget on the issue of budgetary control.

PRIOR EVALUATIONS

At the behest of the Office of Housing, HUD awarded a contract in late 1979 to the National Institute for Advanced Studies to examine first-year program efforts in 48 NSAs in 30 cities. The findings (released in October 1980) focused on identifying the initial condition of the target neighborhoods and their housing and the character of the project designs being developed.[10] Of the 48 neighborhoods sampled, the study found that 19 were targeting NSA units to vacant or predominantly vacant buildings,[11] whereas "about one-quarter indicated a preference for, and seemed to be pursuing a strategy which *gave a preference to small buildings.*"[12]

The sample included a few cases that the researchers characterized as failures. For example, they attributed to local officials in San Francisco the view that Hayes Valley had failed because of "extremely high market demand" that had resulted in a "lack of investor interest in Section 8 rehabilitation."[13] In contrast, they reported that problems with the NSA in Gary, Indiana, were due to a low market demand in the target area which caused owners to be uninterested in participating.[14]

On the whole, the study reached familiar conclusions:

With few exceptions, city officials and HUD Area Office staff noted problems associated with adapting the Section 8 program to smaller buildings owned by small-scale investors. Several local NSA officials indicated that because the program provides no administrative resources, they are unable to provide the extensive technical assistance small property owners need in order to participate in Section 8 rehabilitation. Long processing time and difficulties in obtaining financing were two of the most commonly reported reasons for relying on experienced developers. . . . From the local perspective, it was safer and easier to target Section 8 units to larger properties, attract experienced developers and be more sure of meeting these production goals than to try targeting to small buildings and small investors and risk not meeting production goals.[15]

Early in 1980, HUD began the process of contracting for another evaluation of the program, this time to be based on the accumulated program experience of three years. Internal negotiations at HUD over the terms of the study went on so long that the contract was not awarded until late in the year. A sample of 30 neighborhoods located in 20 cities (drawn from the same sample used in the earlier evaluation) was used. The elaborate research design circulated early in 1981 held out promise of enormous effort.[16] The report itself was completed in the summer of 1982 but was never formally published by HUD; instead, a summary was issued in October 1983, allegedly after considerable disagreement within the department over what was to be done with it.[17]

That HUD was not prepared to attach much significance to the study, was evident from the brevity of the summary and the fact that it covered only a small portion of the ground proposed in the research design. Emblematically, the foreword was signed by an acting assistant secretary for HUD's research office who characterized NSA simply as being "helpful" in the transition to the department's "newest housing initiative, the proposed Rental Rehabilitation Block Grant."[18]

The study estimated that from the outset only three of the cities surveyed proposed measures that would have met 100 percent of the needs of their NSAs. On the average, their original designs covered 47 percent of the total housing needs of the target areas. The researchers attributed this to three factors:

(1) certain cities had selected overly large neighborhoods; (2) many cities lacked significant locally based housing programs to supplement the limited Federal resources provided by the demonstration; and (3) a minority of cities participated in the demonstration solely to obtain Section 8 units and were not committed to securing additional resources for the demonstration.[19]

Comparing neighborhood conditions near project sites in 1981 with those that existed in 1979, the study developed a measure of improvement on the basis of which it reported 18.4 percent improvement in NSAs "where more than half of the projects had reached at least the start of construction, as contrasted to only 5 percent improvement in those NSAs where "less than half of the projects reached construction. . . ."[20] While projects that had tried to make use of small structures and inexperienced owners had not been successful, the study argued that NSA projects represented some advance over what had gone on earlier under the Section 8 Substantial Rehabilitation Program.

This was supported by the finding that almost 25 percent of the individual NSA projects contained ten or fewer units, although the average NSA project contained 31 units. The latter situation, they argued, still represented an advance over the earlier program approach when projects averaged 77 units. Equally impressive, at least as contrasted to the previous experience, NSA developers included "smaller firms, [with] fewer years of experience in the development field, [who] had previously built fewer multifamily housing units than other Section 8 developers."[21] In general, the study also found that "two-thirds of the sites showed at least a moderate increase in their ability to manage a neighborhood revitalization program."[22]

One of the more interesting arguments the study advanced (echoing a criticism made by the USCM during the program development process) was that the large size of the demonstration might have been useful in building a political constituency for the program but tended to confuse local participants about the program's goals. The authors wrote, in that regard:

The large number of applicants resulted in the selection of certain cities only marginally committed to the demonstration's goals and weakened the experimental value of the demonstration. Monitoring and providing technical assistance were also hampered by the size of the demonstration, since the small administrative staff could not give the intensive oversight necessary in a program of this kind.[23]

On the whole, the study questioned whether Section 8 was an appropriate vehicle for rehabilitating small structures since it had taken over 27 months to process applications for a typical Section 8 unit. This resulted from the finding that neither the required technical assistance nor the financial incentives for small-scale owners were present to expedite projects.

While not attempting to draw any conclusions about the ultimate success or failure of the NSA program, the evaluation recognized that programs like NSA would work best in neighborhoods which were only marginally worse than average—a point, of course, that the designers of the program had stressed from the outset. At the same time, localities had not used the program as an opportunity to stimulate substantial additional investment. As they suggested, "for the most part, cities were not innovative in developing other program strategies to supplement the modest level of Federal resources available in the demonstration."[24]

Finally, the reviewers' recommendations reaffirmed their concern about the wisdom of taking on such a large-scale demonstration program. The lessons learned for the design of future programs were stipulated as follows:

(1) keeping it sufficiently small so that it can be closely monitored, (2) limiting participation to those applicants who are appropriate and truly committed to the demonstration's objectives, (3) narrowing the demonstration's objectives to a small set of important coherent goals, (4) simplifying and expediting the demonstration so that it can be completed within a relevant time frame, and (5) building sufficient flexibility into the demonstration design and administration to allow it to respond quickly to changing conditions.[25]

As an adjunct to this evaluation, a panel of local government officials involved in NSA administration was put together by HUD with the assistance of Public

Technology, Inc. (PTI), a research unit associated with the National League of Cities. That panel's functions included reviewing the evaluation design and then serving as consultants to the evaluation. In October 1982, a separate report was issued by PTI which drew on some of the NSA experiences of members of the panel, but the report was essentially geared to serving, as its title indicated, as a *Guide to Local Multifamily Rehabilitation Programs*, rather than as an assessment of NSA.[26]

These participants were more critical of some aspects of the program than some were in interviews done for the present study, as the following sentence from the report suggests: "The Section 8 Substantial Rehabilitation Program was a rigid program that was not entirely appropriate for many of the buildings and/or neighborhoods where it was used during the demonstration." However, the panel argued that since no additional projects would be authorized, "no purpose will be served here by a detailed analysis of why that was the case."[27]

NSA AS A NATIONAL PROGRAM

In terms of making resources available to local governments to promote well-articulated plans for providing assisted housing in combination with neighborhood revitalization, the NSA program met with only partial success. Thus, Section 8 units were reserved early and in substantial numbers by HUD for some NSAs where local governments had only a limited interest in pursuing a meaningful neighborhood revitalization strategy. Even those few communities that bothered to estimate their assisted housing needs with relative care (including some that doubled their requests originally expecting that they would be cut to a lower figure) could not complain about the generosity of the federal government. Where things began to go wrong, of course, was in converting those reservations into projects.

At least three considerations set obstacles in the way of rapid achievement of even that dimension of program success involved in targeting structures for rehabilitation: (1) the inability of the HUD national bureaucracy to dominate its own field staff; (2) the unwillingness of state housing finance and development agencies to get involved in projects that targeted resources to small structures or that involved scattered sites; and (3) the incapacity of HUD and of the Carter administration to influence a money market that was experiencing unfavorable interest rates.

Despite such blockages, what was equally impressive was how much the program did succeed in achieving its goals: marginal neighborhoods were targeted for help; local governments which had never systematically assessed the problems involved in revitalizing neighborhoods took on that responsibility and approached it quite seriously; local organizations—including NBOs and APOs—which had not been previously involved in rental rehabilitation programs honed their skills to the point where they developed significant administrative capacity.

Even before January 1981, various implementation problems were apparent.

First, negotiations between local interests and HUD field offices became more contentious as the program's entrepreneurs faded from the scene. Second, what had been given to local governments was merely somewhat greater influence in a complex administrative and political process that already involved many actors. It had not meant, as occasional talk of block grants suggested, that the ultimate authority would rest with the local government. That is not to suggest that the way local governments would have exercised such responsibility would have been intrinsically better. Rather, it only indicates that NSA was an exceedingly constrained form of program decentralization, albeit one that required the activation of considerable program entrepreneurship if projects were to be implemented.

What the ungainly NSA implementation process did permit local governments to do in particular was to make selections from two sets of dubious options: (1) to choose neighborhoods that were not likely to experience the general turnaround that the program proclaimed as its goal, either because of the size of the area or because of its prior condition; and (2) to select structures to receive NSA resources that some observers might have regarded as questionable parts of meaningful neighborhood revitalization strategies: the conversion to housing of nonresidential structures, or the reliance on professional developers to rehabilitate smaller structures as part of scattered-site designs.

If NSA was not a true block grant in the era of the Carter administration, in an odd way it was both something less and something more under Reagan. The new administration was little committed to the concept and strongly opposed to the expensive Substantial Rehabilitation (Sub Rehab) component of Section 8. It regarded both Sub Rehab and New Construction as unnecessary in a housing market it saw as adequate for meeting the housing needs of low- and moderate-income households.[28] Its goal was to get out of Section 8 construction commitments (including NSA) as quickly and inexpensively as possible.[29]

NATIONAL PROGRAM PLANNING AND LOCAL ACHIEVEMENTS

As the 1983 evaluation indicates, the way HUD distributed resources for NSA makes evaluation of program outcomes and impacts extremely difficult to do. Given proposals that ranged from conversion projects involving a single nonresidential structure in a predominantly nonresidential area to others that attempted to reach small structures in large, badly deteriorated residential areas, it is impossible to develop an analysis of "success" or "failure" based on uniform standards. It is even more questionable whether measuring success in terms of the ratio between the number of Section 8 units allocated to an NSA and those completed would be appropriate, given the hasty manner in which program designs were put together.

Furthermore, where neighborhoods already included a healthy mix of owner-occupied and rental units, to "flood" them with assisted housing was not the route to revitalization. Thus, where HUD field offices did not pay serious attention to limiting the concentration of assisted housing, introduction of NSA units might simply take advantage of neighborhood acquiescence to "dump" Sub Rehab units. That might serve the laudable goal of providing housing opportunities to low- and moderate-income households, but might not serve as the vehicle for neighborhood revitalization that it was supposed to be. Indeed, it might contribute to an anomalous situation where rehabilitation of units under federal sponsorship was potentially in conflict with an understanding of what a neighborhood needed either to maintain existing stability or achieve revitalization.

Contrary to the original conception of the program, only in a few cases did NSA come along at a time when a locality was already engaged in efforts to target neighborhood structures for rehabilitation. More were wrestling with problems that had been left over from previous federal programs, particularly urban renewal or Model Cities. The presence of incomplete neighborhood redevelopment activities was expected by the designers of the NSA program to be commonplace, especially to the extent that local governments were planning to promote housing improvements in low- and moderate-income neighborhoods under the Community Development Block Grant Program. In practice, however, little of the preliminary planning that would have been necessary to meet the expectations that lay behind the NSA program occurred. For some participants, such planning began only after designation for program participation.

It would have been useful to be able to distinguish systematically between those neighborhoods that proceeded from deterioration to stability as a result of NSA as against those where the use of Section 8 either created or reinforced a dependent character on the part of resident populations.[30] We were unable to make such distinctions in the present study, although we touch on this issue in chapter 10. Instead, whether it was the large North Woodlawn neighborhood in Chicago, or smaller target areas in Hartford or Troy, or public housing projects that qualified for NSA treatment in Syracuse or Atlanta, the operational definition of "success" in those areas consisted of making them more pleasant places for the low-income persons who already lived in them—a reasonable goal in its own right, though different in character from the anticipated achievements of the program.

In a dramatically different sense, marginal improvement was also the goal of those programs that sought to reinforce the "pleasantness" of places that already had many positive features (like Greenbelt, Maryland or Burlington, Vermont). However, we must be cautious in treating such projects on the same terms as those where nonresidential structures were converted to housing often for senior citizens as an entering wedge in repopulating an area. Whether the result would be improved neighborhood life for such "urban pioneers" is problematic.[31]

Of course, there is a significant difference between rehabilitating the housing component of a neighborhood to a point where residents were reasonable satisfied with their housing conditions and actually "turning a neighborhood around" so that changes occur in investment patterns. We address questions of these neighborhood changes more fully in chapter 10.

One measure that was discussed in great deal during the program design period was the degree of private investment that would be attracted into the neighborhoods either in the form of housing loans (mainly for owner-occupied structures) or for commercial or institutional upgrading. In practice, relatively few neighborhoods experienced the kind of private investment that would have mixed classes and produced a vibrant neighborhood life—at least according to the ideals identified by writers like Jane Jacobs.[32]

Instead, property owners in neighborhoods already embarked on gentrification saw little value in getting involved in a program that required a long-term commitment to assisted housing. Where project proposals were advanced for such neighborhoods, the result was considerable warfare, sometimes ending either in total defeat for NSA projects or a very uneasy peace among residents from different socioeconomic backgrounds.

And yet to point to tensions created in the course of neighborhood revitalization is not necessarily to point to failures, for what was most impressive about so many of the project efforts is that they were undertaken with considerable seriousness by localities or their agents. Many of these local actors were inexperienced in negotiating with HUD, with various state agencies, with neighborhood groups, and with lending institutions. Even where not much was ultimately accomplished, a qualified case can be made for the achievements of NSA. Compared with some of the demonstration programs that preceded it, especially Model Cities, NSA realized a good deal in many places in terms of stimulating local actors to think and act seriously about revitalizing neighborhoods. And in fact many informants argued that they had learned a great deal from the experience—what was worth trying in the future and what was not.

Before becoming too rhapsodic about such successes, however, we need to recognize that a calculus framed purely in terms of neighborhood improvement and enhanced administrative capacity may be insufficient. A fairer representation of the situation must also take into account the costs of the program relative to other possible uses of national resources, and the time and effort expended by various actors in attempting to implement the program through the awkwardly articulated intergovernmental system. We shall reserve a discussion of those dimensions of the program's outcome to the final chapter.

Before dealing with such issues, however, the next chapter provides a more detailed sense of the range of program achievements.

NOTES

1. Interview, Lawrence B. Simons, Washington, D.C., 13 April, 1981.

2. These data were provided by HUD's Management Information System Division, 30 November, 1983.

3. In January and February 1982, the U.S. Conference of Mayors surveyed 100 of its members to determine their attitudes toward the NSA program. Of the 100 localities, 91 responded to an item asking them to rate the NSA program. The Conference summarized the results as follows,

Among the surveyed communities, 56 gave the Section 8 NSA program a very high rating, while 22 communities rated it a moderate success and 13 communities gave it low ratings. . . . Among those who cited difficulties in the program and give it a lower rating, high interest rates, unpredictable financing, strict HUD-FAA [sic] regulations and lengthy HUD processing delays were cited most often as the causes of frustration at the local level.

(U.S. Conference of Mayors, "Section 8 Neighborhood Strategy Areas: Progress in Meeting Goals—An Assessment of Unmet Needs for Substantial Rehabilitation," March 1982, 4.)

4. Interview, Paul C. Brophy, Director of Housing, City of Pittsburgh, 6 August, 1981.

5. Interview, Manuel Mirabal, Assistant Commissioner, City of New York, Department of Housing Preservation and Development, 18 January, 1984.

6. John Gunther, Executive Director of the USCM, wrote to mayors on 30 March, 1982, that the USCM hoped to employ Congress as a means for holding the administration to the original commitment. Gunther urged mayors to write to their senators on the issue. Little came of that effort. It appears that fewer than a dozen cities submitted letters in support of the program .

7. Interview, John Sheehy, Former Chief, Rehabilitation Division, Office of Multifamily Housing Programs, HUD, Washington, D.C., 13 January, 1984.

8. Barry Zigas, Housing Director, USCM, to David Bley, U.S. House of Representatives, Appropriations Committee, Subcommittee on Housing, 23 April, 1982.

9. Interview, Sheehy.

10. National Institute for Advanced Studies, *Neighborhood Strategy Areas: Neighborhoods and Programs 1979*, Washington, D.C.: Office of Policy Development and Research, Department of Housing and Urban Development, October 1980. An examination of the field reports produced by the National Institute's staff reveals that in many instances only the most preliminary of project analyses were completed by the time the reports were compiled.

11. Ibid., 45.

12. Ibid., 46. The figure overstates the percentage of localities that *succeeded* with such an approach. Among those counted were localities which dropped out of the program because they could not make the strategy work.

13. Ibid., 60. The study appears to have confused Hayes Valley with Upper Ashbury where rapid gentrification made participation in the NSA program unattractive to property owners.

14. Ibid. That argument does not account for the willingness of professional developers to become involved in projects even in unattractive neighborhoods. In fact, a professional developer emerged in Gary subsequently to do units in large structures.

15. Ibid.

16. Urban Systems Research and Engineering, Inc., "Evaluation of Section 8 Neighborhood Strategy Area (NSA) Demonstration: Evaluation Design," Prepared for the Office of Policy Development and Research, Department of Housing and Urban Development, 9 March, 1981.

17. The summary report was issued by Kenneth D. Bleakley, Mary Joel Holin, and Laura H. Fitzpatrick, Urban Systems Research and Engineering, Inc., and Laurent V. Hodes, Office of Policy Development and Research, U.S. Department of Housing and Urban Development, "A Case Study of Local Control over Housing Development: The Neighborhood Strategy Area Demonstration," Washington, D.C.: U.S. Department of Housing and Urban Development, January 1983.

18. See, Benjamin F. Bobo, foreword, "Case Study of Local Control."

19. Ibid., 2

20. Ibid., 3

21. Ibid.

22. Ibid., 5.

23. Ibid., 6.

24. Ibid., 17.

25. Ibid., 19.

26. Donna L. Sorkin and Nancy B. Ferris, *Guide to Local Multifamily Rehabilitation Programs: Lessons Learned from the NSA Demonstration*, Washington, D.C.: Public Technology, Inc., 1982.

27. Ibid., 33.

28. The administration's position is indicated in the following statement:

With the exception of the Section 8 Existing Housing program, Federal housing assistance programs were more suited to addressing the problems of housing availability and adequacy than housing affordability. They aimed to increase housing supply through subsidies for new construction and substantial rehabilitation. These programs proved to be extremely expensive and inefficient ways to address the housing problems of this country. A healthy economy with low inflation and moderate interest rates is the best prescription for the ills which plague housing production today.

(*The President's National Urban Policy Report: 1982*, Washington, D.C.: U.S. Department of Housing and Urban Development, August 1982, 32.)

29. The USCM made an additional effort to focus attention on the needs of NSAs in connection with passage of the Housing and Urban-Rural Recovery Act of 1983. That act provided resources to initiate new Rental Rehabilitation and Housing Development Grant programs. The only concession made to the NSA program was a requirement that HUD provide Congress with a report on the results of the program within four months of passage of the act. (U.S. Conference of Mayors, "Summary of Housing and Urban-Rural Recovery Act of 1983, "*Federal City Reporter*, 6 December, 1983, 14). That report was still not available in early 1985.

30. The danger was that the latter type of neighborhood might remain a "reservation" or "sandbox." On the arguments associated with these metaphors, see George Sternlieb, "The City as Sandbox," and Norton E. Long, "The City as Reservation," *The Public Interest* 25 (Fall 1971), 14–21, 22–38, respectively.

31. The creation of "ghettoes" for the elderly was a tendency fostered by the NSA program. An extreme example occurred in Waterbury, Connecticut, where 400 units of elderly housing were placed in five large nonresidential structures in a business district. To make matters worse, other developers were using different federal housing programs to construct additional units of elderly housing in the same area.

32. Jane Jacobs, *The Death and Life of Great American Cities* (New York: Vintage, 1961).

10

MICRO-EVALUATIONS: THE IMPACTS OF NSA PROGRAMS

A major difficulty in analyzing program-induced changes is arriving at a proper understanding of where each neighborhood began as well as where each wound up. Some target areas for the Section 8 Neighborhood Strategy Area (NSA) Program were in extremely poor condition at the outset of the program while others were in reasonably satisfactory condition. The latter lacked only a small measure of investment in public facilities or in a few particularly bad structures to qualify them as stable.

Unfortunately, no set of quantitative measures were developed for the present study that could be used to compare satisfactorily the preprogram condition of one neighborhood against another. Nor can one realistically do so when comparing the condition of different kinds of neighborhoods—large ones like the badly deteriorated Bedford-Stuyvesant NSA in New York City or the densely populated North of Market NSA in San Francisco as against low-rise, low density, but marginally deficient NSAs in cities like Burlington, Vermont, or Pittsfield, Massachusetts.

Nevertheless, we can still take account of what informants felt were major deficiencies at the outset of the program and contrast those perceptions with program results. We have checked these perceptions against such factors (where information was available) as: (1) the public resources (besides Section 8) that went into improving the housing stock and neighborhood conditions; and (2) the private investment attracted into the area.

While I have relied principally on materials provided by informants for the analysis that follows, part of my visits to NSAs involved personal observations of NSA activities—a basis for comparison that was particularly useful when two or more visits were paid to localities early and late in the course of program development.

Questions still arise as to how to view program impact. In some situations, the greatest local effort and the provision of considerable resources to neighborhood improvements may still yield only minor results. Elsewhere, a few well-targeted resources may have much greater impact. Rather than emphasizing that investment distinction per se, I have chosen to stress the degree and direction of change. With that in mind, I examined twenty NSAs in sixteen cities that I visited or revisited during 1983–1985, at a time when the effects of NSA might have been expected to be visible.[1] The results are summarized in figure 10.1. With three exceptions, I have avoided treating local designs that emphasized the conversion of nonresidential structures to elderly housing in predominantly nonresidential areas. Instead, I have focused most of the following discussion on NSAs that began as predominantly residential areas.

It should be noted at the outset that none of the observed changes were associated with neighborhood decline. Thus, even if neighborhoods did not appear to prosper from participation in NSA, the short-run evidence is that they did not get worse. To speak either of neighborhood decline or of more positive changes is different, however, from treating matters of program success or failure. For the most part, this section treats program successes, albeit in some instances of a fairly marginal quality. Indeed, I would contend that the NSA program experienced only a small number of full-fledged failures in the sense of instances where a serious investment of time and energy (and money) were made and yet produced little or nothing for the locality.

Even by those standards, there were some program failures. Three types of failure may be identified. First, a relatively small number of NSAs (about a dozen) dropped out of the program when local jurisdictions experienced a lack of owner or developer interest. These we may identify as intrinsic program failures—instances where there was an inability to fit the terms of the program to local circumstances. Some localities altered their program plans at that point to make them work better, or they negotiated to shift resources to other neighborhoods where Section 8 could be used to better effect.

There was no necessary relationship between this kind of program failure and neighborhood decline. The most obvious example would be the Upper Ashbury neighborhood of San Francisco which prospered as a major haven of Yuppiedom in the wake of its departure from the NSA program. The argument could well be made that the program failed, especially since major displacement occurred in that instance, even as the neighborhood improved.[2]

A different form of intrinsic program failure was experienced by the suburban community of Greenbelt Maryland, which mobilized considerable technical and political support to do battle with HUD over technical issues involved in extending Section 8 to resident-owners. After fighting unsuccessfully over issues until early 1982, the cooperative withdrew from the program and proceeded to work out alternate financial arrangements for successfully rehabilitating its housing units. Under the circumstances, one might argue that the NSA program failed because the community forfeited 325 units of Section 8. Yet, by 1984, major investment had occurred in housing rehabilitation and infrastructure improvements were in place.[3]

Second, political failures occurred in cases where neighborhood groups defeated NSA program efforts. These included Hamilton Park in Jersey City and Hayes Valley in San Francisco, instances reviewed in chapter 6, where neighborhood-based opposition to NSA was strong enough to terminate the program. In other cases, a neighborhood could become so enmeshed in intergroup controversy early in implementation that even the commitment of units to one project might serve as the death knell of the local NSA program rather than being a mark of program success.

Third, one may speak of failures of program impact—Section 8 projects carried out with little noticeable effect upon target areas. We shall touch upon several such cases in this chapter. Nevertheless, to speak of impact failure with respect to a given neighborhood is not to say that a project did not positively affect the lives of particular households.

Independent of the issue of success or failure, it is necessary to restate a point made earlier with respect to the quality of outcomes. At a minimum, high utilization rates of Section 8 may simply mean that the housing stock of a target area was in such poor condition at the outset that large vacant buildings were readily available to developers. Instead of quantity, then, the judicious use of Section 8 might be a better measure of program performance—using just enough program resources to make the kind of impact upon a neighborhood that would contribute to its revitalization but not "flooding" the neighborhood with so many units of assisted housing that the NSA became a "reservation" either for the elderly or for low- and moderate-income families. This sensitivity to the potential absorptive capacity of a neighborhood is a consideration highlighted in several of the cases that follow.

A TYPOLOGY OF IMPACTS

Consistent with the approaches of authors like Downs, and Goetze and Colton, the following presentation is organized in terms of six sets of neighborhood conditions: (1) stable; (2) marginal; (3) submarginal; (4) deteriorated; (5) substandard; and (6) volatile.[4] We employ these categories to examine the direction of change neighborhoods experienced during NSA implementation.

Stable neighborhoods contain a relatively healthy housing stock, reasonably sound support services, and a satisfactory physical infrastructure. Because such neighborhoods tend to have a high percentage of owner-occupied properties (and because of potential opposition from such residents to assisted housing), such neighborhoods were not usually targeted for NSA. Nevertheless, for the few neighborhoods of that kind included, the goal of program involvement was generally the reinforcement of stable conditions at a level that would maintain the existing residential population in a supportive environment.

Marginal neighborhoods were experiencing some deterioration at the outset of the NSA program, but the program was designed specifically to meet their needs; the expectation was that a reasonable investment of public resources (that might engender some private investment) would counter deterioration.

Neighborhoods in deteriorated conditions were those in which disinvestment was occurring in both housing and support services. Inadequate sums were being put into maintaining neighborhood infrastructure. Nonetheless, the neighborhood might still contain features that would merit public investment. The selection of such neighborhoods for NSA was risky, but a good number were chosen. For the most part, the investment of public resources improved conditions, though perhaps not as substantially as might have been hoped.

In a few instances local governments selected areas that were substandard— marked by a great variety of problems for which NSA appeared to be little more than a placebo. Numerous residential structures were uninhabitable; very little owner occupancy was present to provide some core to reinvestment efforts; services were largely absent or inadequate to sustain the needs of those who lived in the area; the physical infrastructure was in poor condition. Even substantial amounts of public investment might not make these areas sufficiently attractive to move them into more desirable end states.

For the purposes of this analysis, I have also introduced two notions related to conditions after participation in the program. Submarginality relates primarily to situations where NSA raised the housing stock to a satisfactory level but left other significant neighborhood problems unresolved either because of the limited potential of the target area or because of characteristics of the local population mix, or both. In contrast, a volatile neighborhood was experiencing radical changes in public or private investment either as a result of NSA or independent of it. This situation is associated with the experience of gentrification but it also applies to other major changes in a neighborhood that altered its basic character without promoting gentrification.

CASES IN NEIGHBORHOOD CHANGE

Figure 10.1 arranges the twenty NSAs examined in this chapter with respect to where they started in 1978 and where they appeared to be by 1983–1985. (Variability in the latter dates reflects differences in the time of the last visit to the locality.)

From Stable to Stable

The two examples of persistent stability presented here involved cases where projects had relatively little impact upon the continuity of life in the target neighborhoods. Both involved the conversion of nonresidential structures to elderly housing.

The working-class Beachmont neighborhood in Revere, Massachusetts, was

Figure 10.1
Patterns of Change in NSAs: Selected Cases, 1978–1983/85

PRE-NSA CONDITION	POST-NSA CONDITION			
	STABLE	MARGINAL	SUB-MARGINAL	VOLATILE
STABLE	Revere New Bedford/ North End			
MARGINAL	Rochester Burlington Flatbush Pittsfield Hollywood			
DETERIORATED		Washington Heights Niagara Falls Sunset Park Washington, D.C. Lewiston New Britain Bedford-Stuyvesant		North of Market
SUB-STANDARD			Syracuse New Bedford/ North Bedford Worcester Troy	Hartford

highly congested but well maintained and relatively stable both in 1978 and 1983. Rather than focusing NSA resources on the existing housing stock, the city targeted its NSA allocation to two small vacant schools which were to be converted to elderly apartments. This allayed neighborhood concern that low-income families would be introduced into the area and that pressures on parking would increase. By the spring of 1983, Beachmont had two occupied Section 8 structures.[5]

Aside from making loans and grants available to home owners in the neighborhood and doing some minor street improvements, the city supported construction of a senior citizen center on one of the project sites. There were few other changes in the neighborhood linked directly to NSA.

New Bedford, Massachusetts, designated its north end as one of three NSAs. The area contained a substantial number of small low-rise residential structures located on small lots. Even before NSA, the city had engaged in an improvement program supported by resources from its Community Development Block Grant (CDBG) which upgraded the sewer system and water lines in the neighborhood. The city also made public investments in the neighborhood's commercial strip. Its primary purpose in entering the NSA program, however, was to convert a derelict textile mill on the fringe of the neighborhood into 151 units of elderly housing. A developer was selected for that $5 million project early in 1979 and the Massachusetts Housing Finance Agency (MHFA) assured financing. As a result, conversion of the mill was completed by 1982. The project contributed to stabilizing a generally stable area if only by removing a blighting influence.

From Marginal To Stable

Sensitivity to the needs of small-scale neighborhoods was evident in many NSAs but no more than in the cases of Rochester, New York, Burlington, Vermont, and Pittsfield, Massachusetts. The Burlington and Pittsfield NSAs were described in chapter 8, so that our emphasis here will be on Rochester, though we will also briefly refer to the two others. In addition, some material on NSAs in Flatbush in New York City and Hollywood in Los Angeles are included as examples of residential areas in larger cities; in both of those instances, the NSAs were essentially low-rise neighborhoods of a kind more commonly associated with smaller municipalities.

Rochester, New York

The Edgerton neighborhood was a predominantly white working-class area in 1977–1978 that was beginning to experience some deterioration, but residents fell only slightly below median income for the city. The key route through the NSA, Lake Avenue, is a major artery leading to downtown; in the Edgerton portion of that avenue, vacancies in residential and commercial properties were occurring increasingly during the 1970s. The bulk of the neighborhood's 4,100 dwelling units were in 1–3-unit structures located on residential streets off Lake Avenue. Both these smaller structures and the somewhat larger multifamily structures along Lake Avenue required attention. Thus, according to a 1976 survey, 3,500 units needed attention although about 3,100 of these required only cosmetic improvement. About 400 units required intermediate improvements of the kind associated with Section 8 Moderate Rehabilitation (Mod Rehab); no more than 100 units were deteriorated to the point of calling for Substantial Rehabilitation (Sub Rehab).

By 1978, efforts were underway in Edgerton to establish a Neighborhood Housing Services (NHS) program which could be used to reach the owner-occupied units (about 35 percent of the total structures) with loans and grants. The city also committed $4 million in public improvements for a variety of street resurfacing and park upgrading projects.

From the outset of the program, the city sought to attract experienced developers to vacant structures along Lake Avenue. With that in mind, Rochester advertised its NSA allocation of 100 units in January 1979, and selected three developers. The developers eventually undertook a total of 110 units in 6 structures.[6]

While financing problems delayed the start of construction and contributed to the withdrawal of one of the original developers from the program, the local public housing authority issued an 11(b) bond for about $3 million in the fall of 1980 that assured financing for the program. The city also assisted one of the developers in reaching financial feasibility for his project by subsidizing him at the rate of $1,000 per unit from a citywide housing development Urban Development Action Grant (UDAG). Once financing was secured, the project proceeded expeditiously to completion so that they were occupied in the spring of 1981.

By that time, too, the activities of the NHS were well advanced. A 1982 report claimed the organization had conducted 4,300 code inspections in the neighborhood (including reinspections), 546 properties had been brought into code compliance, and 366 mortgage loans involving more than $6.7 million had been granted. One measure of success was that in August 1979, there had been 67 vacant structures in the NHS area; by 1982, only 17 remained. According to the report, of those 17 "only three are not in the process of being rehabilitated."[7]

In addition to these activities, the city used Mod Rehab to upgrade housing in the NSA. Most of the promised neighborhood improvements had also been made by 1982. Finally, efforts to stabilize commercial uses in the area succeeded so well by 1982 that there was virtually no vacant commercial space available. As a result, the city estimated that housing values in the NSA had increased 24 percent between 1978–1981 as contrasted to 16 percent citywide. Under the circumstances, it was possible for one local government official to characterize the overall impact as early as 1982 as highly successful: "The buildings look great, and we have local developers whose management of the units we can control."[8]

Similarly, looking back in mid–1983 at the impact of NSA in Burlington, both the local government official in charge of the program and the former executive director of the city's neighborhood revitalization corporation were highly satisfied with the results. The latter described the changes that had taken place in the following terms:

Visually, there has been a big change and a lot of spinoff. It may be just my impression, but King Street [the NSA] now enjoys a reputation in the rest of the city that it would not have had without this program. Now when you mention King Street, people think of buildings that have been revitalized, painted, are looking better. There has also been a tremendous demographic change in the neighborhood. I don't think you could call it gentrification, but we took a lot of vacant space and re-created it or added on to it.[9]

After Pittsfield Neighborhood Associated (PNA) was forced to drop out of the Pittsfield program, it appeared that plans for scattered-site rehabilitation might fail. However, the city found a private firm willing to acquire and rehabilitate some of the structures PNA originally had targeted. The result was that by March 1983, the developer had completed work on the first phase of an NSA project that involved 32 units in eight structures, and he was in the process of construction on the second (and final) phase, which would cover another 25 units in two buildings.[10] In order to include all of the structures, the city negotiated with HUD to move the NSA boundary twice.

Pittsfield was also able to make rehabilitation loans and grants in the area, so that by 1983, a local government official remarked, "We have pretty much addressed anyone who wants a grant in the NSA."[11] Commenting on the public improvements done by the city, the head of the local advocacy planning organization (APO) remarked, "The city has created an impact by rebuilding a number of the city streets in the NSA, a number of the sewer lines and water lines and sidewalks, so it has really beefed up the infrastructure."[12] Both he and the city official in charge were enthuasiastic about what NSA had achieved. The former summed up the city's experience in the following words:

Comparing the accomplishments to the goals of four or five years ago, most of those have been accomplished. The city has pledged its money, has done the public improvements. It has demolished the worst buildings—the four or five that weren't salvageable. That has created an impact [of its own]. I think of the scattered-site structures that we fixed up—of the first eight, seven of them were the worst buildings that we were aiming at . . . [among those that were] still structurally sound—so it . . . really transformed the worst buildings into the best ones.

New York City's Flatbush

In its original application, New York City described the Flatbush neighborhood in Brooklyn as containing approximately 38,700 dwelling units; 10 percent required rehabilitation. Of those, the city estimated about 1,200 would need substantial rehabilitation. Most of these were in the 700 multifamily structures that made up a significant portion of the neighborhood housing stock. At the same time, abandonment was limited to no more than 200 units. In some ways, one might have characterized Flatbush with its predominantly lower-middle-class and upper-working-class population as laying closer to stability than marginality even in 1978.

Efforts to foster both public and private investment were underway before the approval of the NSA. 68 units had been approved for Section 8 Sub Rehab (including 48 under the Demonstration Rehabilitation Program); another 658 units in 21 buildings were being targeted for other city rental rehabilitation programs. The area had also been targeted both by Citibank and a separate consortium of banks for rehabilitation finance.

A leading role in coordination of revitalization activities was played by a vigorous neighborhood-based organization (NBO), the Flatbush Development Corporation (FDC).[13] Organized by resident homeowners in 1975–1976 because of a concern about neighborhood disinvestment, the FDC provided a variety of services, including housing-related services for tenants, but its greatest efforts were focused on processing applications for rehabilitation loans for home owners. According to its claims, in the period leading up to 1983, the organization had helped complete processing for rehabilitation loans for 51 buildings involving 2,000 units. Loan applications for an additional 104 buildings containing 3,300 apartments were being processed in late 1983.

The city initially targeted 275 units to Flatbush under NSA. However, only two project proposals were approved: one involved 20 units in an area near the boundary with neighboring Crown Heights, an NSA where the same developer had been designated for three other projects; the second Flatbush project was originally expected to involve development of 194 units in 11 buildings, most of which were vacant. However, the HUD area office objected to the distance among the structures and forced the developer to scale back to a plan involving approximately 128 units in 7 buildings clustered in 2 subareas.

Because of the high costs of construction and the relocation costs which the city insisted the developer absorb, the firm was reluctant to move ahead with the project. Meeting with the developer early in 1981, NBO representatives urged the firm either to act or drop out of the project so that another might be chosen. The developer decided on the latter course, but no other firm came forward. This left the FDC in the position of either assuming the role of developer (without any experience in that role) or letting the project die. At the last possible moment, the FDC discovered National Housing Partnerships (NHP) as a potential resource. With their involvement, a project package was put together and approved by HUD before the end of the year. The project was completed and occupied by February 1983.

Sub Rehab was only a small part of the considerable revitalization activity that was helping to stabilize the neighborhood by early 1984. Not only had a variety of rental programs been heavily used but there had been noticeable improvement in the character of owner occupancy. Equally important, the executive director of the FDC noted a change in the quality of landlords acquiring rental properties:

Previously, all that we were getting were the low end of the line—the guys that were going to milk [the properties] . . . because there was no point in doing anything else from their point of view. . . . But now we are getting owners in who are serious managers of buildings. . . . [14]

After summarizing the contribution of the NSA program to the stabilization of the neighborhood, he described an impact on the neighborhood similar to the one in Pittsfield:

[I]t allowed us to rehabilitate buildings that it would have been impossible to do otherwise, and to generally uplift the areas in which those buildings were located. The seven buildings that have been done have really been important to other landlords in the area who used to point to those buildings—and to others . . . that weren't as bad—when we went to them about rehabilitating their buildings . . . In essence, we eliminated two cancers in the area that were inhibiting other things from happening. . . . There are now probably [only] ten abandoned buildings in the [whole] neighborhood.

Hollywood

The NSA designated by the city of Los Angeles included a population estimated in 1977 at over 21,000 covering 150 blocks. The city proposed to place 800 units of Sub Rehab into this ethnically heterogeneous section of the city. While the housing and the neighborhood were shabby, vacancy rates were low in the low-rise 5–20-unit structures that made up the area. 85 percent of the 11,600 dwelling units were rental. Of those, about 20 percent were estimated to require some rehabilitation.

The initial emphasis of the city's program design was on 160 units of new construction based on the argument that those units would serve as a major relocation resource. In the second year of the program, Los Angeles began to lobby for another 100 units of new construction. In the end, the city completed approximately 220 units of new construction under NSA, though not all of these units came directly from the program; 60 units were from a special allocation made by HUD to the Southern California Association of Governments which then passed them on to Hollywood.

At the outset, Los Angeles attempted to target Sub Rehab units to small-scale owners but found this difficult to do; as a result of a first round of advertising for proposals in 1979, only one 71-unit project (in two buildings) emerged. An arrangement was then worked out under which several small owners formed a joint venture that was expected to develop one or more projects. This approach ran into financing problems and difficulties with FHA insurance requirements. At that point, the owners traded their interests in the project (including their project number) to professional developers who paid them, in effect, by making them nominal partners in the projects.

The result of all this activity was 123 units in Sub Rehab carried out under the aegis of the Hollywood Revitalization Corporation, a city agency based in the neighborhood.[15] In addition, the corporation promoted small-property sub-sidized loans for 1–4-unit buildings administered by local lending institutions. The city also made a limited number of public improvements in the NSA, ranging from tree plantings to street lights and work on sewers.

While the range of public investment was not large given the size of the NSA, by early 1985 there appeared to be reasonable improvement in the neighborhood. Thus, in evaluating the condition of the area, a corporation official remarked:

[P]roperty values have increased substantially. In the final analysis that is the test of the program effort. . . . It just seems things are better. . . . I think the same kind of impact would not have occurred if we hadn't had the Section 8.[16]

From Deteriorated to Marginal

On the whole, the condition of NSAs in this category were considerably worse at the outset of the program than those of the neighborhoods already described. The "success" of these NSAs may be best understood in terms of raising these neighborhoods to a better condition than they had been and giving them brighter prospects, though they were still faced with the real possibility they could regress to their troubled pasts.

While the seven cases included in this category are not formally ranked, they are presented in a rough approximation in figure 10.1 in descending order of improvement. For discussion purposes, we will consider only two cases: Washington Heights as a case involving a greater degree of change, and Bedford-Stuyvesant as a neighborhood that changed less.[17]

New York City's Washington Heights

The area designated by New York City as its Washington Heights NSA contained a large (139,000) and complex cross section of Manhattan population located in 54,000 dwelling units. According to 1977 estimates, as many as 37,000 of those required some renovation with 13,860 expected to need only cosmetic improvements. Approximately 2,400 units might still have merited treatment under Sub Rehab, but the Neighborhood Preservation Office (NPO) requested only 500 units under NSA.

The city had targeted the area for participation in a variety of planning and neighborhood governance programs beginning in the 1960s.[18] Thus, unlike Sunset Park or Bedford-Stuyvesant, which did not get their NPOs until 1980, an NPO was in place in Washington Heights in 1975 that had been working to upgrade many of the area's deteriorated units through a variety of publicly financed programs even before NSA came along. The result, according to an NPO estimate for the period covering 1 January, 1975 to 30 June, 1983, was that $142.8 million (much of it in public funds, including NSA units) had gone into housing improvements. The result, the NPO claimed, was that 12,351 units had been upgraded by the later date—approximately one-third of the stock needing attention.[19]

When the city advertised for developers for the NSA units in June 1979, it received proposals for 6 projects that would have involved about 405 units—all of them targeted for families. With subsequent HUD-imposed cutbacks, the actual production was in the range of 337 units. Even this "shortfall" was not as substantial as it might appear, since initial discussions about NSA had included conversion plans for an abandoned hospital. Instead, that project was undertaken by the city's public housing authority and was in construction by 1984 as an elderly project of 247 units. Finally, the city committed approximately $20 million in site improvements from CDBG and its capital budget to neighborhood projects.

City officials took considerable pride in what had been achieved in Washington Heights. As the senior city official overseeing the NSA program remarked, "All of the major areas of blight in Washington Heights have been covered. Whole blocks of buildings have been put back on line with public funds."[20]

Somewhat more hesitantly, the director of NPO remarked:

It looks good to us. . . . There is some interest beginning in co-oping; there is more interest in investment. We have maintained a good flow of rehab loan monies. Landlords find that they are able to attract a somewhat higher income population. . . . Some landlords who were downtown type landlords—the kind who advertise in *The New York Times*—are now starting to move into the area. Rents are going up.[21]

Abandonment also had slowed, as it had citywide, and the city was gradually putting such structures into various programs. The NPO director estimated that 2 percent of the stock was still abandoned and problems remained. Nevertheless, she was quite positive about the "very visible" impact the NSA program had made and was hopeful that Washington Heights was in the process of being stabilized.

New York's Bedford-Stuyvesant

The portion of Bedford-Stuyvesant included in the NSA program was the better part of that large deteriorated section of Brooklyn.[22] The NSA was "confined" to 76 blocks containing about 37,000 people; the area included attractive brownstones occupied increasingly by middle-income black people as well as substandard structures occupied by poorer households. Indeed, one of the notable features of the target area was a 60 percent rate of owner occupancy even before NSA. It also included a historic district. According to the local NPO director, the area was not so much being "gentrified" as being populated by young black professionals who had grown up in the neighborhood and then left it for other locations—people who were moving into structures that had been abandoned, so that there was no problem of displacement.

The NSA also included the area surrounding the headquarters of the Bedford-Stuyvesant Restoration Corporation, a major community development corporation created in 1967 with the help of federal resources and foundation grants.[23] As late as the coming of NSA, persons associated with redevelopment efforts in the neighborhood had complained about the limited attention the city had given to the area, allowing the corporation to pursue outside funding as much as possible. While organizational claims may be exaggerated, a summary report issued by the corporation in 1982 suggests some positive results:

Restoration and its subsidiaries and affiliates have directly generated over a quarter billion dollars for the benefit of Bedford-Stuyvesant, including investments of over $100 million of debt and equity capital. This highly leveraged redevelopment program has successfully combined public and private capital with the energies of local residents to aid over 130 local businesses, develop 1,500 units of quality housing, beautifully renovate the exteriors of 4,200 homes on 150 blocks, provide over $40 million in mortgage financing to 1,600 homeowners, weatherize 500 apartments, induce the IBM Corporation to construct a new $13 million manufacturing plant in the community, and convince several private corporations to enter innovative joint ventures.[24]

The corporation was influential in having the neighborhood targeted for the NSA program. However, when the city advertised for developers, the corporation was the only group to come forward; it became the lead force in redeveloping 278 units. In addition, other housing investment was going into the NSA or into nearby areas of Bedford-Stuyvesant. These included a 74-unit 235 project consisting of single-family homes that would be marketed for $60–65,000, and senior citizen projects involving a total of approximately 600 units. Unlike the NSA projects, the Restoration Corporation was not involved as the sponsor or developer of any of these.

While prospects for a thoroughgoing turnaround in the larger Bedford-Stuyvesant area were poor, both the city official in charge of the NSA program and the director of the local NPO were hopeful about what was happening in the NSA. As the latter remarked in response to a question about how the target area was doing, "It's moving. Some incredible things have happened since the [NSA] designation."[25] Elaborating on that point, she argued:

It's not just buildings, but the city was also mandated to do some focusing [of other resources] within the area. They also designated the same area—or a little bigger area— to put certain services in—a real commitment, a real focus. [One thing was to place the NPO in the neighborhood] which is an ongoing thing. . . . So I really think it played a major role in the turnaround.

From Substandard to Submarginal

The four cases included in this category in figure 10.1 illustrate instances where significant public resources were committed to improving the housing situations of low- and moderate-income households or elderly persons and some improvements were made in the physical condition of the areas targeted. Yet, prospects for enhancing the viability of the areas were limited.

In attempting to identify NSAs that fell into the marginal category earlier, I argued that such neighborhoods were in a position to generate some private investment in housing and commercial activities. In contrast, two of the cases identified as submarginal (Syracuse and New Bedford's North Bedford) did not appear to have that potential. In the third case (Worcester, Massachusetts) only the small historic district within the NSA seemed to achieve a degree of stability; the remainder of the area was in considerable difficulty because of problems of social disorganization. Here we will briefly deal with the first two cases and provide some detail on Worcester. Troy might well have been included in the marginal category discussed in the previous section save for certain program impacts that continued to cause concern about levels of potential intergroup conflict in the neighborhood.

Syracuse and New Bedford

The area selected by the city of Syracuse as its NSA centered on a rather isolated section of the city that contained two large public housing projects of approximately 200 units each. The thrust of the design involved "privatizing" the two projects and rehabilitating them with the help of NSA. Renovation was completed by the spring of 1982.

In addition to the housing, the city and developer contributed funds to making improvements in the vicinity of the project. These commitments were modest. Promises that had been made by the city at the outset of the program to upgrade the limited commercial services available were not realized, so that residents of the newly rehabilitated structures—particularly those without cars—continued to be isolated from other parts of the city. In sum, while the housing was rehabilitated and the immediate environment was somewhat improved, given the questionable character of the area as a "neighborhood" at the outset, its future remained shaky.

New Bedford's design for its North Bedford NSA targeted an industrial and commercial zone separated from the nearest residential area by an expressway. One small NSA project involved the rehabilitation of old factory housing built in support of a local textile mill; a second project located housing for the elderly in a building formerly used by the Order of Eagles; a third converted an historic trolley barn (known locally as the Car Barn) into elderly housing. The last project was the largest (114 units). Approved for financing by the MHFA late in 1979, it was completed in 1981.

While informants agreed that the Car Barn and the two smaller projects made a positive contribution to the city's housing supply by adding 164 units of needed assisted housing, they differed in their perspectives on the NSA program's impact. Given the location of the NSA projects in the midst of an essentially unattractive nonresidential area, one local informant questioned the "neighborhood" character of the area:

It is the drug capital of the area. It's cleaned up and then [it gets back to what it was before]. It's under I–95. It's *great* for an elderly woman with respiratory problems. There *is* a market across the street, but that is it. It's also on a bus route, but [that area] is New Bedford's answer to the Combat Zone.

A representative of the principal developer conceded that the area had a bad reputation but insisted that the Car Barn, in particular, had proven to be popular among residents. However, his remarks also exposed the NSA's negative reputation:

I was at the Car Barn last night and the people who reside there just love it. We do have a problem when there is a vacancy because people immediately think of the area in which it is located but once you get them there—once you have the opportunity to show them some of the apartments and the setting and the courtyards and the community building and the social services that are available and they have an opportunity to talk with the best salesmen for the building—the tenants—our ratios go way, way up.[26]

Unfortunately, it remained doubtful whether the target area would ever entirely escape its history and environment.

Worcester, Massachusetts

In contrast to the rather limited project designs in Syracuse and North Bedford, the city of Worcester selected a large area partially encircling the city's central business district (CBD). Sub Rehab units were targeted to two distinct subareas: the Wellington neighborhood; and an area immediately adjacent to the Crown Hill Historic District. One can argue that there was a measure of improvement in both areas as a result of NSA but it was still unclear in 1983 what the long-term prospects for either of the two subareas would be.

Wellington had a YMCA and a community college set in the midst of sub-standard multifamily structures of various sizes. The inclusion of the area in the NSA program reflected the city's concern that the two institutions might move out unless problems such as a high crime rate and a high concentration of abusers of alcohol and drugs were reduced.

At the time plans for the NSA program were broached, the city was already investing heavily in the target areas using CDBG and a variety of other federal and state program resources. In addition to operating through the local government, these efforts were funneled through the Worcester Cooperation Council, Inc. (WCCI), an APO originally created to implement some of the programs left behind as the Model Cities Program dried up.

As one local government official recalled, it was WCCI that had approached the city about the NSA program. The program had made sense to him at the time:

[The] city has a large number of masonry structures which could be rehabbed. . . . It was a coincidence that the city was looking for some means to finance making use of those structures at the same time as . . . WCCI was looking for more programmatic activity and HUD came along with NSA.[27]

From the outset, the city government and WCCI sought skilled developers to use the city's 375-unit NSA allocation. Indeed, the two prime developers—the Winn Corporation and the Beacon Company (both of Boston)—expressed an interest in working in the area even before NSA. As a result, by April 1979, the local government had designated Winn as the developer of 180 units of housing in the Wellington area and Beacon as developer for 165 units in the area between Crown Hill and downtown.[28]

In the latter area, one of the city's goals was the conversion of two abandoned warehouses to elderly housing. Plans also included new units for the elderly on the same site as the warehouses and 57 townhouses for families on cleared land nearby. These plans were greeted, particularly as far as the family units were concerned, with considerable suspicion by residents of Crown Hill. Many were recent investors who were in the process of upgrading large, older homes—some from the 1840s and 1850s—that had fallen into disrepair.

One of the major sources of continuing irritation to Crown Hill residents was Conway Gardens, a 50-unit Section 236 project designed for large families that had been built in the 1970s under the sponsorship of a local church. WCCI had gotten involved in the management of that project in 1976 when the original contractor defaulted and disappeared, leaving the project incomplete. Members of the Crown Hill Association, the group representing the new home owners, had not accepted matters at Conway Gardens quietly. A member of the association described one of their early protests:

At one point we went down to City Hall, took [along] 5x7 black-and-white photos of the [Conway Gardens] yard: the broken windows, the trash, and the mattresses in the yard. We said, "Look. We were promised that this place was going to be upgraded and it is a dumping ground, and we are furious about it." And we passed the photographs around. The head of WCCI stood up and said it wasn't the trash from Conway Gardens residents, that it was from adjoining neighbors who dumped into their yard, that they weren't responsible and that we were doing a disservice to the Conway Gardens residents. *But* the following day, there were cleanup crews and the place was cleaned up.[29]

These events took place before NSA, but they contributed to the distrust with which gentrifiers greeted project plans for assisted-housing units. Another resident recalled their concerns:

We wanted fewer family units and more green space; more parking space; more play space for the children; we wanted front door and back door access for the units and better fire protection. In other words, we said if we have to have these units, we want a quality thing which will be safe for the residents and we want decent residents and stringent screening of who you get into that place and we want it well managed and well maintained.[30]

Local politicians were not necessarily supportive of the attitudes of Crown Hill residents. Indeed, one member of the city council was quoted by the local newspaper as attacking the "snobs" of Crown Hill.[31] Thus, despite the association's expressions of concern before the city council in March 1979, and then before the city's zoning board of appeals, both bodies approved the project. At the same time, Beacon entered negotiations with MHFA for financing; it was approved in June of that year.

Even though the designs were approved, negotiations continued between the neighborhood and the developer throughout the summer spurred on by a lawsuit filed by the association in July. The result was an agreement that reduced the number of large-family units in the project from 57 to 48. The developers also agreed to move a tot lot and to buy additional land in order to provide 10,000 square feet of green space.[32] Once this agreement was reached, the project moved toward implementation and was fully rented by 1983.

In comparison with this battle the proposal for Wellington involved little political conflict with the local population but more questions about the future viability of the area. Essentially, the Winn Company undertook to provide 180 units of housing—129 units of family housing (although 45 of these were only

one-bedroom) in 13 existing buildings and 51 units for the elderly and handicapped in a newly constructed structure. The MHFA financed the project for
which ground breaking took place in February 1980. Not only did Winn take
on responsibility for the Wellington project, but as work on that project proceeded
they became concerned about the condition of an adjacent 70-unit project managed by WCCI and undertook management of the project as well.

A senior executive in the company admitted that he had been naive to believe
that Winn's work could turn the area around when Wellington was "synonymous
in the city with murder, rape and drugs."[33] While the rehabilitation effort was
going on, in fact, three murders occurred in the neighborhood. In response,
Winn developed a reputation in the neighborhood for "tough management."
The developer was willing to accept that reputation: "We . . . found ourselves
in Worcester taking over roominghouses full of people who were drug pushers,
prostitutes. We had staff stabbed, threats on the lives of people who worked for
us." The firm was insistent, therefore, in being in total control of the rental and
management process (within the parameters permitted by HUD and the MHFA),
despite occasional opposition from WCCI and public advocacy groups.

Additional problems resulted from a city decision to locate an alcoholism
center across the street from the project. Thus, at the same time that Winn was
trying to rent their units, they were regularly finding "guys sleeping and urinating
on the front lawn." The developer had several meetings with the city manager
and the chief of police on that issue which led to extra patrols The company
also beefed up its own security services. As the developer insisted, it was a part
of their philosophy that "[Y]ou either maintain control over the property from
the outset or you lose it. . . . "

Despite the difficulties experienced working in the neighborhood, not only
were the rehabilitated structures having some impact on the immediate area
around the Wellington project by 1983 but some limited institutional reinvestment
was also being made. Both the YMCA and the community college had decided
to stay in the neighborhood rather than move to the suburbs.

In summary, in the Worcester case, it is possible to argue that both sections
of the NSA were marked at the outset by conditions that ranged from substandard
to deteriorated while Crown Hill was becoming a pocket of substantial private
reinvestment. With the heavy infusion of assisted-housing resources into Wellington, that area improved but only to a point where it now had a chance of
becoming a better maintained but still substandard "reservation" for a predominantly dependent population. This situation resembled the one in Syracuse.

The Crown Hill area's fate remained less clear. Private investment in the
historic district continued to be challenged by Section 8 development nearby,
albeit a large portion of the new residents would be elderly. Under the circumstances, it would be inappropriate to characterize the area as a whole as still
substandard in its physical condition but it had not quite attained a "marginal"
status.

From Deteriorated to Volatile

The densely populated section of San Francisco known as the ''Tenderloin'' to residents but as ''North of Market'' to city planners is an area of densely packed 6–10-story hotels and apartment buildings. While only an estimated 280 units were done directly under the NSA program—180 units of rehabilitation in 5 structures; 100 units of new construction—changing demand in the housing market and pressures from commercial development were strongly felt in the area by the 1980s. Matters were further complicated by an influx of Southeast Asian families.

One of the consequences of these pressures was the formation around 1979–1980 of an APO, the North of Market Planning Coalition. Organized by representatives of social service agencies that worked among the area's large population of senior citizens and Asians, one of its major efforts involved getting the city to institute ''mitigation payments'' by developers of tourist hotels. The latter were required to contribute to the rehabilitation of some of the single-room occupancy (SRO) hotels in the NSA in return for permission to build.[34] Some negotiations, for example, involved the construction of a Ramada Hotel which agreed to pay $169,000 a year toward rehabilitation activities up to a total of $8.5 million.

In 1977, local groups had just begun to put together nonprofit housing development corporations to rehabilitate and manage rental structures. Organized citywide through the Council of Community Housing Organizations and aided at critical points by the Catholic Church, these APOs drew upon CDBG and other resources to acquire properties and rehabilitate them.[35] As a result, where there were estimated to be only 300–400 dwelling units under nonprofit sponsorship in 1977, by 1985 that number had increased to approximately 2,400 in the NSA. About 1,600 units were covered by various forms of Section 8, though how much overlap there was between the two sets of units is not clear.

Given the great demand for housing in the city, there were few vacant structures in the NSA by 1985 in contrast to the numerous earlier units. One of the consequences of the heated housing market, according to the executive director of the planning coalition, was a rapid increase in rents:

Four years ago you could rent an SRO here for $60–80 a month. Now it is $250–300 a month for a room without bath. Studios that rented four years ago for $250 are now going for $450–500. As more and more of the city becomes even more expensive than that, this neighborhood remains one of the best deals for housing in the city.[36]

Although more than 85 percent of the housing stock in the neighborhood consisted of studio, SRO, and one-bedroom units, one of the area's major concerns was the many Southeast Asian families that had moved into those small units. The city government chose to ignore its housing codes, in this case with the general support of neighborhood activists. However, densities made units ineligible for family Section 8. At the same time, the Planning Coalition and nonprofits worked with Asian-American design groups to develop living arrangements that would maximize the space available in small units consistent with the values of the immigrants.

Overall, the direction of change in the NSA was improvement in the quality of the housing stock, though the coalition director was pessimistic about the ultimate impact these changes would have on current residents:

Our . . . argument from the beginning is that we can't stop displacement. There will be gentrification of this neighborhood eventually. The question is whether we can stretch it out long enough, so it is not going to be an abrupt change, and in a way that is going to allow as many of the current residents to stay as possible.

A leading neighborhood-oriented activist in the city suggested, in any case, that there was probably a limited time during which Asian families would continue to use the Tenderloin as a zone of first settlement. He was more concerned that the remaining population would have problems maintaining a foothold in the fact of incursions by developmental interests:

San Francisco has an unusually high percentage of single-person households—not only the elderly, but young people and the middle aged. . . . There is clearly a need for that kind of housing. In practical terms it is much easier . . . to achieve that kind of housing in the Tenderloin than it is for families. Unless and until the pace of commercial office buildings can be slowed, we . . . are all living on borrowed time.[37]

From Substandard to Volatile

The Clay Hill neighborhood of Hartford was one that was readily classified as "too bad" at the time NSA applications were reviewed (see chapter 5). Despite reservations about its potential, the HUD central office committed 199 units of Section 8 to the area. Hartford officials then proceeded to select a developer who attempted to design a project without linking up with neighborhood groups. Unhappy about their limited participation in the planning process, residents organized protests against the developer. That opposition figured less in the implementation problems of the developer, however, than difficulties related to finance.

For nearly two years, the project was in limbo—neither completely dead nor quite alive—until early 1982 when a new mayor came into office and insisted that action be taken. With the support of the city council, the first developer was decertified and a new one selected who submitted a proposal to do 156 units in 26 structures. The project was financed by a bond issued by the state's department of housing (rather than its HFDA).

Because of the devastated nature of the area, neither Mod Rehab nor assistance to home owners was appropriate, but the city did encourage the construction of seventeen new units under Section 235 for owner-occupancy. Those units were completed in the fall of 1982 on vacant lots in the neighborhood.

As a result of these efforts, a local government informant looked forward in 1983 to a major alteration in the neighborhood:

In effect, the whole neighborhood is being changed in a period of 2–3 years, so it won't look anything like it used to look. . . . It is like creating a whole new neighborhood because the population will have increased significantly. With the fifteen vacant buildings [out of the 26 targeted for NSA units] and with the 17 moderate-income [home owner] families, there will be more people in the neighborhood and the average income of the people is likely to be higher.[38]

Although the area had pulled back from the brink of complete abandonment, the level of stability it was likely to achieve was uncertain. Whatever happened. the area would be very different from the way it was in 1978.

CONCLUSIONS

In this chapter, we have attempted to assess the impacts of NSA in a selection of neighborhoods, most of which were visited both early in the history of the program and during its final months. At least among a majority of these NSAs, important changes occurred during the period of the program: most target areas fell somewhere in the deteriorated to marginal range initially; almost all experienced a measure of improvement.

In certain instances (e.g., Syracuse; New Bedford's North Bedford) considerable federal investment was made with relatively little impact in promoting improvement in neighborhood life. Still, it might be argued that even in those cases and the ones in Revere and New Bedford's North End, NSA provided assisted-housing opportunities in structures which might otherwise have continued to be blighting influences.

More troubling were the designs for North Bedford and Worcester, where elderly housing was placed in substandard areas with the hope that such construction would contribute to area upgrading. To do so without providing adequate support services and a reasonable positive environment is cause for concern. Indeed, the general question may be raised whether using elderly housing projects as developmental vehicles in troubled neighborhoods is wise.

Furthermore, both with respect to projects for the elderly and for families, substantial federal resources were committed to some NSAs without considering whether those resources were being used to achieve the principal goal of the program—neighborhood revitalization—or simply to establish or reinforce the "reservation" quality of an area. That problem is most clearly present in Syracuse and similar cases where public housing projects were privatized and rehabilitated.

Similar issues might be raised in instances like Worcester's Wellington area Private development does not make "projects" any less concentrated in character, though it may permit management firms to be more selective in their choice of tenants than would be true when such projects are run by public housing authorities.

Presumably, the scattered-site projects undertaken with the support of NSA were more helpful in that regard, though even then assisted housing did not necessarily blend easily into the local environment. In NSAs like North of Market or Washington Heights, where high density or high-rise living was already the norm, or where the socioeconomic position of assisted households did not differ radically from that of older residents, intraneighborhood conflicts were likely to be less serious. When problems of life-style differences were reinforced, as they were in Crown Hill or in areas near other gentrifying neighborhoods, greater possibilities existed for future difficulties.

Given the relatively favorable near-term impacts that most projects made upon the areas in which they were placed, it is not unreasonable to conclude that these local program efforts examined and others made under NSA helped both to enhance housing opportunities and to improve the areas into which they were put—thereby realizing a substantial portion of the goals the NSA program was designed to achieve.

NOTES

1. Of the twenty NSAs treated in this chapter, three were visited only once and then only in 1983: the two in New Bedford, Massachusetts, and the Bedford-Stuyvesant NSA.

2. A similar case took place in Federal Hill in Providence, Rhode Island, though that was much less an instance of gentrification than of incumbent upgrading.

3. Interview, Shekhar Narasimhan, General Manager, Greenbelt Housing, Inc., 13 January, 1984.

4. Anthony C. Downs, *Neighborhoods and Urban Development* (Washington, D.C.: Brookings Institution, 1981), esp. 61–71; and Rolf Goetze and Kent W. Colton, "The Dynamics of Neighborhoods: A Fresh Approach to Understanding Housing and Neighborhood Change," in *Neighborhood Policy and Planning* edited by Phillip L. Clay and Robert M. Hollister (Lexington, Mass.: Lexington Books, 1983), 57–76.

5. One of the schools was destroyed by fire in January 1981. The remaining one was completed and occupied in early 1982. The developer used the opportunity provided by the fire to convert the allocation for the other site to new construction.

6. HUD approved the city's request for ten additional units without any difficulty, a change easier to achieve early in the history of the program than later. On the numbers, see Appendix B.

7. Neighborhood Housing Services of Rochester, Inc., "Annual Report, 1981–1982," May 1982, no page.

8. Interview, Julie Everitt, City of Rochester, Department of Community Development, 17 May, 1982.

9. Interview, Michael Richardson, Director of Community Development Operations, State of Vermont, Montpelier, Vermont, 12 July, 1983. Richardson was Executive Di-

rector of the King Street Neighborhood Revitalization Corporation in Burlington at the time of my earlier visit in September 1980.

10. The use of 57 units for the scattered-site program exceeded the original NSA allocation to Pittfield by five. The difference was made up by the Boston area office.

11. Interview, Richard Hamblin, City of Pittsfield, Office of Community and Economic Development, 20 March, 1983.

12. Interview, Peter J. Lafayette, President, Berkshire Housing Development Corporation, Pittsfield, Massachusetts, 20 March, 1983.

13. See Gary Meo, "Flatbush Development Corporation," *Neighborhood* 6 (Summer 1983), 26.

14. Interview, Robert Blank, Executive Director, Flatbush Development Corporation, Brooklyn, New York, 19 January, 1984.

15. One informant claimed that a total of 571 units had been done in conjunction with the NSA program, but other data suggest the figures were somewhat lower.

16. Interview, Don Bodnar, City of Los Angeles, Community Development Department, Hollywood Neighborhood Strategy Area Program, Housing Division, 13 January, 1985.

17. In some ways, the New Britain program was even more problematic than the one in Bedford-Stuyvesant. Plans for placing 100 units of elderly housing into a vacant school at one end of the NSA and the remaining allocation (98 units awarded; 86 units used) into smaller structures were realized after enormous difficulty. I have not described that NSA in greater detail because the scattered-site project was still in the process of construction at the time of my visit in March 1983, but the overall effort did not appear likely to constitute a solution to the problems of a substantially deteriorated neighborhood. At best, NSA might upgrade the area to marginality.

18. See Ira Katznelson, *City Trenches* (Chicago: University of Chicago Press, 1981), esp. chap. 7.

19. Washington Heights Neighborhood Preservation Office, "Summary of Neighborhood Activity, Washington Heights-Inwood, January 1, 1975–June 30, 1983," June 1983, xerox.

20. Interview, Manuel Mirabal, Assistant Commissioner, City of New York, Department of Housing Preservation and Development, 18 January, 1984.

21. Interview, Barbara Leeds, City of New York, Washington Heights Neighborhood Preservation Office, 19 January, 1984.

22. For a hopeful view of the neighborhood situation even prior to NSA, see Edward K. Carpenter, "Good News from Bed-Stuy," *Design and Environment* 7 (Summer 1976), 34–39.

23. See Bedford Stuyvesant Restoration Corporation, "The Bedford Stuyvesant Restoration Corporation: After Fifteen Years, A Vital Community Institution," May 1982, xerox.

24. Ibid, no page.

25. Interview, Priscilla (Pat) Cyrus, Director, City of New York, Bedford-Stuyvesant Neighborhood Preservation Office, 19 January, 1984.

26. Interview, Peter Rioux, Claremont Company, New Bedford, Massachusetts, 22 June, 1983.

27. Interview, David Kean, Community Development Coordinator, City of Worcester, City Manager's Department of Community Development and Planning, 22 August , 1980.

28. A third developer was selected to rehabilitate three smaller structures near the

Wellington complex in order to use the 32 remaining units of the city's NSA allocation. After many difficulties, those units were in construction by March 1983.

29. Interview, Valentine O'Connor, Crown Hill Association, Worcester, Massachusetts, 10 May, 1983. A WCCI official conceded that many of the complaints about Conway Gardens were warranted: "[T]he density was too high. . . . You just have people hanging out all over the place; the rubbish was bad" (Interview, Nancy Pelser-Richard, Senior Housing Development Specialist, WCCI, Worcester, Massachusetts, 22 August, 1980).

30. Interview, Christopher Carlaw, Crown Hill Association, Worcester, Massachusetts, 12 June, 1983. Professionally, Carlaw was Deputy Director of Development for the Boston Redevelopment Authority.

31. *Worcester Telegram*, 19 May, 1979.

32. *Worcester Telegram*, 11 November, 1979.

33. Interview, Roger Cassin, Winn Corporation, Boston, Massachusetts, 15 June, 1983.

34. By early 1985, a major controversy had erupted over the quality of the management done by the firm designated to run the first structures rehabilitated under the program. See Rob Waters, "City-Funded Tenderloin Hotels a Mismanaged Mess, Critics Say," *The Tenderloin Times* January 1985.

35. See Susan S. Fainstein, Norman I. Fainstein, and P. Jefferson Armistead, "San Francisco: Urban Transformation and the Local State," *Restructuring the City* edited by Susan S. Fainstein et al. (New York: Longman, 1983), esp. 235–38; and Chester Hartman, *The Transformation of San Francisco* (Totowa, N.J.: Rowman and Allanheld, 1984), esp. 231–60.

36. Interview, Brad Paul, Executive Director, North of Market Planning Coalition, San Francisco, California, 18 January, 1985.

37. Interview, Calvin Welch, San Francisco Information Clearinghouse, 18 January, 1985.

38. Interview, Edward Williams, Housing Production Coordinator, City of Hartford, Department of Housing, 29 March, 1983.

11

THE NEIGHBORHOOD STRATEGY
AREA PROGRAM IN THEORY AND
PRACTICE

In conclusion we shall review four sets of issues: (1) the usefulness of the models of intergovernmental relations (IGR) introduced in chapter 1 in understanding the way the Section 8 Neighborhood Strategy Area (NSA) Program worked; (2) the organizational arrangements under which the program was generated and the problems associated with its administration; (3) lessons learned about the policy process from an examination of the program; and (4) the consequences for urban policy of the collapse of the program coalition that supported the creation of the NSA program.

NSA AS A CASE IN INTERGOVERNMENTAL RELATIONS

At the outset of this study, we derived five descriptive models from an examination of the IGR literature: (1) a conflict model in which governments within the American political system have distinct political and programmatic interests that they pursue independently of each other, coming together to battle out their differences only when interests overlap; (2) a pork barrel model in which transactions in IGR are premised on distinct institutional actors valuing participation in material exchanges but with the expectation that recipients will do only those things minimally necessary to satisfy donors while otherwise limiting the ability of donors to constrain their behaviors;[1] (3) a bargaining model related to the first two which recognizes the presence of elements of conflict among governmental actors but assigns to actors the capacity to work together toward resolving differences in order to achieve common ends; (4) a sharing model which assumes that intergovernmental transactions proceed on the basis of like-mindedness in policy and program goals and means; and (5) a control model which borrows from hierarchical images of governmental and bureaucratic relations to emphasize tendencies toward federal domination over the way state and local governments take part in IGR.

Each of these models may be used to describe some aspects of the formulation and implementation processes associated with the NSA program, but none is adequate for understanding the history of the program as a whole. Indeed, while we may speak of certain tendencies highlighted by the models operating at different stages of the program development process, within those stages, we can identify a complex mixture of intergovernmental behaviors.

Thus, the creation of the NSA program initially had a controlled character—centered, as it was, in the ideas of a few program entrepreneurs in the Washington office of HUD. Yet, the program was created as part of the efforts of the Carter administration to create a national urban policy that reflected a sharing approach.[2] There is a certain irony in that situation, but that irony should not be exaggerated, for any expectations by program entrepreneurs that they would shape local programs and projects were tempered from the outset by recognition that their designs would be exposed to the vagaries of the intergovernmental system in the course of macro-implementation.

Seen from a longer-term perspective, NSA was merely the last in a line of national coalition building efforts that emerged out of earlier bargaining relations among housing-related interests in which pork barrel was a consideration in drawing together public agencies and private interests. What was new was the addition of general purpose local government officials to those coalitions but this was hardly a radical step, coming as it did after several years' experience with the Community Development Block Grant (CDBG).

Of course, the original program design allowed considerable room for local government discretion in such matters as the decision to participate in the program, in the choice of NSAs, and in the definition of how interests with a stake in the program were to be managed. Indeed, in the early phase of local program development, HUD's role was envisioned by program entrepreneurs as primarily that of supporting local endeavors rather than being directive. If not avowedly paternalistic, the mission of HUD was conceived of primarily as providing "technical assistance" to localities to help them in understanding what their best interests were within the constraints imposed by the program design as well as by statutory and regulatory requirements.

Control over the selection of localities for program participation might have given considerable scope to HUD to direct the program's operations. Instead, the department decided to serve a variety of other political and bureaucratic purposes: (1) promoting as widely as possible a commitment among local governments to neighborhood revitalization; (2) benefiting Section 8-eligible households; (3) protecting the department's considerable budgetary stake in the Section 8 Substantial Rehabilitation (Sub Rehab) Program against pressures for restraint that were building under the Carter administration; (4) constructing a political constituency among local governments and neighborhood organizations in support of both HUD's budget and its housing programs; and (5) shoring up support for HUD among those political and developmental interest (members of Congress; developers; construction unions; lending institutions) that participated in the housing and community development subgovernments.

NSA, then, can be seen as a means of combining the political interests of an activist agency concerned with strengthening its political base with a means of meeting its policy goals which included providing housing opportunities for low- and moderate-income segments of society and promoting neighborhood revitalization. Those goals had wide acceptance in the Democratic Party's national coalition by the time of the Carter administration; indeed, until the 1980s they were also present in the policies of Republican administrations.

Local governments were attracted to the NSA program by the ideological, power-related and pork barrel aspects of the program. Not only would benefits flow directly to occupants of the structures rehabilitated and to the targeted areas in which they were located, but gains in administrative and political influence would accrue to local governments from their roles in designating NSAs and in selecting the developers who would undertake particular projects. In exchange for these benefits, the locality was expected to exert its administrative energy to bringing about necessary physical or social improvements in the selected area, but either these were not regarded as unreasonably burdensome by prospective participants or they believed there was sufficient room for them to maneuver their way out of such commitments.

Given unhappy experiences with prior HUD programs, however, few localities were willing to prepare planning documents that fully met program entrepreneurs' expectations. This reflected local ambivalence—a desire to participate in the pork barrel of NSA, and sharing in the general goals of the program, but diffidence about becoming involved in program designs that might be financially, administratively, or politically demanding. Indeed, for many local participants, project planning was held in abeyance until HUD crossed their collective palms with Section 8 commitments. At that point, they were guided by their own political and administrative needs that were reflected in such choices as focusing resources on large vacant structures (in order to avoid problems with relocation) and making use of professional developers.

Where differences over such matters surfaced between HUD and the locality during the review process, they occasioned some of the "conditional approvals" we reviewed earlier. Both in such instances and in cases where conflicts did not become apparent until after Section 8 awards were made, these differences led to negotiations which varied from those marked by a high degree of intensity to others that were amicable in character. Taken as a whole, however, local designs were generally accepted by HUD without substantial revision.

Once these awards were made, the responsibility for translating local programs into projects began. At that point, the nature of IGR changed. Having acted the part of the fly during the preliminaries to the selection process and in some of the negotiations over conditional approvals, HUD officials became the spider. In part, this reflected the major role assumed by FHA and housing "technicians" in reviewing individual projects for financial and structural feasibility. Implementation at this stage was further complicated by a need to meet such federal or state requirements as historic preservation and environmental impact. Intergovernmental bargaining over such matters of "detail" could be difficult.

For a time, particularly while NSA program entrepreneurs continued to run the program, localities that experienced problems with HUD technicians could appeal to the central office. By early 1980, however, several critical figures in program development were gone and the small remaining NSA staff was in a less effective position to play the role of "fixer" among conflicting forces.[3] As a result, even during the Carter administration, relations between HUD technicians and representatives of local interests sometimes took on an edge, but that edge became more pronounced during the Reagan administration. Considerable local energy was then expended simply in attempting to get HUD to live up to the commitments supposedly made at the outset of the program. In a sense, the larger intergovernmental program "bargain" began to come unglued.

Given the Reagan administration's goal of removing the federal government from housing production, the preconditions for intergovernmental sharing or even for bargaining were severely weakened. Some members of the central office NSA staff were sufficiently committed to the program that they continued to support completion of as many projects as possible, but their efforts were viewed largely as a mop-up operation.

While sharing never fully characterized any stage of the process, bargaining proceeded initially from a base of some common interest in program achievements. With the installation of Reagan, whatever goals had been held in common substantially evaporated to be replaced by a more conflictual relationship. One major consequence was the need of localities to expend enormous energy to implement even those past bargains they thought they had already struck.

For many local governments, therefore, the feeling by 1983 was akin to the one Charlie Brown regularly has when he is lured by Lucy's offer to hold the football while he kicks it: they had been coaxed into playing HUD's game again only to find themselves kicking into empty air. The inevitable crash landing occurred, at least for those participants who had not been sufficiently lucky or cautious. By that time, however, most local jurisdictions were willing to take the situation lying down either because they had already realized their major program goals or they saw little to be gained by making additional efforts. What was more impressive, perhaps, was that a few got up and fought for the resources promised to them, though enormous political energy had to be expended to gain those resources.

From a theoretical perspective, whatever the utility of the descriptive models employed above, each of the models of IGR is inadequate for capturing the complexity and the dynamism of the inter- and intra-organizational relations associated with the NSA program. Even the bargaining model, which captures best the flavor of federal-local program relations, is marked by certain deficiencies. Thus, NSA suffered from what might be described as a lack of synchronization of enthusiasms between federal and local officials which resulted in officials talking past each other a good deal of the time. At the outset, the efforts of central office staff made the program possible but there was only a small measure of involvement by local governments. Subsequently, when local governments became enmeshed in program commitments to their target neighborhoods, the federal government's interest waned.

Pressman and Wildavsky note in their classic study of implementation that it is commonplace for a program that receives special attention by an agency in its early phases later to become routinized with negative consequences for implementation.[4] In the case of NSA, the problems the program faced after 1980 went beyond routinization. Reflecting changes in national administrations, the behavior of HUD came increasingly to be characterized either by indifference or antagonism to past program commitments.

As I have suggested elsewhere, one of the hallmarks of many routine exchanges in IGR is the indifference of critical actors in responding to others in the policy process.[5] This arises from the way actors based in different institutional settings are engaged in quite distinct personal and organizational "games."[6] That being the case, it is relatively easy for an intergovernmental policy process to fall victim to various forms of temporizing and delays unless one party to the transaction is sufficiently motivated to pressure the other to keep the process going. In the NSA case, the actions of local governments and their developers were essential to maintaining momentum the program had after 1981, particularly after the large "easy" projects were approved and moved into construction. This left the small-owner or scattered-site projects as the chief material of increasingly difficult federal-local relations.

Along with indifference, complex intergovernmental transactions are frequently marked by a high degree of uncertainty. Such uncertainty may allow for bureaucratic purism—insistence by bureaucrats on close adherence to procedures either defined in statutes or regulations, or associated with administrative routines. Purist behaviors may arise out of commitments to the values associated with particular programs or the procedures operative within a particular bureaucracy. They may also reflect bureaucratic reluctance to take risks in a political environment where to do nothing may be less dangerous than to take a particular course of action.

Unfortunately, the Carter administration's commitment to the special character of the NSA program began to wane just at the point when many local projects were coming to the implementation stage. The result was that field officials were increasingly inclined to delay decisions which might commit substantial resources in a way that could put them personally or organizationally at risk. One common response to uncertainty was to demand changes in project plans which imposed additional burdens on developers, not the least of them being time.

NSA AS A PROBLEM IN BUREAUCRATIC BEHAVIOR

One of the greatest weaknesses of IGR models is their tendency to overlook intragovernmental differences in the behaviors of participants in policy processes.

The problem is well illustrated by the inability of HUD's NSA program leadership to mobilize effectively both its field staff and technicians within the central office. Thus, the Office of Housing's NSA staff attempted to reach an agreement with personnel from FHA at the outset that would have resulted in expediting projects.

Specifically, the FHA would have set a value on properties targeted for NSA projects that took into account the anticipated value of those properties after rehabilitation rather than relying on existing property values. Such a procedure would have deviated from FHA's normal valuation method, but it would have eased considerably the problem of qualifying deteriorated properties for mortgage insurance at a level that would have underwritten the high construction costs of many projects. No intra-agency agreement was ever forged, however, with the result that those field personnel responsible for mortgage reviews approached each property valuation with all the skepticism at their command.

To some extent, the problem might have been dealt with through the effective institutionalization of the position of NSA coordinator within the field offices. Unfortunately, that position did not function as anticipated. Instead of acting as "fixers" to smooth the way for local program designs and project implementation efforts, coordinators were unable to exercise meaningful control over other participants.

These problems resulted from the unwillingness of program entrepreneurs to confront directly the characteristics of their own organization. Instead, they assumed that their bureaucratic equals within HUD and their organizational subordinates would accommodate to their program purposes and would function either according to some sense of shared goals or in keeping with notions of hierarchical control. Instead, many field officials lacked enthusiasm for the program from the outset and were unwilling to approve projects they regarded as risky, whatever the urgings of the Assistant Secretary for Housing.

No doubt, some of the concerns of HUD technicians were warranted. Many of the projects proposed were risky; methods of proper valuation were uncertain given the limited experience HUD had working in inner-city rehabilitation. What is more at issue is that agency personnel had a variety of bureaucratic tactics for handling relations with localities and project developers when they were forced unwillingly to deal with such projects—tactics which operated outside the boundaries of organizational control. They could allow review processes to drag on for months; documents could be repeatedly misplaced or "lost".

The idea that someone designated as an NSA coordinator could successfully overcome such resistances quickly dissipated. To make matters worse, as the result of a major field reorganization individuals left the coordinator position and were either not replaced or if they were replaced it was done by an equally low-status person within the office who was unable to command the authority necessary to mover projects forward expeditiously.

An effort by the central office to formally designate area managers as NSA coordinators and the coordinators as the managers' deputies proved equally ineffective. In many offices, NSA was seen as simply one among many chores dumped on the housing section of the office; nominally passing responsibility upwards in the field office hierarchy did not effectively change that situation.

The bureaucratic purism of field office personnel during the project review period also reflected a concern with "covering their own asses." Memories of the FHA scandals that had rocked several field offices—sending some HUD employees to jail—were still relatively fresh among middle-level officials. Constant changes in programs also contributed to great cynicism even during the period of program growth under Carter.

To recognize that organizational problems existed is not to come up with a reasonable solution to them. One of the weaknesses of NSA was the administrative halfway house that was created, under which the program was neither fully centralized nor fully decentralized. As a result, HUD technicians had a continuous opportunity to exercise major influence on the project approval process, frequently avoiding the necessity of saying "No" through their control over procedural details. Such organizational evasiveness might have been overcome if the highest levels of the central office at HUD had been able and willing to focus more time and energy on developing organizational solutions to procedural problems, but they were not so inclined. Another possibility might have been to promote more participation by field office personnel at the outset of the program. Instead, the central office engaged in relatively brief "training" sessions for field personnel which proved to be ineffective in mobilizing their support.

Still another approach might have been to attempt to impose greater discipline upon the field staff by monitoring its actions on a regular and systematic basis and, in extremis, removing persons who failed to meet centrally set standards of performance. As desirable as movement toward a more centrally controlled bureaucratic decision-making approach might have been, it was simply not available as a realistic option. While high-level political appointees might occasionally take notice of the way a field office was relating to local jurisdictions and attempt to overcome frictions—as in the Buffalo area office problem discussed in chapter 7—during the Carter administration no one was prepared to move toward a more centralized model of internal program control The political and financial resources to do so were largely unavailable. Such an initiative might have worked better under the Reagan administration, given its general distrust of the federal bureaucracy, but that administration's attitudes toward program reforms in housing made the point irrelevant.[7]

To place a share of the blame on the field office is not to overlook the role of central office actors, for part of the problem in expediting projects came from the unwillingness of the same Assistant Secretary for Housing whose office generated the NSA program to force FHA officials to adopt special procedures for NSA. If coordination between two units of the same agency was difficult, promoting greater coordination in matters like historic preservation (which came under the Department of the Interior) or environmental concerns (under the Environmental Protection Agency) were equally troublesome.

Having failed to mobilize sufficient support for the program from federal officials, the NSA program staff preferred to use what organizational resources it had to generate program commitments from localities. In many instances, that approach worked reasonably well, though it involved sometimes difficult intergovernmental bargaining and took a toll on the enthusiasm of local participants and developers.

NSA AS A PUBLIC PROGRAM

This study has provided an opportunity to follow the life history of a public program as it proceeded from conception to death. NSA was conceived of as a "demonstration program," partly because of uncertainties about how some of its features might work and partly because of what were thought to be the political advantages involved in avoiding congressional review during its formative period. Even in its somewhat truncated life, one of the things that NSA demonstrated was the inevitable strain that operates in the process of converting a program conception into an effective program.

At the time that this study got underway, Pressman, Wildavsky, and others had been engaged for nearly a decade in efforts to suggest that governmental attempts to design and implement effective social programs—especially through the intergovernmental system—are doomed to failure.[8] The history of programs in housing and community development was particularly replete with such examples: urban renewal, Model Cities, conventional public housing, new towns— all were pointed to (though in different ways) as examples of the gap between well-intended public policies and program interventions that soured—some in the short run, some over the longer term.[9]

One's perspective on federal program making need not be quite as bleak as some of the critics of program interventions suggest.[10] The achievements of the Section 8 Existing Housing Program, CDBG, the Urban Development Action Grant (UDAG) Program, and Neighborhood Housing Services (NHS) may be subject to debate but they are not so easily dismissed as program failures pure and simple.[11] Similarly, the Section 8 New Construction and Sub Rehab programs both in their original forms and through the NSA program achieved their major purposes: the provision of housing opportunities to low- and moderate-income households at affordable costs.

In the case of the NSA program, specifically, questions may be raised about a second goal: the extent to which neighborhood revitalization was achieved. The picture is not a simple one, but at least among the cases reviewed in chapter 10, we found that some neighborhoods were significantly benefited by NSA.

Given the limited life of NSA, it is difficult to address the long-term implications of the program. However, we can highlight some issues related to the disjunction between program conception and program achievement. It is important to note that there were clearly tradeoffs in the way the NSA program was formulated. What the program gained in conceptual clarity from the manner of its design by a small group of persons within HUD may have been lost in terms of preparatory groundwork in various political and bureaucratic arenas. Three issues are particularly relevant.

To begin with, it is problematic whether working more directly through Congress would have made a difference in building and sustaining political and financial support for the program. Even though HUD retreated from its initial commitment to providing Section 8 subsidies entirely out of a special allocation from Fiscal Year 1978, only a few communities complained about the ''sellout'' involved and there was no congressional feedback on the issue. Whatever congressional unhappiness resulted from that decision may have been outweighed by the resources that were widely spread among localities.

The lack of sufficient Section 8 resources was not the critical issue initially; rather financing for the rehabilitation of projects was. Here greater federal appropriations to vehicles like the Government National Mortgage Association might have been in order from the outset, or other special funds might have been set aside to make the program less of a hostage to prevailing interest rates. Yet, as many local participants appreciated by 1981, this was an exceedingly expensive program because it relied both on Section 8 subsidies and associated tax expenditures to assure developer interest. Whether Congress could or should have done more to guarantee these resources is a matter of debate.

Equally important, despite the fact that program designers emphasized their desire to reach owners of small numbers of rental units, little provision was made in the NSA implementation process for supporting such efforts. A substantial number of local governments tried to encourage such participation; on the whole, these attempts failed. Participation by small-scale landlords was also discouraged by HUD technicians and state financing agencies. Thus, contrary to the original program intent, NSA became a program primarily for large-scale professional developers or for more skillful advocacy planning organizations (APOs) or neighborhood-based organizations (NBOs) that assumed the role of developer.

Second, the NSA staff at HUD did much less than it might have done to draw state agencies into the NSA design process. While a few state agencies became deeply involved in financing projects, most backed away. This left local governments and their developers in financial difficulty. Localities themselves, however, failed to bring effective pressure on state agencies to upgrade their involvement in neighborhood revitalization and housing rehabilitation. That, in turn, placed a greater processing burden on HUD field offices.

Third, while the U.S. Conference of Mayors and National League of Cities were given an opportunity to comment on elements of the NSA design as it proceeded through the regulation and notice-writing stages at HUD, they were not in a position to play the role of negotiator for local governments that might have upgraded the quality of the designs ultimately submitted. Indeed, the position taken by these organizations before the program design was settled upon was that the resource distribution approach should be made analogous to the one adopted under CDBG so that the need for a competitive design phase would be diluted.

During the formulation stage, there were also three important constraints on HUD's program design staff that prevented them from imposing a truly competitive categorical grant system on NSA. These were: (1) HUD staff did not want to get bogged down in a lengthy planning process; (2) the resources intended for the program supposedly had to be obligated no later than 30 September; and (3) procedures for applying could not be so onerous that they would dissuade localities from taking part.

In connection with the first point, if the designers of the NSA program thought they had learned anything in particular from the past, it was that programs like urban renewal and Model Cities had been mortally wounded by delays in moving from program planning to project implementation. Model Cities, in particular, was widely condemned for the way it emphasized a careful and, therefore, lengthy local planning process. If anything, NSA program entrepreneurs were inclined to err in the opposite direction—pushing ahead perhaps too rapidly toward project implementation.

In retrospect, the decision to move quickly did permit the program to achieve as much as it did. If HUD had given localities more time to plan, some of the later negotiations might not have been required, but that approach might also have left many localities even further behind than they were by the time the full brunt of escalating interest rates and later, the Reagan administration's antipathy to the program were felt.

Whatever the problems in maintaining a degree of clarity of purpose and organizational direction during the formulation phase, the programs that were ultimately implemented were not quite the ones that had originally been promoted by HUD. HUD might have held fast to its original model. That would have yielded a truer opportunity for final evaluations of the connection between program designs and variations in neighborhood revitalization efforts. Instead, the leadership of HUD determined that the political benefits that flowed from the program should be maximized by including as many participants as possible even if local designs strayed markedly from the national model.

The program process went seriously askew at this point. This indicates the critical role of the conversion process in program development—the bridging activity required between the presentation of program guidelines and the initial stages of project design and implementation. In this case, the majority of local officials or their agents were only prepared to implement program designs that were acceptable to local political interests; this was, of course, a function of the decentralized form of program making characteristic of this country. In only a few places were local officials not astute enough to head off local opposition by the choices they made. In those places, their programs either failed or required substantial revision.

Nevertheless, many localities invested considerable energy in implementing the major goals of the program even after HUD's interest waned. In the course of doing so, however, important steps were taken in converting what started out as a single national program into 155 programs intended to affect the character of 155 target areas—perhaps a desirable object in its own right, but one somewhat at odds with the concept of developing a limited repertoire of approaches to the revitalization of certain kinds of target areas. Still, for what the program was and what it became, its achievements were reasonable. Within a larger scheme of national urban policy, however, questions can be raised about the value of NSA. A few such questions will be considered in the final section.

NSA AS A REFLECTION OF NATIONAL URBAN POLICY

NSA evolved as a variant on established policies in housing and community development. It was the product of a subgovernmental system that bridged ideological differences by providing housing assistance to low- and moderate-income households using the construction and financial industries as important intermediaries, thus assuring the political support of those interests if not their ideological commitment.

At the outset of the NSA program, the subgovernment concerned with assisted housing included specialized local government agencies—primarily public housing authorities—as well as builders and bankers, interested members of Congress, and those at HUD with responsibilities in the area. General purpose local government officials (mayors, city managers, and members of local councils) had few occasions to participate; even more limited were the positions of NBOs and residents of affected neighborhoods, though occasionally well-organized NBOs or APOs assumed developmental roles.

From 1974 on, a community development subgovernment emerged which involved HUD, general purpose local governments, and neighborhood interests. In a sense, NSA was designed to extend this participation into assisted housing. At the same time, local governments would gain political resources by playing a major role in selecting project developers and in working with the owners of smaller structures to achieve a measure of improvement in targeted neighborhoods.

As it turned out, many projects were actually done by professional developers. For the most part, local governments felt comfortable entering into relations with those developers whether they were locally based or, just as likely, companies located elsewhere. The result was a re-creation of the progrowth coalitions between local governments and developers that had existed under urban renewal.

What was more problematic was the relationship that developed between those coalitions and residents of the target areas and NBOs. For, while the Carter administration claimed an interest in promoting the participation of neighborhood residents and their organizations in national urban policy, each NBO (or APO) had to work out arrangements with its own local government rather than participating collectively in the NSA implementation process. In some instances, such organizations played a major role in attaining designation of a particular target area for inclusion in the program and then proceeded to exercise substantial influence in the implementation not only of the housing component but of other aspects of neighborhood revitalization. In other cases, neighborhood groups (sometimes representing middle-class gentrifiers; sometimes reflecting the concerns of working-class white populations) were influential in excluding NSA projects from "their" neighborhoods or in shaping projects so that the population served was predominantly elderly.

To indicate that neighborhood organizations were not consistently part of local program coalitions is not to suggest that local governments were not concerned about neighborhood response to NSA plans. Indeed, for that very reason, many local governments placed NSA projects in areas that were either nonresidential or were so deteriorated that residents were likely to favor any commitment of resources.

Whatever the particular scenario for local program development, the reality is that the NSA program was one of the last of a dying breed of programs fostered by a coalition of interested groups—including an activist federal agency—intended to serve the housing interests of the poor through a complex series of plans, applications, reviews, grants, and other institutional commitments. At the same time, the distribution of program benefits (including subsidies provided to construction, real estate, and banking interests) made the program an expensive one. The addition of local governments and, in some places, neighborhood organizations to the coalition of participants only made the process more complicated and expensive.

Aside from the case that could be made for seeking other means for providing housing assistance to the poor (at least in those localities where a reasonable vacancy rate existed), one of the more interesting aspects of the study is how much it illustrates the fragility of the assisted housing subgovernment and local progrowth coalitions in confronting the Reagan administration.[12] For, while a few localities used political initiatives to achieve their project goals even after 1981, NSA and the Section 8 Sub Rehab Program on which it was based were targets of an unusually effective ideological and budgetary onslaught at the outset of the administration. Although it is easy enough to point to the critical role played by the president and his advisors in this, it is more difficult to explain why the intergovernmental coalition of interests reinforced by resources from the Carter administration collapsed so readily in the face of Reagan's assaults.

The suggestion advanced by Mollenkopf is that the Republican coalition of suburban and Sunbelt interests was little wedded to sustaining such programs.[13] This argument has some appeal, but it overlooks the fact that programs like CDBG and Section 8—as well as the General Revenue Sharing and the Comprehensive Employment and Training Act—were products of the Nixon–Ford presidencies which drew support from that same coalition. Admittedly, the liberal Congresses of the time moderated the effects of the coalition forces identified by Mollenkopf. At the same time, Section 8, in particular, served the interests of builders, bankers, and real estate firms who were as likely to be Republican as Democratic.

Perhaps the weakness of the subgovernment simply reflected the timing of the NSA program which coincided with high rates of inflation, escalation of interest rates, and major changes in the banking industry. These factors contributed to making investment in housing, particularly assisted housing, a low priority item.

Equally important, divisions within HUD over implementation of the NSA program may have weakened support for intergovernmental programs by local officials and developers. Thus, while the latter welcomed the housing resources, they recounted tales of procedural nightmares that had taken enormous effort on their part to resolve. The result was a feeling by the time that the Reagan administration took office that assisted housing was still a desirable public good in principle but that other policy instruments would be necessary to achieve that goal. This weak display of support for NSA contrasted with the attitudes of local officials toward the political and financial benefits that CDBG and UDAG brought them. They were clearly prepared to fight for retention of those programs, as their continuing existence in 1988 attests.

The Reagan administration's hostility toward housing construction programs leaves unattended the problem that in a growing number of places dwelling units do not exist in sufficient number and at sufficiently affordable costs for low- and moderate-income households. A limited attempt has been made through congressional pressures to encourage a modest amount of rehabilitation of deteriorated units.[14] However, there is no evidence the Reagan administration or budgetary deficits would support larger scale endeavors.

For more than forty years, a succession of moderate Democratic and Republican administrations played basically on the same theme of government support to housing efforts, though they varied in the resources they were willing to commit. This was by no means an entirely altruistic perspective. Both parties received considerable financial support from the construction and financial industries, and moderate Republicans as well as liberal Democrats gained electoral benefits from keeping those industries happy by expanding housing construction activities. Countercyclical theories in vogue from the 1930s until the late 1970s also justified such expenditures.

To a large extent, the particular set of Republicans who came to office in 1981 did not share that perspective and its associated political loyalties with the result that one of the first things the Reagan administration saw fit to do was make significant cutbacks in direct housing subsidies, perhaps for reasons having as much to do with political ideology as with the nature of the interests forming the Reagan coalition.

In the same way that there was a retreat from the notion that the national government had a role to play in the supply of housing, the Reagan administration adopted an essentially noninterventionist attitude toward urban redevelopment, in general, and neighborhood revitalization, in particular. It is a matter of considerable debate how much earlier federal interventions like urban renewal contributed to realizing that goal. Common wisdom has it that early efforts at urban renewal destroyed more than they revitalized neighborhoods. Nonetheless, the urban renewal program went through major modifications in the 1960s that put a greater accent on revitalization. Later, one of the more interesting phenomena of the 1970s was the mood swing that occurred with respect to how people began to perceive central cities. While nirvana had not come, the idea that older cities were not inherently unlovable began to be bruited about. How much this swing in moods reflected the successes of government policy is a matter of conjecture.

Urban renewal projects like Harborplace in Baltimore and Quincy Market in Boston enlivened not only those cities' downtowns but encouraged residential activity in those and other central cities. Cities began to rebuild themselves using UDAG funding and various forms of revenue bonds, as well as CDBG. While visions of an urban renaissance may have been overstated, downtowns and other central city target areas *were* being revitalized. Programs begun under the Nixon and Ford administrations were supported by Carter which promoted reinvestment in older central cities including their neighborhoods. The creation of NSA was consistent with this effort.

Nevertheless, it could well be argued, as the Reagan administration has done, that federal investment to reverse processes of suburbanization, urban decline, and regional movements out of the Frost Belt are an unnecessary investment of limited federal resources in comparison to investment in economic growth.[15] Indeed, even prior to the Reagan administration, a report to Carter on federal urban policy took the national government to task for continuing to invest heavily in trying to fight market forces by putting substantial resources into "place-oriented" programs. The argument of these critics was that such social programs as the federal government invested in should be directed principally to promoting the development of human resources, allowing people to decide for themselves where and how they wished to live.[16] This perspective was the harbinger of the Reagan administration's urban policy—letting the processes of the marketplace work their will upon urban areas.

If cities, as a whole, have receded as an area of national concern, a policy interest in neighborhoods has become even more remote. Save for occasional rhetorical support for voluntary action, the Reagan administration has done nothing to strengthen the fabric of neighborhood life. This contrasts with the organized neighborhood-based political activity that appeared to be at its high-water mark at just about the time that the Carter administration came into office and was encouraged by that administration. NBOs and APOs became the beneficiaries of a variety of federal programs provided directly to them or siphoned through state and local governments.

Where we stand at the moment in terms of the quality of neighborhood life is difficult to estimate.[17] Whether the years of the Reagan administration have actually witnessed a reversal in efforts to revitalize neighborhoods is problematic. Some cities continue to maintain healthy housing markets and neighborhoods which have become increasingly attractive places in which to live, despite cutbacks in federal programs. Local governments and neighborhood groups have continued to strive to find means of "creatively" financing neighborhood improvement programs, sometimes using federal resources like CDBG and UDAG to achieve their goals.

What kinds of urban policies we *should* have is another matter. The creation of horizontal inequities in the housing market where a small percentage of households in need of assistance (and a disproportionately large share of the elderly) are housed well—but very expensively—in a limited number of assisted units does not appear to be the way to go. Programs which promote the moderate rehabilitation of existing structures (including the conversion to housing of non-residential structures where the costs of such conversions are not inordinately high) are perhaps in order. At least in those housing markets where the supply of units is comfortable, the emphasis should be on such an approach.

More troublesome are the tighter rental markets in both the older and newer sections of the country where construction assistance may well be warranted. Here combinations of tax expenditures and direct developer subsidies may be called for, though not on the lavish scale associated with Section 8. At the same time, the need for differential national investment in housing markets suggests the need for the generation of a different approach to national housing programs—a targeted redistributive approach—something which is inconsistent with American intergovernmental history.

Furthermore, it is uncertain where the boundaries of responsibility for urban policies and programs *ought* to be drawn. To the extent that the NSA program sought to target resources to a few areas in each city, it may have been a mistake to retreat from this approach. In a world of limited resources, reason may require that cities face up to their own possibilities by making choices about areas where public investments make the most sense. Despite the poor reception that "triage" arguments received, there is a case to be made for a vision of the scaled-down city—particularly in those urban centers where population decreases have been significant both in relative and absolute terms.

At some point, then, it is not unreasonable that persons with national political responsibility be forced to make choices about where public investment in housing and community development is sensible and where it is not.[18] While few cities have been willing to make such policies explicitly, in practice both the pressures of fiscal necessity in the last decade and the political realities associated with the better organization of some neighborhoods than others has resulted in some targeting of resources. Unfortunately, it is unlikely that residents in an area targeted for staged disinvestment would ever willingly accede to such a course of action.

In conclusion, the approach followed in the Neighborhood Strategy Area

Program had much to recommend it in terms of producing housing opportunities for low- and moderate-income households, and especially for the elderly, but it did not begin to represent part of a well-articulated national plan for neighborhood revitalization. Nor did it provide incentives to local governments of sufficient attractiveness to force them to make the decisions that would have encouraged the development of systematic policies toward their neighborhoods. Instead, it provided a few opportunities in a few places for more modest goals to be achieved: making housing opportunities available to a small number of households in a variety of somewhat improved settings.

NOTES

1. In that connection, see Jeffrey L. Pressman, *Federal Programs and City Politics* (Berkeley, Calif.: University of California Press, 1975), esp. chap. 5.

2. See *A New Partnership to Conserve America's Communities: A National Urban Policy*, The President's Urban and Regional Policy Group Report, Washington, D.C.: U.S. Department of Housing and Urban Development, April 1978; and *The President's Urban Policy Report*, Washington, D.C.: U.S. Department of Housing and Urban Development, August 1978. While "sharing" may have characterized the procedural goals of these policy efforts, the reality was one of considerable infighting within the administration. See Eric L. Stowe, "Defining a National Urban Policy," in *Urban Revitalization* edited by Donald B. Rosenthal (Beverly Hills, Calif.: Sage, 1980), 145–63.

3. See Eugene Bardach, *The Implementation Game* (Cambridge, Mass.: MIT Press, 1977), esp. 55–58.

4. Jeffrey L. Pressman and Aaron Wildavsky, *Implementation*, 2d ed. (Berkeley, Calif.: University of California Press, 1979), esp. 113–24.

5. Donald B. Rosenthal, "Bargaining Analysis in Intergovernmental Relations," *Publius* 10 (Summer 1980), 5–44.

6. Bardach, *Implementation Game*.

7. For an examination of the means by which the Reagan administration gained control of the federal bureaucracy but at the cost of significant morale problems, see Irene S. Rubin, *Shrinking the Federal Government* (New York: Longman, 1985).

8. Pressman and Wildavsky, *Implementation*. Their study was only one of many produced by a line of neoconservative scholars who held that government was essentially incapable of designing and implementing effective programs. Other works that set the tone for that literature were Daniel P. Moynihan, *Maximum Feasible Misunderstanding* (New York: Free Press, 1970); and Edward C. Banfield, *The Unheavenly City* (Boston: Little, Brown, 1970). Their perspective was strongly adopted by the Reagan administration.

9. In addition to materials cited in chapter 2, see, William Alonso, "The Mirage of New Towns," *The Public Interest* 19 (Spring 1970), 3–17; and Martha Derthick, *New Towns In-Town* (Washington, D.C.: Urban Institute, 1972).

10. In that connection, see Marshall Kaplan and Peggy Cuciti (eds.), *The Great Society and Its Legacy* (Durham, N.C.: Duke University Press, 1986); Paul E. Peterson, Barry G. Rabe, and Kenneth K. Wong, *When Federalism Works* (Washington, D.C.: Brookings Institution, 1986); and John E. Schwarz, *America's Hidden Success* (New York: W. W. Norton, 1983).

11. Much depends on the criteria that one employs in making those judgments. For CDBG, see the series of volumes issued by the U.S. Department of Housing and Urban Development and through the Brookings Institution by Paul R. Dommel and associates. For NHS, see, *Creating Local Partnerships*, Washington D.C.: U.S. Department of Housing and Urban Development, March 1980; and Phillip L. Clay, *Neighborhood Partnerships in Action*, (Washington, D.C.: Neighborhood Reinvestment Corporation, 1981); for a recent negative view of the achievements of NHS, see Richard C. Hula, "Markets and Redevelopment," *Urban Affairs Quarterly* 21 (June 1986), 461–83.

12. The Reagan administration's perspective is presented in U.S. Department of Housing and Urban Development, *The President's National Urban Policy Report, 1984* Washington, D.C., August 1984, esp. 58–59.

13. John H. Mollenkopf, *The Contested City* (Princeton, N.J.: Princeton University Press, 1983).

14. For a useful summary of the principal features of the Housing and Urban-Rural Recovery Act of 1983, for example, see U.S. Conference of Mayors, *Federal City Reporter*, 6 December, 1983. For recent evidence of a resurgence of interest in assisted housing, see Carol F. Steinbach and Neal R. Pierce, "Picking Up Hammers," *National Journal* (6 June, 1987), 1464–1465, which highlights efforts made by state and local governments and nonprofit groups to produce housing for low- and moderate-income households in the absence of federal support.

15. Yet, federal policies continued to reward investment in the preservation of sites designated as historically significant. In that connection, see U.S. General Accounting Office, *Information on Historic Preservation Tax Incentives*, Report to the Joint Committee on Taxation (Washington, D.C.: U.S. Government Printing Office, 29 March, 1984); and U.S. General Accounting Office, *Historic Preservation Tax Incentives* (Washington, D.C.: U.S. Government Printing Office, 12 August, 1986). The latter study estimated that a total of $1.3 billion in tax credits were granted for 1982 and 1983. The Tax Reform Act of 1986 continued these benefits by providing a 20 percent investment tax credit for rehabilitation of certified historic structures and a 10 percent credit for nonhistoric buildings built before 1936.

16. See the Report of the President's Commission for a National Agenda for the 80s, *Urban America in the Eighties*, Washington, D.C., 1980.

17. Despite recent monitoring studies that deal with the impacts of cutbacks and other changes in federal system programming, there is little clear understanding of the impacts those changes have made on neighborhoods. See, for example, George E. Peterson, "The State and Local Sector," in *The Reagan Experiment* edited by John L. Palmer and Isabel V. Sawhill, (Washington, D.C.: Urban Institute, 1982), 157–217.

18. If one accepts the argument of Paul Peterson that local governments are unable to generate the resources and make the variety of redistributive decisions involved in financing assisted-housing programs, it becomes even more clearly the responsibility of the national government—and, to some extent, state governments—to assume leadership in these matters if public action is to be taken at all. See Paul E. Peterson, *City Limits* (Chicago: University of Chicago Press, 1981).

Appendix A

PERSONS INTERVIEWED

Provided below is a summary of the kinds of informants included in this study. They are categorized by program role at the time of their most recent program involvement. Thus a person who served in a HUD field office when the NSA program was developed but was working for a professional developer at the time of the interview would be listed in the latter category. In contrast, a former HUD field official who had since gone to work for a municipal housing authority is listed in the former capacity.

Tabulating the number of "interviewees" is complicated by two factors. First, 35 persons were interviewed twice, seven three times, and four others four times. These interviewees are not double counted, even though different persons who served in other places in the same position at different times were counted separately. A second concern involved sixteen interviews in which more than one person participated. In each case, only one "interviewee" was counted.

It may be incomplete to list interviewees without indicating something about the number of local governments or other organizations they represented. Therefore, I have listed separately in the table below the number of organizations included. Since the main purpose of this exercise is to provide the reader with some sense of the diversity as well as the number of interviewees, the attributed numbers are less important than the range.

Table A-1
Number of Interviewees and Types of Organizations

Government Officials:	Individuals	Organizations
Federal Officials -- HUD Central Office	13	--
HUD Field Offices	28	17 [a]
Congressional Staff	2	--
State Government Officials	10	8
Local Officials	142 [b]	88
Professional Development Organization	18	13
Advocacy Planning Organizations	35	29 [c]
Neighborhood-Based Organizations	27	22
Others [d]	9	9
TOTAL	286	

a The number of field offices where interviews were conducted.

b Includes one elected person; the remainder were administrators.

c Includes Neighborhood Housing Services and Legal Service
   Corporation units.

d Includes academics, planners and observers not directly
   involved in program design or delivery.

Appendix B

PROJECT ACTIVITY

This appendix identifies the local program participants and the various project activities undertaken in Section 8 Neighborhood Strategy Areas (NSAs). It includes a complete list of all NSAs approved either conditionally or unconditionally by the Department of Housing and Urban Development (HUD) in 1978. It also lists several NSAs which were approved subsequently. In some instances, the latter were expected to use Section 8 units not already obligated to other NSAs within the same jurisdiction; in other cases, the units represented additions by HUD to the original allocation. HUD varied in the extent to which it left to local discretion decisions about shifting units among NSAs in the same city. In order to deal with the confusion this may cause in reading the materials, in such cases, I have supplied a summary number (in parentheses) for the city as a whole in columns 3 and 4 as well as providing figures for each NSA individually.

In column 1, I have listed dates when interviews were conducted in particular localities. (This data says nothing about the dates of interviews held elsewhere which touched on project activity in the NSA in question.) In cases where more than two visits were made, the first and last dates are cited. Where a locality was not visited, I have marked a "n.a." in parentheses next to the name of the locality. In a few cases where sufficient information about a particular NSA was not available even within a city where other interviewing was done, I have marked an "n.i." next to that particular NSA.

In column 2, the general character of the NSA is identified. I have divided NSAs into three categories: R (predominantly residential); NR (non-residential); and M (mixed). The last includes cases where residential units were already present in an area that contained substantial non-residential uses. This information was drawn from interviews and personal observation as well as HUD analyses of local government applications when personal data-gathering was not possible.

Column 3 lists the number of units initially awarded (with some exceptions indicated in the section notes). Column 4 estimates Section 8 units used. This estimation involves a mixture of data sources. Where visits were made and detailed interviews were conducted about the projects implemented, those data were the primary source. Since field research began in 1978, and was conducted in some places only through 1981, uncertainties remained about the fate of many projects. In those instances, I made use of data drawn from a monitoring survey done by HUD for the Fiscal Year ending September 30, 1981. In some of these instances, this data was not collected separately for each NSA within a municipality, so that it was not possible to refine the utilization figure further than the municipal level. For Fiscal Year 1983, HUD produced a survey of housing production figures for all field offices; this survey included data on the number of NSA projects and total units in various stages of implementation (projects and units "reserved," "started" and "completed"). Unfortunately, these figures were not disaggregated below the field office level. Nonetheless, they are useful for three purposes: they represent the outer limits of production for the particular field office as of September, 1983; secondly, where a HUD field office contained only one NSA, they served as a check against data gathered by other means; thirdly, by providing data on the number of projects within a field office jurisdiction, they helped provide further evidence of the fates of particular projects.

In column 5, several features of projects completed or expected to be completed are listed. First, where the information was available, I have indicated what kind of project it was. The majority of projects involved rehabilitation ("R") of existing residential structures. Many others saw the conversion of non-residential structures to residential use. I have marked such conversions with a "C". In those few cases where a project involved the rehabilitation of a public housing project under private auspices, I have indicated it as "R(PH)". Finally, I have identified a project as "NC" where substantial new construction was involved. In some instances, a project involved mixes of rehabilitation and conversion or new construction. In such cases, I have tried to provide information on the nature of the mix.

Where information was also available on the nature of the population the units were designed to serve, I have marked them either "E" (elderly) or "F" (family) in column 6. In a very few instances, information was also provided on special set-asides of units for the handicapped (marked as "H"). When no marking is provided next to the number of units in a project it means that the information was not available.

REGION I

Boston Area Office

	(1) Interview	(2) Character	(3) Allocated	(4) Used	(5) Features	(6) Residents
Boston:	9/80; 5/83		(510)	(429)		
Chinatown		NR	155	54[a]	2C	54F
Dorchester		R	88	73[a]	1R	73E
Franklin Field		R	97	83[a]	1C&R	83
Sav-Mor (Roxbury)		R	170	139	1C	41E
					1R	98
(1980)South End		R[a]	117	80	1R	80F
Chelsea	8/80; 4/83	M	265	213	1C&R	120E & 33F
					4R	60
Chicopee	8/80; 3/83	NR	155[b]	155	2C	155E
Fall River	6/83	NR	100	124[c]	2C	105E&15H
Framingham	8/80; 6/83	M	200	172	1NC	40E
					2C	99E
					3R	33
Lowell:	8/80; 6/83		(370)	(228)		
CBD		NR	270	228	1C	228E
Lower Belvidere		R	100	n.i.		n.i.

Lynn	8/80; 5/83	M	250	302[d]	3C	151E
					1NC&C	65
					2R	60E;26 E&F
New Bedford	6/83:					
North End		M	150	150	1C	150E
North Bedford		NR	163	164[e]	2C	114E & 25
					1R	25E
South Central		R	50	n.i.	1CI	31[f]
Pittsfield	8/80; 3/83	M	153	162[g]	2C	105E
					2R	32F & 25
Revere	8/80; 3/83	R	50	40	1C	40E
Somerville	8/80		325	212	2NC	65E & 85
					5R	23E & 39
Springfield	8/80; 3/83	R	395	395	4R	226E;127F&42
Taunton	6/83	M	129	129	1NC	49E
					1C	75E
					2R	5F
Waltham	8/80	NR	108	108	1C	108E
Worcester	8/80; 6/83	M	375	375	1NC&R	129F&51EH
					1NC&C	90E&73F
					1R	20E&12F
Boston Area Total			3805	3358[h]		

[a] This NSA involved the transfer of 88 unused units from Chinatown, 15 from Dorchester and 14 from Franklin Field.
[b] Chicopee originally applied for and received 150 units but shortly thereafter requested and received an additional five units.
[c] Fall River received an allocation of 100 units to do one project, then was given an additional 24 units to complete a second one.
[d] Lynn was originally approved for only 250 units. It received later an additional allocation of 57 units when developers showed an interest in doing more projects. The number of units actually used, however, was apparently only 302..
[e] North Bedford received an additional units from HUD to complete its approved projects.
[f] Informants in June, 1983 claimed that a conversion project was underway in the NSA after numerous false starts, but there was disagreement about how many units of Section 8 would go into the project. One source suggested that only 31 dwelling units in the project would be subsidized through Section 8.
[g] Additional units provided by HUD.
[h] HUD's 1983 summary figures: 66 projects involving 3304 units completed or in production. In addition, 29 units had been reserved for three projects still not in construction.

Hartford Area Office

	(1)	(2)	(3)	(4)	(5)	(6)
Hartford	9/80; 3/83	R	199	156	1R	156F
New Britain	1/81; 3/83	R	198	185	1C	100E
					1R	85F
New Haven	1/81	R	422	264	1C	144E
					1R	120
New London	n.a.	M	165	145	1C	145E
Stamford	1/81	R	360	124[a]	2NC	28;60
					3R	21;12;3
Waterbury	9/80	M	400	393	5C	377E
					1R	16E
Hartford Area Total			1744	1267[b]		

[a] By June, 1982, HUD was under considerable pressure to release 186 units not already reserved for projects in Stamford's NSA. Washington-based informants suggest that 174 units may have already been committed by that date to projects and that others were produced.
[b] HUD's 1983 figures: 13 projects involving 946 units completed or in production. 23 units for two other projects were reserved but not in construction. HUD's figures probably understate production in Hartford, New Britain and Stanford.

Manchester (NH) Area Office

	(1)	(2)	(3)	(4)	(5)	(6)
Lewiston, Me. 10/80; 6/83		M	300	278	1C&R	22
					4R	40E;94F&122
Portland, Me. 6/83		M	375	- -		
Congress Square		M		248	1NC	44E
					3C	160E; 23F
					1R	21F
(1980) India Street		R[a]		60	1C	60E
Burlington, Vt. 8/80; 7/83		R	350	- -		
King Street		R		199	1C	88F
					9R	111F
(1981) Old North End		R[b]		48	1NC	36E & 5F
					1R	7F
Winooski, Vt. 8/80		R	120	117	1C	100E
					1R	15F
Manchester Area Total			1145	950[c]		

[a] The India Street NSA was created in 1980 based on units unused in the Congress Square NSA.
[b] The Old North End NSA was created in 1981 based on units left over from the King Street NSA.
[c] HUD's 1983 figures: 26 projects for 959 units.

Providence Service Office

	(1)	(2)	(3)	(4)	(5)	(6)
Providence	6/83					
Elmwood		R	130	42	1R	42F
Federal Hill		R	100[a]	WITHDREW		
Lower South		R	113	193	1R	193F
Providence Total			343	235		

[a] Units not used in Federal Hill were transferred to Lower South.

REGION I Total   7037   5810*
----

* HUD's 1983 figures: 107 projects involving 5444 units completed or in production. Another 52 units were reserved for five projects still not in construction at that time.

REGION II

Buffalo Area Office (12/78; 6/80)

	(1)	(2)	(3)	(4)	(5)	(6)
Amsterdam	11/79; 1/83	R	44	13	2R	13F

	(1)	(2)	(3)	(4)	(5)	(6)
Cohoes	11/79; 1/83	M	300	307[a]	2C	230E
					1R	77F
Erie County	12/78; 6/82	R	125	77	5R	77F
Hudson	6/80; 7/82	M	35	35	1R	35F
Niagara Falls	2/79; 5/84	M	120	121[a]	1C&R	70
					3R	20E & 30F
Rochester	2/79; 5/82	M	100	110[a]	2R	110F
Schenectady	11/79; 2/83	R	200	145	2R	75E & 70F
Syracuse	6/80; 5/83	R	412	393	1R(PH)	393F
Troy	11/79; 2/83	R	40	120[b]	1NC&R	80F
					1R	40F
Utica	6/80; 4/83	M	250	263[a]	1NC	84E[c]
					3C	179E
Buffalo Area Total			1626	1584[d]		

[a] Additional units provided by HUD.
[b] Troy formally applied for and received 80 additional units in 1979.
[c] Utica originally designated a vacant nursing home for rehabilitation. A suspicious fire demolished the structure. The city then received a special waiver from HUD to undertake an equivalent number of new construction units on the site.
[d] HUD's 1983 figures: 25 projects involving 1580 units.

Caribbean Area Office

	(1)	(2)	(3)	(4)	(5)	(6)
San Juan	n.a.		250	184[a]	n.i.	
Caribbean Area Total			250	184		

[a] HUD 1983 data: 184 units in seven projects.

New York Area Office (12/80; 3/81)

	(1)	(2)	(3)	(4)	(5)	(6)
Beacon	n.a.	R[a]	75	WITHDREW		
			50	WITHDREW		
Mount Vernon	1/80; 1/81	R	361	104	2R	104
New Rochelle	12/80; 1/81	R	279	211	1NC&C	211E
					1R	24F
(1980) Hugenot Street[b]			75	n.i.	n.i.	
New York City	1/80; 1/84		(5000)[c]	(4066)		
Bedford-Stuyvesant	1/84	M	500	278	1NC	72F 2R 206F
Crown Heights	1/81	R	750	1000[d]	16R	1000F
Far Rockaway		R	300	367	1R	367F
Flatbush	1/81; 1/84	R	275	148	2R	148F
Gateway to Harlem	1/81	R	750	408	1NC	183F
					3R	225F
Hamilton Heights	1/81; 1/84	R	625	577	1NC&R	131F
					5R	446
Kingsbridge-Bedford Park	1/81	R	300	79	1R	79F
Manhattan Valley	1/81	R	500	539	5R	539
Sunset Park	1/81; 1/84	R	500	333	1NC&2R	333F
Washington Heights	1/81; 1/84	R	500	337	1NC	109F

	(1)	(2)	(3)	(4)	(5)	(6)
					4R	228
White Plains	1/80; 1/81	M	250	101[e]	2C	101E
Yonkers	1/80; 6/80:					
Glenwood		R	60	62[f]	1R	62
Ludlow-Morris		R	144	58	1NC&R	58
New York Area Total			6219	4602[g]		

[a] Beacon was approved for allocations of 50 and 75 units for two NSAs. Shortly after designation, the city withdrew from the program.

[b] New Rochelle received permission in the Spring of 1980 to create a second NSA. Sources disagree as to whether 75 additional units from HUD were applied to buildings or units simply tranferred from elsewhere. Data collected by the US Conference of Mayors in 1982 indicate that more than the 211 units project in the first NSA were used by the city but exactly how many is unclear.

[c] The Area Office allowed the city to move units among NSAs with great ease. Figures listed in column 4 are those agreed upon as a result of negotiations over removing the conditional status of the ten NSAs in the city.

[d] It was impossible to get more precise figures on units used in Crown Heights.

[e] According to 1982 data collected by the US Conference of Mayors, 201 units were reserved for projects by that time.

[f] Additional units provided by HUD.

[g] HUD data for FY 1983: 56 projects in production for 4432 units. An additional 688 units were reserved for seven projects not yet in production. Interviews conducted subsequently indicate that several of those projects were implemented.

Newark Area Office

	(1)	(2)	(3)	(4)	(5)	(6)
Atlantic City	n.a.	R	471	321	1NC	168E
					1R	153
Hoboken	1/80; 4/81	R	500	138	2R	82F;56
Jersey City	1/80; 4/81:		(520)	- -		
Greenville		R	100	WITHDREW		
Hamilton Park		R	295	WITHDREW		
Van Vorst		R	125	125	n.i.	
(1980) Audubon Park		R[a]	145	n.i.		
Newark	3/81	M	611	299	1NC&R	220F
					1R	79E
New Brunswick	3/81; 3/82	R	287	216	1C	132E
					2R(PH)	84F
Paterson	1/80; 1/81:		(100)			
Essex		NR	100	146[b]	1C	146
(1980)Barbour Park		R[c]	480	n.i.		
Trenton	3/81	R	335	285	1C	285E
Newark Area Total			2824[d]	1530[e]		

[a] HUD approved the creation of this NSA and the transfer of 145 units from Hamilton Park NSA when the former failed.

[b] Additional units provided by HUD.

[c] This NSA was approved for 480 units in 1980. In the 1982 US Conference of Mayors survey, Paterson was still hoping to get 200 units to complete projects.

[d] This figure does not include the 480 units for Paterson's Barbour Park.

[e] HUD's 1983 figures: 15 projects in production for 1616 units. Another three projects (involving 183 units) were reserved but not under construction.

```
-----------------------------------------------
REGION II Totals              10919    7900*
-----------------------------------------------
```

* HUD's 1983 figures: 7812 units in 103 projects completed or in production. 871 units were reserved for ten additional projects.

REGION III

Baltimore Area Office (12/79)

	(1)	(2)	(3)	(4)	(5)	(6)
Baltimore 12/79; 10/80:						
Barclay-Greenmount	R		280	n.i.		
Mt. Clare-Poppleton	R		280	n.i.		
Baltimore Area Total			560	513[a]		

[a] Based on HUD's 1983 data which indicates five projects were undertaken in the city of Baltimore.

Philadelphia Area Office

	(1)	(2)	(3)	(4)	(5)	(6)
Allentown	3/81	M	125[a]	166	1C&R	81
					2R	85
Bucks County	3/81	R	100	97	1R	97F
Easton	3/81	R	100	94	6R	9E & 85
Harrisburg	n.a.	R	300	297	2NC	131
					2R	166
Luzerne County	n.a.	R	65	42	1C	42E
Montgomery County	3/81	R	30	3	1R	3
Philadelphia	3/81	R	125	85	1R	85
Reading	3/81	R	75	0		
Williamsport	n.a.	R	50	n.i.		
York	3/81	R	200	75	1NC&R	75F
Wilmington,Del.	10/80; 3/81	R	350	146	3NC&R	90F & 56
Philadelphia Area Total			1520[b]	1005[c]		

[a] The city applied for 125 units under the NSA program and also received an allocation of 85 units through the Pennsylvania Housing Finance Agency. Activities under both allocations were later combined in HUD calculations. Thus, a HUD summary for Fiscal Year 1981 listed 151 units committed even though the same source indicated only 125 units.
[b] This includes the original Allentown request.
[c] HUD's 1983 figures: 833 units in 12 projects in production; units for two more projects involving 106 units were reserved but not in production.

Pittsburgh Area Office (8/81)

	(1)	(2)	(3)	(4)	(5)	(6)
Butler	8/81	R	75	14	3R	14F
Pittsburgh	8/81	R	75	28	1C&R	28F
Pittsburgh Area Total			150	42[a]		

[a] This figure accords with HUD data for 1983.

<u>Richmond</u> <u>Area</u> <u>Office</u> (7/80)

	(1)	(2)	(3)	(4)	(5)	(6)
Norfolk	7/80; 6/81	R	175	10	2R	10
Portsmouth	7/80; 4/81	R	141	88	1NC	88E
Richmond	7/80; 4/81:					
Central Wards		R	70	18	1R	18F
Randolph		R	230	n.i.		
Richmond Area Total			616	116[a]		

[a] HUD 1983 data: one project containing 49 units was in production within the Area; 165 more were reserved for four others.

<u>D.C.</u> <u>Area</u> <u>Office</u> (12/79)

	(1)	(2)	(3)	(4)	(5)	(6)
Greenbelt	7/80; 1/84	R	325	0[a]		
Washington, DC	10/79; 1/84	R	521	403[b]	4R	122E&F; 404
Washington, D.C. Area Total			846	403[b]		

[a] Greenbelt dropped out of the program after three years spent in unsuccessful negotiations with HUD.
[b] There is a considerable discrepancy betweeen's HUD's figures and those provided by city personnel. HUD listed two projects involving 171 units in production by 1983 and one in planning; city officials accounted for at least three projects totaling 403 units completed by June 30, 1983 with a fifth (involving 123 units) still in planning. I have not counted the latter in the total.

   REGION III Totals   3692   2074*
----

* HUD's 1983 totals: 1608 units in production in 25 projects; another 328 were for seven projects.

REGION IV

<u>Atlanta</u> <u>Area</u> <u>Office</u> (4/81)

	(1)	(2)	(3)	(4)	(5)	(6)
Atlanta	4/81; 6/81					
Edgewood		R	300	305	1R(PH)	305F
West End		R	300	148	2R	148F
Savannah	4/81; 7/81	R	500	233	1NC	44
					2R	189F
Atlanta Area Total			1100	686[a]		

[a] HUD's 1983 figures: 709 units committed to 14 projects either in construction or completed.

<u>Columbia</u> <u>Area</u> <u>Office</u>

	(1)	(2)	(3)	(4)	(5)	(6)
Charleston	4/81	R	150	18	2R	18
Columbia Area Total			150	18[a]		

[a] HUD's 1983 figures show only one 12-unit project in production.

Greenboro Area Office (4/81)

	(1)	(2)	(3)	(4)	(5)	(6)
Raleigh	4/81	R	50	26	2R	26F
Winston-Salem	4/81	R	90	44	5R	7E; 37
Greensboro Area Total			140	70[a]		

[a] HUD's 1983 figures: eight projects involving 96 units had been completed or were in construction.

Jacksonville Area Office

	(1)	(2)	(3)	(4)	(5)	(6)
Dade County	4/81:					
Liberty City		R	214	100	1R(PH)	150
S. Miami		R	48	n.i.		
Miami	4/81	R	500	480	15R	448E; 32F
Miami Area Total			762	580[a]		

[a] HUD's 1983 figures: 20 projects involving 604 units.

Nashville Service Office (6/81)

	(1)	(2)	(3)	(4)	(5)	(6)
Memphis	7/81	R	250	32	1R	32F
Nashville Area Total			250	32[a]		

[a] This figure is the same as HUD's 1983 data.

Louisville Area Office (7/81)

	(1)	(2)	(3)	(4)	(5)	(6)
Covington	7/81	R	130	80	1CS&R	40E & 8F
					2R	16F & 16E
Louisville	7/81:					
Old Louisville		R	350	136	5R	136
Shawnee		R	150	52	2R	52
Louisville Area Total			630	268[a]		

[a] HUD's 1983 figures: 12 projects for 297 units.

REGION IV Totals   3032   1654*
. . . .

* HUD's 1983 figures: 56 projects involving 1750 units.

REGION V

Chicago Area Office (11/80)

	(1)	(2)	(3)	(4)	(5)	(6)
Chicago	4/80; 11/80	R	382	57	1R	57
Lake County	10/80	R	40	WITHDREW		
Chicago Area Total			422	57[a]		

[a] HUD's 1983 figures: two projects underway for 97 units.

Columbus Area Office (7/81)

	(1)	(2)	(3)	(4)	(5)	(6)
Akron	7/81	R	500	348	1NC	100E
					1C	68E
					5R	82E;35F;63
Athens	7/81	R	281	178	1NC	44F
					3C	100E; 30
					1R	4F
Cleveland	8/81:					
Glenville		R	214	210	1NC	36
					2R	174F
Near West Side		R	125	14[a]	1R	14F
Columbus	7/81; 8/81	R	325[b]	356	1C&R	41F & 34E
					5R	281
East Cleveland	7/81	R	141[c]	166	2R	166
Montgomery County	7/81	R	25	WITHDREW		
Toledo	n.a.:					
North Toledo			860	433	2NC&R	230F & 195E
					4R	46F
(1980) Old West End		R	500[d]	160	1NC&C	160E
Columbus Area Total			2471[e]	1865[f]		

[a] These are the combined figures for the Columbus Area Office and the Cleveland Service Office. 48 units for two other projects were still reserved.
[b] When the NSA for the Near West Side proved largely unworkable, the city attempted in 1981 to create a new NSA in the Forest Hills neighborhood in 1981. I have no reliable information about the fate of that NSA proposal.
[c] The city received 215 units of Section 8 units in 1979 under an innovative grant in addition to its NSA allocation. Local accounts indicated that some of the former units were included in HUD's 1983 NSA tabulations for the city.
[d] The city's allocation was increased to 178 units to cover structures targeted by developers designated by the city.
[e] The city received designation for the second NSA for which an extra allocation of 500 units was approved.
[f] This figure does not include the extra units acquired by Columbus or East Cleveland or the 500-unit allocation to Toledo's second NSA.
[g] HUD's 1983 data: 34 involving 2178 units.

Detroit Area Office

	(1)	(2)	(3)	(4)	(5)	(6)
Detroit	n.a.	NR	610	349[a]	3C	349E
Grand Rapids	n.a.	M	300	n.i.		
Jackson	n.a.	R	120	30	n.i.	
Kalamazoo	n.a.	R	120	48	n.i.	
Lansing	n.a.	M	250	n.i.		
Detroit Area Total			1400	427[b]		

[a] 349 units completed in the jurisdiction of the Detroit Area Office according to HUD's 1983 data. Six projects involving 472 units fell within the Service Office jurisdiction. HUD data for 1981 indicate that at least 30 units had been used in Jackson and 48 in Kalamazoo by that date.

[b] Includes data for the Detroit Area Office and the Grand Rapids Service Office.

Indianapolis Area Office (7/81)

	(1)	(2)	(3)	(4)	(5)	(6)
Gary	11/80	R	750	533	1C	64E
					2R	469
Indianapolis	7/81	R	250	86	1C&R	33
					6R	53
Indianapolis Area Total			1000	619[a]		

[a] HUD's 1983 data indicates only four projects completed or in construction but for 659 units -- a marked discrepancy.

Milwaukee Area Office

	(1)	(2)	(3)	(4)	(5)	(6)
Beloit	11/80	R	20	31[a]		
Eau Claire	n.a.	R[b]	125	34[c]	n.i.	
Milwaukee Area Total			145	65[d]		

[a] By late 1980, there appeared to be little prospect of making the program work in Beloit. Local officials regarded it as unofficially dead. Nonetheless, according to HUD figures for 1981, 31 units were in construction.
[b] Eau Claire applied for and received 125 units for two areas of the city near its Central Business District.

[c] This figure is listed in HUD's 1981 summary.
[d] HUD's 1983 figures: two projects involving 52 units.

Minneapolis/St.Paul

	(1)	(2)	(3)	(4)	(5)	(6)
Mankato	n.a.	M	110	108[a]	3C	108
Minneapolis	n.a.	R	400	n.i.		
St.Paul	n.a.	NR[b]	225	n.i.		
Minneapolis Area Total			735	108[c]		

[a] 1981 survey indicates 108 units already under contract.
[b] A HUD official indicated in January, 1984 that St. Paul had so much difficulty implementing its NSA proposal that it received permission to divide its original allocation and to create two new NSAs based on that allocation. He did not have information on program achievements.
[c] HUD's 1983 data: six projects involving 330 units were completed; 47 units in two other projects were still reserved.

REGION V Totals   6173*   3110+
----

* Excludes additions made to the original allocations for Columbus, East Cleveland and Toledo, Ohio.

+ HUD lists 57 projects involving 4137 units as completed or started. Another four projects involving 95 units were reserved.

REGION VI

Dallas Area Office

	(1)	(2)	(3)	(4)	(5)	(6)
Waco	n.a.	R	152	152	1R	152F
Dallas Area Total			152	152[a]		

[a] The city applied to rehabilitate a former subsidized housing project. HUD data for 1981 indicate that the project was already under construction.

Houston Service Office

	(1)	(2)	(3)	(4)	(5)	(6)
Beaumont	n.a.	R	45	n.i.[a]		
Houston	n.a.		350	0		
Houston Area Total			395	0[b]		

[a] 1981 HUD data indicate two units may have been committed to a project in Beaumont.
[b] 1983 data suggest no projects were carried out either in Beaumont or Houston.

San Antonio Area Office

	(1)	(2)	(3)	(4)	(5)	(6)
Austin	n.a.	R	500	153	n.i.	
San Antonio Area Total			500	153[a]		

[a] The Area Office 1983 survey data attributed 13 projects involving 153 units to the city of Austin.

| REGION VI Totals | 1047 | 305* |

* This figure is derived directly from HUD's 1983 data.

REGION VII

Des Moines Service Office

	(1)	(2)	(3)	(4)	(5)	(6)
Burlington, Ia.	n.a.	R	138	134	1R	134F
Des Moines Area Total			138	134[a]		

[a] Burlington applied to rehabilitate a deteriorated subsidized housing project. 1983 HUD data suggest that plan was carried out.

Kansas City Area Office

	(1)	(2)	(3)	(4)	(5)	(6)
Kansas City	n.a.:					
Santa Fe		R	310	n.i.		
S. Hyde Park		R	450	n.i.		

```
        Kansas City Area Total              760        418ᵃ
```

ᵃ According to 1983 HUD data, 418 units were used in Kansas City in
18 projects.

Omaha Area Office

	(1)	(2)	(3)	(4)	(5)	(6)
Omaha	n.a.	R	10	10	1R	10F
Omaha Area Total			10	10ᵃ		

ᵃ The city applied for only ten units and committed those units by
1981.

St. Louis Area Office (7/81)

	(1)	(2)	(3)	(4)	(5)	(6)
St. Louis Midtown						
Medical Ctr.	7/81	M	110	60	1R	60
Murphy-Blair	n.a.	R	40	0		
Soulard-Benton						
Park	7/81	R	170	125	1C	100E
					1R	25
Union-Sarah	7/81	M	140	97	1R	97F
Page-Goodfellow	n.a.	R	53ᵃ	0		
St. Louis Area Total			500	282ᵇ		

ᵃ This NSA was based on units not used elsewhere in the city.
ᵇ HUD's 1983 data: five projects were completed or in process for 350
units.

```
    --------------------------------------------------
    REGION VII Totals              1408       844*
    ..................................................
```

* HUD's 1983 data: 25 projects for 912 units completed or under
construction.

REGION VIII

Denver Regional and Area Office

	(1)	(2)	(3)	(4)	(5)	(6)
Denver	n.a.	R	200	n.i.		
Sioux Falls, SD	n.a.	R	24	n.i.		
Region VIII Totals			224	117ᵃ		

ᵃ This data comes from HUD's 1983 summary.

REGION IX

Los Angeles Area Office (7/79;1/85)

	(1)	(2)	(3)	(4)	(5)	(6)
Los Angeles	7/79; 1/85	R	800	503	3NC	220E
					3R	283
Los Angeles						
County	7/79:					
Maravilla		R	250	0		
Willowbrook		R	250	0		

```
     Los Angeles Area Total              1300        503ᵃ
```

[a] HUD's 1983 summary reports 503 units in eleven projects in some phase of production. I cannot account for the disparity in number of projects.

San Francisco Area Office (7/79;1/85)

	(1)	(2)	(3)	(4)	(5)	(6)
Eureka	n.a.	R	110	36[a]		
San Francisco 7/79; 1/85:						
Hayes Valley		R	245	WITHDREW		
North of Market		M	550	377	1NC	100E
					2C	116E
					2R	161E
Upper Ashbury		R	200	WITHDREW		
San Francisco Area Total			1105	413[b]		

[a] HUD's 1981 summary identifies 36 units under contract in Eureka.
[b] The 1983 HUD data: four projects involving 250 units in production. By 1985 a fifth 100-unit new construction project was also in production in San Francisco.

```
     REGION IX Totals              2405        916*
```

* HUD's 1983 data: l5 projects involving 754 units.

REGION X

Portland Area Office

	(1)	(2)	(3)	(4)	(5)	(6)
Portland	n.a.	M	500	388	n.i.	
Portland Area Total			500	388[a]		

[a] These are HUD's 1983 figures for four projects.

Seattle Area Office

	(1)	(2)	(3)	(4)	(5)	(6)
King County	n.a.:					
Auburn		M	100	n.i.		
Renton		M	75	n.i.		
Seattle	n.a.:					
Chinatown		M	225	n.i.		
Stevens		R	200	n.i.		
Seattle Area Total			600	n.i.[a]		

[a] According to HUD's 1983 figures, there were ten projects involving 195 units completed or in construction.

```
     REGION X Totals              1100        388*
```

* HUD's l983 figures for the region indicate that 583 units were used in l14 projects.

```
-----------------------------------------------------------------
-----------------------------------------------------------------
National Totals                 37,037      23,118*      23,474+
.................................................................
```

* These figures represent the sum of units listed in this column for the ten regions.

\+ HUD's official summary for 1983 lists a total of 420 projects involving 23,422 units either completed or in construction. In addition, 1,347 units were reserved for another 27 projects. In a data sheet prepared by the Management Information System of HUD on January 17, 1984, covering the period through November 30, 1983, 23,421 units were attributed to projects already completed or under construction; another 947 units were listed as reserved for projects not yet under construction.

SELECTED BIBLIOGRAPHY

Ahlbrandt, Roger S., Jr., and Paul C. Brophy, *Neighborhood Revitalization*. Lexington, Mass.: Lexington Books, 1975.

Anagnoson, Theodore J. "Bureaucratic Reactions to Political Pressure: Can a Grant Agency 'Manage' Its Political Environment?" *Administration and Society* 15 (May 1983): 97–118.

————. "Equity, Efficiency and Political Feasibility in Federal Project Selection Procedures." *Policy Sciences* 14 (August 1982): 331–45.

Anderson, Martin. *The Federal Bulldozer*. Cambridge, Mass.: MIT Press, 1964.

Arthur D. Little, Inc., *Project Rehab Monitoring Report: Overview*. Washington, D.C.: U.S. Department of Housing and Urban Development, 1971.

————. *Title I Property Improvement Program*. Washington, D.C.: U. S. Department of Housing and Urban Development, 1977.

Bailey, Robert. *Radicals in Urban Politics*. Chicago: University of Chicago Press, 1974.

Banfield, Edward C. "Making a New Federal Program: Model Cities, 1964–68." In *Social Program Implementation*, edited by Walter Williams and Richard F. Elmore, 183–217. New York: Academic Press, 1976.

————. *Political Influence*. New York: Free Press, 1961.

Bardach, Eugene. *The Implementation Game*. Cambridge, Mass.: MIT Press, 1977.

Barton, Allen H., et al. *Decentralizing City Government*. Lexington, Mass.: Lexington Books, 1977.

Baumer, Donald C., and Carl E. Van Horn. *The Politics of Unemployment*. Washington, D.C.: Congressional Quarterly Press, 1985.

Beer, Samuel H. "The Modernization of American Federalism." *Publius* 3 (Fall 1973): 49–95.

Berman, Paul. "The Study of Macro- and Micro-Implementation," *Public Policy* 26 (Spring 1978): 157–84.

Betnun, Nathan S. *Housing Finance Agencies: A Comparison Between the States and HUD*. New York: Praeger, 1976.

Bierbaum, Martin A. "The Applied Housing Program." In *Housing Rehabilitation*, edited by David Listokin, 225–34. New Brunswick, N.J.: Center for Urban Policy Research, Rutgers University, 1983.

———. "Hoboken—A Comeback City." Ph.D. diss. Rutgers University, 1980.

Blew, Joseph Miller, and Howard H. Stevenson. "How to Understand a Subsidized-Housing Syndication." In *Housing Urban America*, edited by Jon Pynoos et al., 574–84. 2d ed. New York: Aldine, 1960.

Boyte, Harry G. *The Backyard Revolution*. Philadelphia: Temple University Press, 1980.

Caro, Robert A. *The Power Broker*. New York: Alfred A. Knopf, 1974.

Carpenter, Edward K. "Good News from Bed-Stuy." *Design and Environment* 7 (Summer 1976): 34–39.

Christensen, Karen S., and Michael B. Teitz. "The Housing Assistance Plan: Promise and Reality." In *Housing Policy for the 1980s*, edited by Roger Montgomery and Dale R. Marshall, 185–202. Lexington, Mass.: Lexington Books, 1980.

Clay, Phillip L. *Neighborhood Partnerships in Action*. Washington, D.C.: Neighborhood Reinvestment Corporation, 1981.

———. *Neighborhood Renewal*. Lexington, Mass: Lexington Books, 1979.

Clay, Phillip L., and Robert M. Hollister, eds. *Neighborhood Policy and Planning*. Lexington, Mass.: Lexington Books, 1983.

Cobb, Roger W., and Charles D. Elder. *Participation in American Politics: The Dynamics of Agenda Building*. 2d ed. Baltimore: Johns Hopkins University Press, 1983.

Comings, William D., Jr. "Advice to Developers: Multifamily Rental Housing Can be Built." *Journal of Housing* 37 (May 1980): 258–61.

Crenson, Matthew A. *Neighborhood Politics*. Cambridge, Mass.: Harvard University Press, 1983.

Dahl, Robert A. *Who Governs?* New Haven, Conn.: Yale University Press, 1961.

Davidoff, Paul. "Advocacy and Pluralism in Planning." *Journal of the American Institute of Planners* 31 (November 1965): 331–38.

Derthick, Martha. *New Towns In-Town*. Washington, D.C.: Urban Institute, 1972.

Dommel, Paul R., et al. *Decentralizing Urban Policy*. Washington, D.C.: Brookings Institution, 1982.

———. *Deregulating Community Development*. Washington, D.C.: U.S. Department of Housing and Urban Development, 1983.

———. *Targeting Community Development*. Washington, D.C.: U.S. Department of Housing and Urban Development, 1980.

Downs, Anthony C. *Neighborhoods and Urban Development*. Washington, D.C.: Brookings Institution, 1981.

Elazar, Daniel J. *American Federalism: A View from the States*. 3d ed. New York: Harper and Row, 1984.

———. *The American Partnership*. Chicago: University of Chicago Press, 1962.

———. "Cursed by Bigness or Toward a Post-Technocratic Federalism." *Publius* 3 (Fall 1973): 239–98.

———. "Federalism vs. Decentralization." *Publius* 6 (Fall 1976): 9–19.

Fainstein, Susan S., et al. *Restructuring the City*. New York: Longman, 1983.

Feagin, Joe R. "The Corporate Center Strategy." *Urban Affairs Quarterly* 21 (June 1986): 617–628.

Federal City Reporter. "Summary of Housing and Urban-Rural Recovery Act of 1983," 6 December, 1983.

Federal Register. Vol. 41, no. 81, 26 April, 1976, 17488.

————. Vol. 42, no. 20, 31 January, 1977, 5918–5922.

————. Vol. 43, no. 21, 31 January, 1978.

Fish, John Hall. *Black Power/White Control*. Princeton, N.J.: Princeton University Press, 1973.

Fisher, Robert. *Let the People Decide*. Boston: G. K. Hall, 1984.

Frieden, Bernard J. "Housing Allowances: An Experiment That Worked." *The Public Interest* 59 (Spring 1980): 15–35.

Frieden, Bernard J., and Marshall Kaplan. *The Politics of Neglect*. Cambridge, Mass.: MIT Press, 1975.

Gans, Herbert. *People and Plans*. New York: Basic Books, 1968.

————. *The Urban Villagers*. New York: Free Press, 1961.

Genovese, Rosalie G. "Issues in Combining Social Action with Planning: The Case of Advocacy Planning." In *Research in Social Problems and Public Policy*, edited by Michael A. Lewis, vol. 1, 195–224. Greenwich, Conn.: JAI Press, 1979.

Glendening, Parris N., and Mavis Mann Reeves. *Pragmatic Federalism*. 2d ed. Pacific Palisades, Calif.: Palisades Publishers, 1984.

Greenstone, J. David, and Paul Peterson. *Race and Authority in Urban Politics*. New York: Russell Sage, 1973.

Grodzins, Morton. *The American System*. Chicago: Rand-McNally, 1966.

Haar, Charles M. *Between the Idea and the Reality*. Boston: Little, Brown and Co., 1975.

Hartman, Chester. *The Transformation of San Francisco*. Totowa, N.J.: Rowman and Allenheld, 1984.

Hartman, Paul J., and Thomas R. McCoy. "Garcia: The Latest Retreat on the 'States' Rights' Front." *Intergovernmental Perspective* 11 (Spring–Summer 1985): 8–11.

Hawkins, Robert B., ed. *American Federalism*. San Francisco: Institute for Contemporary Studies, 1982.

Hays, R. Allen. *The Federal Government and Urban Housing*. Albany: State University of New York Press, 1985.

Henig, Jeffrey R. *Neighborhood Mobilization*. New Brunswick, N.J.: Rutgers University Press, 1982.

Howard, A. E. Dick. "Garcia: Federalism's Principles Forgotten." *Intergovernmental Perspective* 11 (Spring–Summer 1985): 12–14.

Hudson, William. "The Federal Aid Crutch." *The Urban Interest* 2 (Spring 1980): 34–44.

Hula, Richard. "Markets and Redevelopment." *Urban Affairs Quarterly* 21 (June 1986): 461–83.

Ingram, Helen. "Policy Implementation Through Bargaining." *Public Policy* 25 (Fall 1973): 499–526.

Jacobs, Jane. *The Death and Life of Great American Cities*. New York: Vintage, 1963.

Judd, Dennis R., and Robert E. Mendelson. *The Politics of Urban Planning*. Urbana, Ill.: University of Illinois Press, 1973.

Kaplan, Marshall, and Peggy Cuciti, eds. *The Great Society and Its Legacy*. Durham, N.C.: Duke University Press, 1986.

Karabatsos, Lewis T. "Lowell Reborn." *National Parks and Conservation Magazine* 54 (January 1980): 4–9.

Katznelson, Ira. *City Trenches*. Chicago: University of Chicago Press, 1981.

Keith, Nathaniel S. *Politics and the Housing Crisis Since 1930*. New York: Universe Books, 1973.

Kettl, Donald F. *Managing Community Development in the New Federalism*. New York: Praeger, 1980.

Keyes, Langley C. *The Boston Rehabilitation Program*. Cambridge, Mass.: Joint Center for Urban Studies of Harvard-MIT, 1970.

Kotler, Milton. *Neighborhood Government*. Indianapolis: Bobbs-Merrill, 1969.

Kuttner, Bob. "Ethnic Renewal." In *Neighborhoods in America* edited by Ronald H. Bayor, 209–19. Port Washington, N.Y.: Kennikat, 1982.

Legates, Richard. "Can the Federal Welfare Bureaucracies Control Their Programs?: The Case of HUD and Urban Renewal," *The Urban Lawyer* 5 (Spring 1973): 228–63.

Listokin, David, ed. *Housing Rehabilitation*. New Brunswick, N.J.: Center for Urban Policy Research, Rutgers University, 1983.

Long, Norton E. "The City as Reservation." *The Public Interest* 25 (Fall 1971): 22–38.

Lovell, Catherine, and Charles Tobin. "The Mandate Issue." *Public Administration Review* 41 (May–June 1981): 318–31.

Lowi, Theodore J. "American Business, Public Policy, Case Studies and Political Theory." *World Politics* 16 (July 1964): 677–715.

McFarland, M. Carter. *Federal Government and Urban Problems*. Boulder, Colo: Westview Press, 1978.

Marcuse, Peter. "The Deceptive Consensus on Redlining." *Journal of the American Planning Association* 45 (October 1979): 549–56.

Marris, Peter and Martin Rein. *Dilemmas of Social Reform*. New York: Atherton, 1969.

Meehan, Eugene J. "The Rise and Fall of Public Housing: Condemnation Without Trial." In *A Decent Home and Environment*, edited by Donald Phares, 3–42. Cambridge, Mass.: Ballinger, 1977.

Meo, Gary. "Flatbush Development Corporation." *Neighborhood* 6 (Summer 1983): 26.

Mollenkopf, John H. *The Contested City*. Princeton, N.J.: Princeton University Press, 1983.

Molotch, Harvey. "The City as a Growth Machine." *American Journal of Sociology* 74 (September 1976): 309–32.

Moynihan, Daniel P. *Maximum Feasible Misunderstanding*. New York: Free Press, 1969.

Nolan, John R. "Innovative Joint Ventures: The Role of Residential Development Agencies." *Journal of Housing* 40 (January–February 1983): 13–19.

Palmer, John L., and Isabel V. Sawhill, eds. *The Reagan Experiment*. Washington, D.C.: Urban Institute, 1982.

Perlman, Janice. "Grassrooting the System." *Social Policy* 7 (September–October 1976): 4–20.

Peterson, Paul E. *City Limits*. Chicago: University of Chicago Press, 1981.

Peterson, Paul E., Barry G. Rabe, and Kenneth K. Wong. *When Federalism Works*. Washington, D.C.: Brookings Institution, 1986.

Petty, Ann E. "Historic Preservation Without Relocation." *Journal of Housing* 35 (September 1978): 422–23.

Pierce, Neil R. "New Life in Spindle City." *Washington Post*, 29 December, 1977.

———"Savannah's Human-Scale Renewal Plan." *Washington Post*, 22 November 1977.

Piven, Francis Fox, and Richard Cloward. *Regulating the Poor*. New York: Vintage, 1971.

President's Commission for a National Agenda for the 80s. *Urban America In the Eighties*. Washington, D.C.: U.S. Government Printing Office, 1980.

Pressman, Jeffrey L. *Federal Programs and City Politics*. Berkeley, Calif: University of California Press, 1975.

Pressman, Jeffrey L., and Aaron Wildavsky. *Implementation*. 2d ed. Berkeley, Calif.: University of California Press, 1979.

Reagan, Michael D., and John G. Sanzone. *The New Federalism*. 2d ed. New York: Oxford University Press, 1981.

Rogg, Nathaniel. *Urban Housing Rehabilitation in the United Sates*. Chicago: U.S. League of Savings Associations, 1978.

Rosenberg, William G. "Downtown Adaptive Reuse Project Signals New Public/Private Partnership." *Journal of Housing* 38 (August–September 1981): 437–43.

Rosenthal, Donald B. "Bargaining Analysis in Intergovernmental Relations." *Publius* 10 (Summer 1980): 5–44.

———. "Neighborhood Strategy Areas." *Journal of Housing* 35 (March 1978): 120–21.

———. *Sticking Points and Ploys in Federal-Local Relations*. Philadelphia: Center for the Study of Federalism, Temple University, 1979.

———. ed. *Urban Revitalization*. Beverly Hills, Calif.: Sage, 1980.

Rothman, Rozann. "The Ambiguity of American Federal Theory." *Publius* 8 (Summer 1978): 103–122.

Rubin, Irene S. *Shrinking the Federal Government*. New York: Longman, 1985.

Sagalyn, Lynne Beyer. "Mortgage Lending in Older Urban Neighborhoods." *Annals of the American Academy* 465 (January 1983): 98–108.

Salisbury, Robert. "Urban Politics: The New Convergence of Power." *Journal of Politics* 26 (November 1964): 775–97.

San Francisco Department of City Planning. *Feasibility of a Rehabilitation Assistance Program and Recommended Alternative Program for Hayes Valley*, March 1979.

Savas, E. S. *Privatizing the Public Sector*. Chatham, N.J.: Chatham House, 1982.

Schill, Michael H., and Richard P. Nathan. *Revitalizing America's Cities*. Albany: State University of New York Press, 1983.

Schoenberg, Sandra Perlman, and Patricia L. Rosenbaum. *Neighborhoods That Work*. New Brunswick, N.J.: Rutgers University Press, 1980.

Schuler, Gregory. "Financing Section 8 Projects: A Section 11(b) Funding Guide." *Journal of Housing* 40 (March–April 1983): 44–46.

Schwarz, John E. *America's Hidden Success*. New York: W. W. Norton, 1983.

Seidman, Harold. *Politics, Position and Power*. 3d ed. New York: Oxford University Press, 1980.

Seligman, Ralph. "Hoboken Rediscovered Yet Again." *New York Affairs* 5 (Summer–Fall 1979): 26–38.

Shashaty, Andre F. "Dial-a-Mortgage System Changed to a Priority-Lottery Plan." *New York Times*, 11 January, 1981.

Smith, Michael P., ed. *Cities in Transformation*. Beverly Hills, Calif.: Sage, 1984.

Sorkin, Donna L., and Nancy B. Ferris. *Guide to Local Multifamily Rehabilitation Programs: Lessons Learned from the NSA Demonstration*. Washington, D.C.: Public Technology, 1982.

Starr, Roger. *Housing and the Money Market*. New York: Basic Books, 1975.

———. "Making New York Smaller." *The New York Times*, 14 November 1976.

Steinbach, Carol F., and Neal R. Pierce. "Picking Up Hammers." *National Journal*, 6 June, 1987.

Sternlieb, George. "The City as Sandbox." *The Public Interest* 25 (Fall 1971): 14–21.

Stockman, Davis. "The Social Pork Barrel." *The Public Interest* 39 (Spring 1975): 3–31.

Stone, Clarence N. *Economic Growth and Neighborhood Discontent*. Chapel Hill, N.C.: University of North Carolina Press, 1976..

———. "Systemic Power in Community Decision Making." *American Political Science Review* 74 (December 1980): 978–90.

Storing, Herbert F. *What the Anti-Federalists Were For*. Chicago: University of Chicago Press, 1981.

Strange, John. "Community Action in North Carolina: Maximum Feasible Misunderstanding? Mistake? or Magic Formula?" *Publius* 2 (Fall 1982): 51–73.

Sundquist, James L., and David W. Davis. *Making Federalism Work*. Washington, D.C.: Brookings Institution, 1969.

Tabb, William K., and Larry Sawers, eds. *Marxism and the Metropolis*. New York: Oxford University Press, 1978.

U.S. Department of Housing and Urban Development. *A Case Study of Local Control Over Housing Development: The Neighborhood Strategy Area Demonstration*. Washington, D.C.: U.S. Department of Housing and Urban Development, January 1983.

———. *Creating Local Partnerships*. Washington, D.C.: U.S. Department of Housing and Urban Development, March 1980.

———. Office of Loan Origination. *HUD/FHA Rehabilitation Program: Multifamily*. 1 May, 1977.

———. *Interim Report to Congress: The Section 312 Multifamily Rehabilitation Loan Program*. Washington, D.C.: U.S. Department of Housing and Urban Development, March 1980.

———. *The Neighborhood Housing Services Model*. Washington, D.C.: U.S. Department of Housing and Urban Development, September 1975.

———. *Neighborhood Strategy Areas: A Guidebook for Local Government*. Washington, D.C.: U.S. Department of Housing and Urban Development, 1978.

———. Neighborhood Strategy Areas: Neighborhoods and Programs 1979. Washington, D.C.: U.S. Department of Housing and Urban Development, October 1980.

———. *A New Partnership to Conserve America's Communities: A National Urban Policy*. Washington, D.C.: U.S. Department of Housing and Urban Development, April 1978.

———. *The President's Urban Policy Report*. Washington, D.C.: U.S. Department of Housing and Urban Development, August 1978.

———. *The Presidents National Urban Policy Report: 1982*. Washington, D.C.: U.S. Department of Housing and Urban Development, August 1982.

———. *The President's National Urban Policy Report: 1984*. Washington, D.C.: U.S. Department of Housing and Urban Development, August 1984.

U.S. General Accounting Office. *Historic Preservation Tax Incentives*. Washington, D.C.: U.S. Government Printing Office, 1986.

———. *HUD Needs to Better Determine Extent of Community Block Grants' Lower Income Benefits*. Washington, D.C.: U.S. Government Printing Office, 1982.

————. *Information on Historic Preservation Tax Incentives*. Washington, D.C.: U.S. Government Printing Office, 1984.

Walker, David B. *Toward a Functioning Federalism*. Cambridge, Mass.: Winthrop, 1981.

Wildavsky, Aaron. "A Bias Toward Federalism: Confronting the Conventional Wisdom on the Delivery of Government Services." *Publius* 6 (Spring 1976): 95–120.

Wilson, James Q., ed. *Urban Renewal: The Record and the Controversy*. Cambridge, Mass.: MIT Press, 1966.

Wolfinger, Raymond. *The Politics of Progress*. Englewood Cliffs, N.J.: Prentice-Hall, 1974.

Wright, Deil S. *Understanding Intergovernmental Relations*. 2d ed. Monterey, Calif.: Brooks-Cole, 1982.

INDEX

About the Author

DONALD B. ROSENTHAL is Professor and Chair of the Department of Political Science at the State University of New York at Buffalo. His areas of scholarly interest include intergovernmental relations and various aspects of urban policy including housing and community development. Among his publications in these areas are *The Politics of Community Conflict*, *Urban Revitalization*, and *Sticking-Points and Ploys in Federal Local Relations*.